FEDERA

Kh...

Arkhangel'sk

Dickson

Novaya
Zemlya

Kara Sea

Stolbovoy

Murmansk

FINLAND

Barents

Sea

Northern Sea Route

SWEDEN

Bukhta
Tikhaya

Tromsø

NORWAY

Arkticheskiy

Franz Josef
Land

Nansen Basin

March 1895
Nansen leaves
Fram towards Pole

Svalbard

Longyearbyen

Spitsbergen

Norwegian Sea

3300m

Cordillera

Basin

Lena Trough

North Geographic Pole
4345m

Ridge

Oodaaq Island
(Northernmost point
of land on Earth)

Greenland Sea

Winter extent of sea ice cover

Summer extent of sea ice cover

ICELAND

Hö

Ward Hunt
Island

Cape Columbia

Lincoln Sea

Challenger Mtns.

Islands

Ellesmere Island

Eureka

Gunnbjørn Fjeld
3700m

Reykjavík

Patreksfjord

G R E E N L A N D

(DENMARK)

Norwegian
Bay

Grise Ford

Qaanaaq
(Thule)

Tasiilaq

Devon
Island

Arctic
Bay

Baffin Bay

Arctic Circle

V U T A

Baffin Island

A

Igloolik

Solo

UT PROSIM

Solo

The North Pole: Alone and Unsupported

PEN HADOW

MICHAEL JOSEPH
an imprint of
PENGUIN BOOKS

MICHAEL JOSEPH

Published by the Penguin Group

Penguin Books Ltd, 80 Strand, London WC2R ORL, England

Penguin Group (USA) Inc., 375 Hudson Street, New York, New York 10014, USA

Penguin Books Australia Ltd, 250 Camberwell Road, Camberwell, Victoria 3124, Australia

Penguin Books Canada Ltd, 10 Alcorn Avenue, Toronto, Ontario, Canada M4V 3B2

Penguin Books India (P) Ltd, 11 Community Centre, Panchsheel Park, New Delhi – 110 017, India

Penguin Group (NZ), cnr Airborne and Rosedale Roads, Albany, Auckland 1310, New Zealand

Penguin Books (South Africa) (Pty) Ltd, 24 Sturdee Avenue, Rosebank 2196, South Africa

Penguin Books Ltd, Registered Offices: 80 Strand, London WC2R ORL, England

www.penguin.com

First published 2004

1

Set in 13.5/16 pt Monotype Garamond
Typeset by Rowland Phototypesetting Ltd, Bury St Edmunds, Suffolk
Printed in Great Britain by Clays Ltd, St Ives plc

A CIP catalogue record for this book is available from the British Library

ISBN 0-718-14710-3

I dedicate this endeavour
to the memory of
my beloved late father,
Nigel Philip Ian Hadow

And I dedicate this book to my wife, Mary,
our children, Wilf and Freya,
and my mother, Anne

Unseen and untrodden under the spotless mantle of ice, the rigid polar region slept the profound sleep of death from the earliest dawn of time . . . Ages passed – deep was the silence. Then in the dawn of history far away in the south, the awakening spirit of man reared its head on high and gazed over the earth. To the south it encountered warmth, to the north cold; behind the boundaries of the unknown it placed in imagination the twin kingdoms of consuming heat and of deadly cold. But the limits of the unknown had to recede step by step before the ever increasing yearning after light and knowledge of the human mind, until they made a stand in the north at the threshold of Nature's great Ice Temple of the polar regions with their endless silence.

(Fridtjof Nansen, *Farthest North*)

Contents

List of Illustrations

Prologue

I flew into Resolute Bay on 26 February 2003 – the point of no return, the last staging post on the way to the North Pole. I was already deep in the tundra, further north than most citizens of the world, past or present, have ever been, but my destination still lay over a thousand miles to the north.

Resolute Bay, also known as Qausuittuq – 'place with no dawn' – in the Inuit language, Inuktituk, is a sheltered bay on the southern shores of Cornwallis Island, overlooking the ice-choked waters of the North-West Passage – the grail that so many seamen lost their lives in seeking. Dependent for virtually all its supplies on an annual 'sea-lift' by a supply vessel escorted by two icebreakers, Resolute Bay is so remote an outpost that no mainland Canadian I have ever met has heard of it, and its very existence is so marginal that it may well expire in my lifetime. It did not even exist as a settlement until the late 1940s, when the Canadian government decided to lay formal claim to all the islands to the north of the mainland and began setting up military installations, airport facilities, weather stations, exploratory oil and gas rigs, and civilian settlements in previously uninhabited areas.

Resolute Bay was one of these settlements and a number of Canadian Inuit living well to the south were encouraged to resettle there on the basis of the dubious promise of rich hunting grounds. It now has around 200 permanent inhabitants together with a number of contract workers who maintain the infrastructure, but the only significant employers are the Polar Continental Shelf Project – an international scientific study centre – and the airport complex, with its air charter operators serving the ultra-remote, outlying communities of Igloolik,

Pond Inlet, Arctic Bay and Grise Fjord, and ferrying travellers and adventurers to the far north.

The permanent population at Resolute mostly live at The Hamlet, a mile from the airfield, in the shadow of the rocky outcrop rearing 500 feet above the town. As I drove down the dirt road in a battered Ford pick-up, I saw the lights of this forlorn, almost pointless village shimmering through the cold, dark haze of the late winter afternoon. Prominent among them was the steeple light of the tiny church. Constructed of wood, painted pea-green, and reminiscent of a chapel high in the Alps, the church lies at the heart of the village – a beacon of hope in a dark, cold place. I pulled up at the side of the dirt road, the wheels crunching on the frozen, wind-packed snow, and hurried into the church. Its wooden interior seemed barely larger than a doll's house, with everything somehow scaled down in proportion. A lovingly prepared sealskin quilt covered the altar, and the prayer and hymn books were in Inuktituk. A tracksuit top lay discarded under a bench and the paintings of the Sunday school children hung on the walls at the back. I had the strong feeling that I had clumsily intruded into a place of childlike faith, but I stayed a while in this oasis of warmth and calm, a refuge both from the frenzy of the final preparations ahead of me and the wildness of the weather outside.

As I left the church, the ferocious cold made me gasp for breath but nonetheless I went for a walk through the village to retune into life up here. At once I bumped into three old friends: Toni and Mavis Manik, and Diane Guy, wife of Gary, my Canadian base manager at Resolute. Toni is a wonderful man for whom I have huge admiration. Brought up 'the traditional Inuit way' on Somerset Island on the southern shores of the North-West Passage, he had hunted fish and fowl, seal and whale, musk ox, caribou and even polar bear throughout his childhood, and was one of the most skilled hunters of his generation. In recent years, he has been hired by an endless succession of TV and film crews to demonstrate the extraordinary skills passed on to him by his elders – and every film unit went away staggered by his skill and artistry – but that has now become a sideline. He is now not only one of the two people responsible for maintaining Resolute's power plant and telephone system, but also the lay vicar for the community, christening, marrying and burying his kinsfolk, and he is in charge of the Canadian military's Arctic Survival School that swings into action at a nearby encampment known as Crystal City every spring. As if all that were not enough to keep him occupied, he has also become a business partner of my great ally, Gary Guy, providing base camp facilities for polar expeditions in the spring and for wilderness travellers in the summer.

His daughter, Mavis, had been a schoolgirl when I'd first met her in 1994, born and bred in Resolute but with dreams of breaking the mould that left the vast majority of her peers dependent on state handouts. When I returned in 1998, she was working as an office assistant for one of the local air charter operators and was hoping to win a scholarship to flight school down south. If she succeeded, she would return to Resolute as the first Inuk pilot in Nunavut. Of all the young people I'd met in Resolute she had seemed the one most likely to succeed, so I was delighted to see her again and intrigued to know whether her dream had been realised. Sadly the scholarship had never materialised and, unable to afford the cost herself, she had had to shelve her ambitions. However, she was still working for the charter operation, and in a more senior position. As we talked, I also noticed a mop of black hair and two dark eyes peering over her shoulder at me from the safety of a papoose. Oh yes, she had a son and was looking forward to more children.

After a few minutes standing still, the cold was penetrating my bones. I left my friends at the church and hurried on through the snow-lined streets, walking fast to try and generate a little body-heat. Surrounding the church was a scattering of squat, single-storey houses, raised clear of the permafrost on stilts and constructed of wood, aluminium siding or sheet metal, painted in muted colours: greys, greens, browns, and muddy yellows. For eight months of the year snow is banked against their walls up to roof height. Dogs are chained outside almost every house, but the teams of huskies that pull the hunters' sleds are kept about a quarter of a mile from the settlement – any closer and the noise of their incessant barking and howling would unhinge the most phlegmatic inhabitant. They also act as an early warning system; when the barking reaches a particularly frenzied peak, it is a signal that a polar bear has entered the bay.

The surplus Arctic char that the Inuit catch in the lakes and the ptarmigan that they shoot are stored on the house-roofs or on hanging lines – nature's deep-freezes – until needed for the table; and the one and only store in Resolute Bay also sells convenience foods like pizza, burgers and even ice cream, alongside rifles and computer software. The Inuit clothing and equipment is a similarly eclectic mixture of ancient and modern, like home-made sealskin coats and the traditionally embroidered double-hooded *armanti* coats – often containing a sleeping infant – set off by luridly coloured shell-suit bottoms. As I hurried on through the settlement, I could see the skins of polar bears and seals, stretched on wooden frames to cure in the frigid Arctic wind, hanging next to the pyjamas and underwear from the weekly wash. The huge old wooden *komatik* sleds, pulled by dog teams and held together by string and skill alone, were drawn up alongside petrol-engined snowmobiles, and kayaks were lashed against the outbuildings alongside upturned boats with outboard engines. And, like children the world over, the Inuit kids were playing football in the street; the only difference was that their 'ball' was a polar bear's foot.

Driving back from the settlement, I hunched over the wheel, barely able to move, my body stiff with cold, my sole focus to get back to the warmth and home-comforts of my base. I was going to be operating in these extreme temperatures and worse for months and at the moment I could hardly cope inside a heated car. But I knew that I would quickly adapt and it occurred to me then, as it has done at the start of every polar season, how remarkable the human body is in being able to adjust to almost any environment – natural or artificial, in peace or in war – for as long as necessary.

A giant Caterpillar bulldozer was clearing newly fallen snow from the nearby streets, charging the drifts, its engine revs suddenly dropping an octave as it buried its head deep into the drifted snow and drove it a few feet further south out of town. In winter it often has to operate twenty-four hours a day, just to keep the road open. An area the size of a football field on the downwind side of the town is used as a dump for the snow cleared from the streets. It is piled there in huge mounds and left for the prevailing winds to carry away across the bay. In the brief summer, the settlement resembles a desert; a dirt-brown dust-bowl with not a single blade of grass to be seen.

The sea is normally icebound from the autumn right through to the summer break-up of the ice the following July, but in recent years, perhaps in response to global warming, the floe-edge – the interface between the immobile sea-ice locked between the islands, and the ice-pans covering the open sea that shift in response to tide, current and wind – has formed closer and closer to Resolute. And this year, almost unprecedentedly, it actually ran south from Resolute Bay. A lead – strictly a navigable channel, but polar travellers tend to use the term for any expanse of open water – had opened in the sea-ice and, once established, the tides, currents and winds kept the ice moving enough to prevent it refreezing completely. The presence of open water so near to the settlement had positive implications both for the local hunters and for me, though for very different reasons.

Simon Murray, a friend who I was to partner on an unsupported expedition to the South Pole later in the year, had also flown in to spend a week camping out on the ice with me. It was a way of building our sledging partnership in an environment similar to Antarctica, in the last polar season available to us before heading south at the end of the year. Simon and I were doing our training between Resolute Bay and Griffith Island, just five miles west of the floe-edge, even though sledging and camping that close to a lead is less than ideal, for where there is open water, seals can come up for air and wherever you have seals, polar bears will inevitably gather, bringing Arctic foxes in their wake. Earlier that year sixteen bears – a record number – had been seen around the rubbish dump at Resolute Bay, and there were bear tracks everywhere around our nightly campsites, of all different sizes: adult males, mother bears and baby bears – all we were missing was Goldilocks. It lent a certain frisson to eating our porridge in our tent every morning. We were easier prey than any seal and we were always on the look-out for any signs of bears as we made our way across to Griffith Island. As a rule, the yellowish tinge to a polar bear's fur makes it relatively easy to pick out from the backdrop of ice and snow, but movement is usually the big give-away.

As we sledged, we paused every fifteen minutes to carry out a 360° visual sweep, Simon covering to our left and behind, and me to the right, with each of us overlapping by 20° behind us to be sure of missing nothing. It was not that easy to do on skis, pulling a heavy sledge, with a huge fur-trimmed hood drawn close around the face and wearing goggles and a full-face mask, but vigilance was essential. At night in our tent – the most vulnerable time – I kept a loaded double-barrelled shotgun by my sleeping-bag, but once asleep, we took our chances; even the use of huskies as guard-dogs or tripwire alarm systems are no guarantee of waking up alive in the morning. But in the event, while local hunters encountered any number of bears, we finished our training programme having seen nothing more alarming than tracks. We had also successfully endured blisteringly cold temperatures – including the wind-chill, it was below −70 °C – and Simon then headed back to warmer climes, leaving me to focus on the mission ahead.

I was elated by the nearby open water and the accompanying thin ice, because it provided a great opportunity to test my polar 'lilo' – a flotation and stabilisation device that we'd designed, that effectively converted my sledge into a boat when crossing open water – and my immersion suit in similar conditions to those that I would soon be encountering on my way to the Pole. Made of a synthetic fabric called Hypalon, the immersion suit had been pioneered by the Norwegian explorer, Borge Ousland, on one of his polar expeditions. It was an ultra-lightweight dry-suit with integral boots, mitts and hood. Bright orange in colour, it weighed only 1.5 kilos and was designed to be worn over all my Arctic clothing, including my ski-boots and fur-trimmed hood, but as a result of its size, a lot of air was trapped inside it. That was great for buoyancy but carried the attendant risk that if I slipped and fell head-first into the water or became inverted for any reason while in the water, the trapped air would form a bubble around my feet, making it almost impossible for me to right myself. I couldn't imagine a more undignified way to die.

Not being an experienced diver, let alone a specialist ice-diver, I was extremely anxious about how this suit and I were going to get on, and I jumped at the chance to test it under semi-controlled conditions with my English base team of Ian Wesley and Martin Hartley ready to come to my aid if needed. My only previous test of the suit had been in the rather less icy waters of the West Dart River near my Dartmoor home. One February afternoon my wife, Mary, was driving back from a children's birthday party with our daughter, Freya, when she spotted our dilapidated Range Rover parked by the river. Strange, she thought, so she pulled over and found our son, Wilf, stripped to the bare essentials, larking about in the shallows. She was about to ask him where I was, when what appeared to be a large orange fertiliser bag hove into view, drifting Eeyore-like downstream and occasionally spinning in the eddies as it headed for the rapids below the bridge. 'Hi, Darling. All well?' I shouted over the roar of the water, before turning on to my front and swimming against the current to the bank. As a result, I knew that the immersion suit fitted me, and that it seemed to be waterproof, but I had to test it in true Arctic conditions before I could feel genuine confidence in it.

With my ever supportive base team around me and snow-mobiles standing ready to whisk me back to our base if required, I was able to test the suit to its limits. I did so at the floe-edge running across Resolute Passage, a stretch of ice and open water with such a fierce current flowing through it that I tied a rope around my waist, so that if I was swept straight under the ice, Ian could pull me back before I drowned. I soon developed an energy-efficient technique for breaking a channel through ice up to two inches thick, using my flailing arms or my body weight to smash through it, a technique that quickly saw me christened 'the human icebreaker' when it was reported in the press. Then I eased my way up onto some slightly thicker ice and tried leopard-crawling to see if it was quicker, and then I started crawling on all fours. It was much faster, but would it eventually wear through the material covering my knees, leaving irreparable, if not fatal, holes? How much abrasion could the Hypalon fabric take? It was a completely new piece of equip-ment to me and I had to be certain that the seams would not give way or the material be shredded – the edges of polar ice are sharp enough to leave unprotected hands covered in blood. All the time I was testing the suit, I was also bringing myself back up to speed since the last polar season, noting the proper-ties of the ice: colour, tone, opacity, surface texture and micro-freezing features, fault-lines, thickness and transition zones, and flexibility (thin ice is rubbery and can flex under your weight without necessarily dropping you through).

Finally I began walking, first on thicker ice, but with ever increasing confidence on thinner and thinner ice until at last the inevitable happened: as if dropping through the trapdoor on a theatre stage, I broke through the ice and fell into the water, the most dreaded sensation for any sea-ice traveller. But with all that air in my suit, I seemed to sink down in slow motion; it was almost fun. After that, I started deliberately falling through the ice. The Inuit hunters passing by probably thought that I was just larking about, but there was a serious purpose to it; boosting my confidence in the suit and also testing how it – and I – would react if the ice suddenly gave way beneath me on the way to the Pole, dropping me into the water. Now I knew that it didn't matter any more if I fell in. As long as I was wearing my immersion suit, I wasn't even going to get wet, let alone suffer hypothermia or worse. The ice, or lack of it, was no longer the threat to success it had always been to me in the past. I snowmobiled back believing that the last big question had been answered: water was not going to be a problem anymore.

I returned to Resolute to make my final preparations for the Pole and make sure that my chartered aircraft was ready and waiting. There's an old saying that yachting is like standing under a cold shower, tearing up £50 notes; if so, chartering flights around the Arctic is like standing naked in a blizzard and throwing £10,000 bundles into the air. Over the previous ten years my flights in and out of Resolute for myself and The Polar Travel Company that I run had cost in excess of £750,000. This year, one company, Kenn Borek Air, had a monopoly on the business, but the astronomical prices they charged were as much a reflection of the vast distances and the appalling conditions as of the lack of competition.

Over the years I had come to know well most of the managers at Resolute and the pilots of the Twin Otter aircraft, some of whom were living legends – I'd even invited a couple of them to my wedding. Aircraft support is crucial to any Arctic expedition. The plane sets you down at the start, collects you at the finish and provides emergency cover during the journey, and a good working relationship based on the mutual respect of the air operator and expedition team is absolutely essential. With lives and aircraft at stake in one of the most challenging environments on our planet, decisions often have to be made in marginal situations, and the partnership between pilot and polar traveller requires both an appreciation of the inherent risks and the professional skills of both parties to assess and report on weather and surface conditions, and to select and prepare airstrips.

I called in at the Borek offices in Resolute Bay to renew acquaintances and make sure that they'd received my banker's draft for CDN $100,000 – the price of two flights, one to drop me off at Ward Hunt Island and the other, with luck, to collect me from the Pole around ten weeks later. I also finalised the dates and timings with the company's duty manager, Bill Gawletz, and the duty pilot, Troy McKerral. We agreed that I would be dropped off at Ward Hunt Island from 13 March onwards, subject to weather. Given that I expected to take sixty-five days to reach the Pole, I should be arriving there around 16 May. Adverse weather conditions could easily make a nonsense of even the most carefully estimated timings, but provided that I arrived there between 15 and 25 May, and made my best efforts to do so in the earlier part of that ten-day window, they both declared themselves satisfied with the proposed schedule.

It would be hard to exaggerate the sheer unending pressure of the last few days before the expedition began. Even with the help of Ian and Martin, there were a thousand tasks to complete and a mountain of equipment to be tested, modified, checked and rechecked. The days passed in a blur and the nights were short and restless. Between Simon's departure on 5 March and the flight north to Ward Hunt Island, I averaged no more than four hours' sleep a night. By the end of this intense period of preparation I had enormous fondness, gratitude and respect for my aides, who had given me a level of support that could not have been surpassed. Even so, the multitude of stresses and strains were taking their toll, and I was exhausted before I'd even set off.

Early on the morning of my proposed departure date, 13 March, Troy dropped by our base to report that poor weather over Ward Hunt Island and the midway refuelling stop at the Eureka High Arctic Weather Station would prevent us from flying that day. Instead, we spent some time over a coffee getting to know each other, swapping a few polar stories, and immersing ourselves in the detail of the weather charts he had brought with him, looking at the possibility of setting off the following day. When Troy had left, Ian, Martin and I seized the unexpected opportunity for a little more fine-tuning, and once more took everything out of the carefully packed sledge. I should have rested, but I was driven by the knowledge, based on painful past experience, that anything that we could do here at base to forestall the need for decision-making and action out on the ice, where even the simplest activity is rendered all but impossible by the cumulative effects of the bone-chilling cold, was time well-spent. So we spent the day tinkering, adjusting, trimming and testing the equipment one more time.

Early the next morning, Friday 14 March, Bill Gawletz phoned to confirm that weather conditions at Eureka and Ward Hunt Island were now satisfactory and we were 'Go' to depart. The moment had arrived. I made a last phone call home to Mary – it was the middle of the night in England, but I'd promised to ring one last time before I set out – and discovered that, the day before, Freya had taken her first hesitant steps – another family milestone that I had missed. Then, accompanied by Ian, Martin and Ginny Dougary, a British journalist, I boarded the aircraft – one of Kenn Borek Air's fleet of De Havilland DHC-6 Twin Otters: 'the workhorses of the North'. On a good strip with a headwind, a pilot can land and take off in as little as 100 metres, using either wheels or skis. Although the aircraft has been out of production for over twenty-five years, the shrinking pool of survivors are rebuilt, repaired and maintained to exacting standards.

We took off at 7.30 in the morning and flew due north for almost three hours, the landscape far beneath us growing ever more barren and threadbare. I'd left the great pine forests of the Canadian north far behind during the flight up to Resolute from Ottawa. Here, even the stunted, scrub Arctic willows and birches, growing no more than a couple of inches above the ground, could not maintain a hold, and we flew on over a landscape as grey and apparently lifeless as a desert. The comparison is surprisingly apt: there is no more rainfall in the Arctic than the most arid of southern deserts and only for a few short summer weeks does the heat of the sun melt the ice bound into the frozen surface of the land. Beneath that thin surface layer is the everlastingly frozen rock and soil of the permafrost.

I spent the first part of the flight deep in conversation with Ian about my mileage plan, my best estimate of the distance I aimed to cover in each part of the expedition. The loud drone of the plane's twin engines made conversation more like a series of shouted word-bursts aimed into the side of each other's heads, and the cabin air was so hot and dry that we both soon started to lose our voices, but somehow we battled on. The first part of the plan was merely a psychological trick: to break the 416 nautical mile distance (1 nautical mile is equivalent to 1.151 statute miles or 1.852 kilometres) into manageable portions – of time as well as distance. I knew that sixty days' travelling should pretty much crack it so, like the minutes of a clock-face, I split the journey down into multiples of five days.

My plan was to average three nautical miles a day over the first twenty days – the hardest in terms of ice and weather conditions, and made even more gruelling because the sledge would then be at its heaviest. 'Sledge' seems to be the term used by the British on expeditions; sleighs get pulled by reindeers and Father Christmas sits on top, sleds are pulled by dogs, and pulks are pulled by Norwegians and other Europeans. I would be travelling for no more than five or six hours a day in the early stages, reflecting the exhausting battle to drag the sledge over jumbled compressed ice and through deep snow-fields in particularly cold temperatures – probably the hardest 'terrain' and the lowest temperatures that I would encounter on my journey to the Pole. But as the weather and ice-conditions improved and the sledge grew lighter, I was aiming to progressively increase the pace and the hours travelled to cover up to ten nautical miles a day, before the final push to the Pole in the perpetual daylight of the polar summer, when I would be travelling for fifteen hours or more a day.

I had to stay positive in the daunting early stages of the expedition, when the day's progress – perhaps as little as a single nautical mile – would seem pitifully small against the vast distances still to be covered; but dwelling on that was the surest way of sapping morale to the point of throwing in the towel. My hard-won knowledge told me that this was how it had to be and I had to focus on the fact that the passing days and weeks would see the conditions improve in step with the reduction of the sledge-weight, allowing me to accelerate dramatically. I could then accept that the low early mileages were not only inevitable but an acceptable part of a realistic master plan. I also needed Ian to be equally positive in our satellite-phone conversations. I would be under immense pressure at the best of times but if my planned mileages began to go awry, I would be especially vulnerable to anything negative – however slight. I felt I had to stress the point because, unless you have been through it yourself, it is impossible to convey how narrow the dividing line can be between success and failure – staying on the ice or abandoning the expedition.

Ian and I also discussed contingency plans if the early targets were not met, for the situation could soon spiral dangerously out of control. There is always a trade-off: the fewer supplies you are dragging behind you, the faster you can travel, but if you pare the weight down too far, you are jeopardising the success of the expedition. The amount of fuel and food I was carrying was finite, and if I was delayed by bad weather or injury, I would find myself having to do the same gruelling work on progressively less and less food and fuel. Life and the expedition would go on without food, but if I ran out of fuel I would have to abandon the expedition altogether, not because I needed heat from the stove to keep warm, but because without fuel, I could not melt snow for drinking water. It takes a huge amount of snow to produce a small amount of water and, apart from the risk of dehydration, if an emergency forces you to try to eat snow in sub-zero temperatures you're likely to die of hypothermia due to the heat-loss as you use your body-warmth to melt the snow. In addition, any serious delays would mean that I would still be trying to cross the ice-cap as the summer thaw broke it up, making travel increasingly difficult and dangerous. The fogs and overcast skies that always accompany the thaw would also hinder both my progress to the Pole and the final pick-up by aircraft.

I gazed down at the familiar landscape as we flew north. It is undulating country at first, blanketed with snow, but further north the landscape becomes much more dramatic: pyramidal peaks and frost-shattered screes, huge glaciated valleys, and densely crevassed glaciers with broad tongues of vivid, azure-blue ice spilling into the frozen sea. Some people talk about the Arctic as a monotonous wilderness of white, but if you open your eyes and really look at the landscape, especially at this time of year, you realise that there are no whites whatsoever to be seen. Everything is in shades and tones of pastel colours – cream, grey, blue, green, yellow, orange, pink – and only in the stark bright light at the height of the polar summer, when the sun is high in the sky, do you begin to see true whites among the other colours.

By now the snow-covered hills of Cornwallis and Devon Island had given way to the featureless sea-ice of Norwegian Bay and then we began the spectacular run up Eureka Sound before landing to refuel at Canada's northernmost civilian outpost, the Eureka High Arctic Weather Station, at 79°59'N on the west coast of Ellesmere Island, 601 nautical miles from the Pole. A three-kilometre gravel road links the airstrip complex, set back from the Sound on higher ground, to the weather station by the shore. We could have twenty minutes of jaw-locking cold for free by walking down the road to the station, but the Officer-in-Charge's warning: 'If you want to walk, don't touch the wolves if they get close to you; they may look friendly but they ain't!' had clearly given the red-coated Ginny cause to remember Little Red Riding Hood's fate. The alternative was to accept a lift in the snug cabin of the O-i-C's pick-up at a price – £100 each way – that took the breath away almost as fast as the cold. To be fair, though, the cost of delivering, maintaining and fuelling anything – people or plant – this far north is so great that even the taxi-fares, and the other similarly surreally priced services at Eureka, do not even begin to cover the cost of providing them.

As we were only on the ground for forty-five minutes while Troy and his co-pilot refuelled the plane, we all squeezed into the pick-up – not easy in our enormous down jackets and cumbersome polar boots – for the world's most expensive taxi ride. In the heart of a frozen desert, the weather station was an oasis of warmth and comfortable normality, albeit with a quirky decor including musk-ox skulls with red pool balls jammed into the empty eye-sockets. We were greeted by an enticing smell of hot food, the murmur of conversation and the flicker of a satellite television from an adjoining room. We walked along a corridor past a labyrinth of bunk-bedrooms, a quiet room, a bar, a lounge with more videos than a high-street megastore, a fitness room, a dining area with a huge kitchen and the reason for the station's existence: a small room, unmanned as we passed, lined with wall-to-wall weather monitoring instruments.

The whole station seemed strangely quiet. So much space, so much heat and so few people. Its heyday, when fifty scientists and supporting staff called this their home-from-home, was long past. The hard-core team – the O-i-C, three meteorologists, three maintenance personnel and a chef, who all work on a three-month rotation with their counterparts – now had the place to themselves, like astronauts in a partially decommissioned space-station. Some of them had worked here for decades. They were part of the fabric of the place and holding out until the end. We had a cup of tea and a cake with the very hospitable duty officer, Al Guadet, and the resident meteorologists. I have some good friends there; I'd got to know them well over the years as I passed through on my various Arctic expeditions, and in some respects it was like a small homecoming – the gateway to the place that I knew and loved so well – but it was also a bittersweet moment, the last taste of civilisation for many weeks to come.

I'd been reasonably relaxed on the flight up to Eureka but I was now rapidly withdrawing into myself. It was deliberate and absolutely necessary. In a few hours the others would be back at Resolute, watching videos, having a drink at the bar and then sleeping in warm and comfortable beds, but I had to prepare myself for the moment when I was left alone on the ice in one of the most isolated and inhospitable locations on earth, at the start of the most important endeavour of my life. As the others chomped away on muffins, I sat alone, staring unseeing into the middle distance.

We stayed no more than half an hour, then climbed back aboard the Twin Otter for the final leg to Ward Hunt Island, a further 185 miles to the north. Although Ginny kept chatting to me all the way, I was lost in my own thoughts and replied only in monosyllables, if at all. For the next ten weeks I had to put the normal concerns and preoccupations – paying the mortgage, changing Freya's nappies, shopping at Sainsbury's –

behind me. I was focusing only on the journey ahead and the ultimate goal that lay out on the ice, and trying to brace myself for the pressure that would be on me from the moment that I watched the aircraft take off from Ward Hunt Island. From then on there would be no one to share the burden or blame, or to bail me out if it all went pear-shaped. My friends at Eureka would be the human beings nearest to me but, if anything went wrong, they would be as powerless as anyone else to help.

I kept going over in my mind what it was going to feel like as I set off and kept telling myself not to worry if things didn't go exactly according to plan. I just had to grind it out for the first few days, knowing that there were bound to be some problems – there always are, often apparently insuperable ones – but I had to be prepared to face them, find a way through them and not get in a flap or panic. Progress north was the only criterion and after all the months of preparation and the help and support of countless individuals and organisations, it was now down to me alone; my success or failure would be my sole responsibility.

We flew on. The scene beneath my frosted window was as grainy as an old silent movie. A forest of jagged mountain peaks clawed upwards out of the ice and snow. Between them, glaciers, their upper surfaces speckled with frost-shattered rock, slithered down to bury themselves in the sea. Everything was sharp and angular, hard and unyielding. This was a region where even the dwarf vegetation of the tundra struggles to survive, a land at the frontier of the habitable earth, stripped to its bare elements: rock, snow and ice. And beyond that lay the Arctic Ocean. In summer its dark waters are littered with ice-floes pocked with aquamarine pools of meltwater; in winter it is held in the semi-rigid embrace of the polar ice-cap.

Some visitors find the raw, elemental quality of the high Arctic landscape disturbing and even frightening; but I love it for precisely those reasons. Virtually no one has ever set foot on the majority of these mountains, let alone climbed to their summits. You could walk for weeks and see crags, hidden valleys and whole vistas that no one has ever set eyes on before. It is desolate country, of course, but has its own subtle and haunting beauty. Much of the exposed rock is chocolate brown in colour and overlaid with a delicate filigree of ice and snow, tracing the contours of even the narrowest fault-line, rock ledge or gully. The steeper slopes have a herringbone pattern caused by the constant action of the wind on the ice and snow over the cycle of the seasons, revealing the texture of the underlying rock like a rubbing of a church brass.

I had stopped even pretending to listen to the conversation now. I was deep within myself, feeling the adrenalin coursing through my body, but a prisoner of my thoughts. This was the worst moment. Despite the unimaginable commitment and costs of getting to this point, I could not have claimed to be excited by what lay ahead. Instead I was filled with dread. The idea of being left alone on the ice bothered me not one jot, but so much was riding on the weeks ahead. It was my third attempt and somehow I *had* to succeed this time. There was such a weight of hope and expectation upon me, but as yet I had taken not a single step north. The tension was almost suffocating. I felt blind-driven to set off but I was dreading those tough first days, trying to haul a near-immovable object over a near-impenetrable terrain.

It took an hour and three-quarters to reach our destination. Ward Hunt Island, three miles off the northern shore of Ellesmere Island at roughly 83°05'N, is no more than a couple of miles long and a mile or so wide. It is dominated by Walker Hill, a conical peak like an extinct volcano rising 1,360 feet from the frozen sea, with a narrow apron of ice-covered rock to the east, enclosing a shallow frozen lake. The island marks the frontier between two worlds. From the summit of Walker Hill you can look south towards a vast land mass extending for 10,000 miles, populated by billions of creatures and encompassing mountains and plains; tundra, grasslands and forests; rivers, lakes and deserts; villages, towns and great cities. To the north lies no land at all, only ice and black, frigid water. A tiny handful of creatures eke out an existence at the margins, but in the frozen heart of the ice-cap there is almost nothing but ice, snow, wind and water.

There are no shades of grey in people's reactions to this ice-world. Some polar expeditioners seem to treat their time there as a torment to be endured, and they curse every step that takes them nearer to their objective but further from the familiar landscapes and civilised comforts of home. They see the Arctic as an enemy to be fought and forced into submission and their language is full of aggressive terms: 'battle', 'conquest', 'victory' and, all too often, 'defeat'. But a few others revel in this strange and beautiful world and are compelled to return again and again for the love of the solitude, simplicity, and contemplation that it engenders.

My own relationship with the Arctic has evolved over fifteen years. Initially I was fearful of it, keeping a safe distance between 'me' in here and 'it' out there, but as I grew more competent in the day-to-day strategies and skills of surviving and travelling, I gradually let down my guard and found myself drawn to its rarefied presence. There are times, alone on the ice towards the end of a long sledging day, when I feel wholly in tune with this world – transcending normal existence, moving over the ice without conscious thought or action. Those are the moments that inform long after they have passed.

Much as I love my family and my home among the beautiful moors and tors of Dartmoor in England, I know that the Arctic Ocean will always exert a powerful pull on me. I'm there by choice, not compulsion, and I tolerate the cold, the hardship, the dangers and the backbreaking effort as a fair price to be paid for the privilege of experiencing life on the frozen ocean and seeing sights that no other human has ever seen or ever will see, for one of the wonders of the polar ice-cap is that it is ever the same but ever different.

It exists not as an immovable mass of solid ice but in a state of constant flux, as the perpetual motion, compression and distortion of the ice opens up fresh leads or crumples the ice-cap like paper. Sometimes imperceptibly, sometimes dramatically, the whole sweep of the frozen landscape changes from hour to hour and day to day, leaving an onlooker doubting the evidence of his own eyes. Two people could set off for the Pole on the same day, but even if they travelled no more than three miles apart, each could have a completely different experience. One could get fog while the other was in bright sunshine, or huge drifts of snow while the other crossed clear ice, or could get stuck in a huge rubble-field of ice, slowing him down by four or five days, while the other just missed the edge of it.

My route from Ward Hunt Island lay due north, to the North Geographic Pole, lying near the heart of the Arctic Ocean, and I would be using a chart rather than a map for navigation because this was an ocean voyage not an overland journey. My sledge was my vessel, and I was its captain, subject to the same forces – winds, tides and currents – that a yachtsman would face. But there was one crucial difference between my expedition to the Pole and a sea-voyage; in a boat you can sit motionless and still travel in the direction you want to go, on this expedition (except on the rare occasions when lucky enough to pick up a few miles of northward ice-drift) every metre of the distance to the Pole had to be won by the sweat of my brow.

There were certain givens. On a straight-line course bearing true north from Ward Hunt Island to the Pole, I knew that, to a greater or lesser extent, I would be encountering open water, rubble-fields and pressure ridges of ice, flat ice-pans and floes, and areas of recently refrozen water. I would never be more than 12 metres above sea level, nor, despite an ocean depth of 4,000 metres at the Pole, more than a metre below it – any more and I would not be coming back. Excluding wind-chill, the coldest conceivable temperature was −55°, though −50° was a more realistic probability, and the maximum +10°, though again, +5° was more likely. The highest winds were not likely to exceed fifty knots and the sea-ice was unlikely to be drifting in any direction faster than one nautical mile an hour, with the maximum drift in a twenty-four-hour period unlikely to exceed twenty miles.

Unlike a mountaineering expedition such as the ascent of Everest, where there are photographs, satellite images, sketches and written accounts of the routes and almost every metre of the way is recorded and can be studied and rehearsed, the chart for the North Pole is essentially a blank piece of paper, but for a point in the middle – the Pole – a series of equally spaced concentric circles around it – the degrees of latitude – and 360 equally spaced lines radiating out from it – the degrees of longitude. There is nothing else to record – no rocky outcrops to be avoided or used as landmarks, no mountains or hills, no islands, shallows or deeps, no shipwrecks, navigational beacons or lighthouses, no permanent features of any sort. I would just step off a beach, almost the northernmost beach in the world, and simply keep heading out to sea until I reached the North Geographic Pole – a pinprick of nothingness in the middle of nowhere.

The location of the Pole is the one constant in this morass of instability and change, but the physical features and the very ice upon which you stand, if and when you reach the Pole, are never the same as they were yesterday or will be tomorrow. Each person's experience of the Pole is therefore unique. In previous years, on other expeditions with clients, I'd found the Pole in the middle of large rubble-fields, in a small pan surrounded by large pressure ridges and, on one occasion, in the middle of a recently refrozen lead that couldn't be crossed because the ice was too thin. We had to wait until the drift had moved that ice away before we could reach the Pole.

In addition to the changing surface features, the whole

ice-cap is continually drifting, driven by ocean currents, tides and winds in an inexorable and sometimes unpredictable pattern. This imperceptible movement of the ice was the despair of dozens of early Arctic explorers. Many have recorded how they trudged endlessly on a northward course throughout a long polar day, only to discover, when they awoke the next morning and took a reading of their position, that the ice-drift had carried them away from their destination so fast that they were actually further from the Pole than they had been when they set out the morning before.

The wind is as great if not an even greater influence on this ice movement than the unseen currents and tides of the Arctic Ocean. Those Arctic gales do not simply howl across the unresisting surface of the ice; they seize on every ice-ridge, boulder and projection on the surface, driving the whole ice sheet before them, ripping it apart into ice-islands separated by leads of black, fathomless Arctic waters, or driving it together with unimaginable force, grinding it into ice-rubble, boulder-fields and mountainous compression ridges.

Those features are particularly severe north of Ward Hunt Island, where the prevailing north-westerlies bring the irresistible force of the wind-driven ice-cap into collision with the immovable shores of the first land this side of the Pole. As a result, the ice is crumpled like a vast sheet of corrugated iron for miles to the north of the island. The resultant forest of pressure ridges makes for a far harder physical – and therefore psychological – journey to the Pole than the crossing from Siberia, where the prevailing south-easterlies tend to drive the ice-sheet away from the land. Once you have completed the difficult first few miles where the ice is only intermittently strong enough to bear your weight, you reach broad expanses of new and relatively flat ice that allow fast progress, even with a fully loaded sledge. And even though it is a longer distance to the Pole from Siberia, you would normally expect to get the extra miles back because, rather like being on a moving walkway, the wind is continually moving the ice in the general direction of the Pole at a rate of about one mile a day. The harder route is from the North American side. No one had ever travelled solo and un-resupplied to the Pole from there, whereas Borge Ousland had from Siberia, so Ward Hunt Island had to be my starting point.

It isn't quite the northernmost point of the North American land mass; Cape Columbia is about ten miles closer to the Pole, but there comes a point where you are too near to Greenland. The sea off the east coast of Greenland is like a 'plug-hole' from the Arctic, and the East Greenland Current swirling down past it produces a very powerful ice-drift. To start from there would be like trying to climb up a down escalator – two steps forward and one back if you're lucky – and it's actually better to start a few miles further from the Pole at Ward Hunt Island, in the middle of a more neutral area in terms of ice-drift.

The Twin Otter forged on to meet its deadline. At this latitude the sun had only peeped over the horizon for the first time this year ten days earlier, and daylight was limited to the two hours either side of noon. Troy had to use the shadow, contrast, perspective and definition offered by that brief period of sunlight to select a suitable landing-strip on the ice. Without it, he would be bringing the plane in blind because there is no runway on the island and the wind is continually reshaping the contours of the snow. Each time they fly there, pilots have to identify a new landing strip. There are two potential sites: an area of roughly level ground and the lake, but both are covered with wind-packed snowdrifts. If a pilot tried to land 'cross-grained' to these, he would hammer the aircraft to pieces within the first few yards, because those steep-faced drifts are up to a metre high and the snow is as hard as concrete.

My first problem was evident before we had even landed. Just before we'd set out that morning, I'd seen the latest meteorological reports and satellite images, taken late the previous day. They had shown calm conditions and an absence of open water, but I asked Troy to fly ten miles north of Ward Hunt before landing, to give me an even more up-to-date idea of the general ice conditions, which can change with disconcerting rapidity. They certainly had on this occasion. I braced myself in the entranceway to the cockpit as we flew due north of the small frozen lake to the east of Walker Hill, following the route I would be taking from my starting point. We had barely crossed the Ward Hunt Ice Shelf separating the island from the polar pack-ice of the Arctic Ocean when things started to go terribly wrong. In contrast to the forecast clear weather, there was a partial overcast with stinging snow showers, and thirty-knot winds, gusting to forty knots, were scouring over the ice, stripping parts of it bare of snow-cover and dumping it in vast drifts on the downwind side of each pressure ridge and boulder-field. That was routine for the Arctic, but what horrified me was the effect that the winds had had on the ice-cap itself. In the slightly murky off-white of the middle-distance a darkening strip was emerging; and as it came into focus, another one, and then a third, appeared in the distance beyond it.

Three vast leads had been opened up by the winds that were now battering the plane. Each was half a mile to a mile across, with the water showing black as ink against the surrounding ice. The first was perhaps five miles north of Ward Hunt, the others at roughly three-mile intervals beyond it. They ran parallel to each other, aligned SSW–NNE across the course I had to follow to reach the Pole, and even looking down from 5,000 feet, I could see no end to them; they extended out of sight in both directions. On the open water between the pans of ice, the gale was ripping the crests from the waves and hurling them downwind in long white streamers of spume and spray. Even supposing I could make progress north in temperatures that, including the wind-chill factor, would be the equivalent of −60 or −70 °C, there was no possibility of circumventing those leads and, even with my immersion suit and my 'lilo' for the sledge, there was no way of crossing the murderously choppy black waters in such a wind. In flat calm conditions I would have struggled to swim half a mile in my bulky immersion suit, dragging my fully laden sledge behind me, but in this maelstrom, I would have been submerged and drowned like a rat in seconds.

It was a devastating blow. One of my operating principles was that I would be taking what was effectively a straight line north. In practice, in the minute-to-minute process of weaving along the line of least resistance for your sledge, you're hardly ever heading true north, and certainly not in big rubble-fields, where you're forced to detour around endless piles of ice-blocks the size of juggernauts, but the few degrees east or west of due north average out over the course of the day. I had been sure that the open water that had caused me such problems on my previous solo expeditions would be at worst an inconvenience; I would simply cross it using the equipment and techniques I had developed and continue on an unwavering line north. I was confident that only huge expanses of ice too thin to ski across and yet too thick to swim through would cause me serious delays. I had evaluated every possibility – or so I had thought – and it had seemed to me that only a right-angle fracture of my leg, coma or death could stop me moving north. Now that conceit had been blown out of the water before I'd even started and I was staring down at not one, but three impassable obstacles.

I tried not to show it to my companions, but I felt sick with anxiety, not helped by the violent lurches of the plane as Troy turned back for the island and began searching for a safe landing strip. It took me several minutes to weigh all these factors and reach my decision. Shortly before I had been gearing myself up, impatient to hit the ice and get some miles under my belt, but now I knew that I could not set off in these conditions and would simply have to wait out the storm. Friends, sponsors and supporters were all willing me on, a *Times* journalist was there to record my departure and now I was going to be sitting twiddling my thumbs until the conditions improved. When the winds fell and the ice technically referred to as 'light *nilas*' had formed (its opacity indicates that it's safe to walk on; 'dark *nilas*', through which the dark water of the ocean can still be seen, tends to be too fragile to bear a person's weight), I would be able to cross the leads and move north but until then, I would simply have to mark time at Ward Hunt Island.

Although it is completely uninhabited, there is a building there, a stout hut, shaped like a recumbent 'D' and weathered to the grey colour of dried sealskin. It was recently renovated by the Canadian National Park Service as a refuge for icebound mariners, scientists, travellers and anyone else in need of shelter in this impossibly remote region, around 2,500 miles north of Ottawa and 1,250 miles closer to the Pole than Anchorage, Alaska. That hut would have to serve as my forward base until the weather relented.

I put the best public face I could on the decision and, as Troy began his final approach, I shouted to my team over the noise of the engine that I'd take the opportunity that the storm was providing for some much needed rest. I'd wait at Ward Hunt Island until the winds abated, acclimatising and getting as much sleep as possible. I was less sure than I tried to sound about how restful life was going to be. Over the previous fifteen years I had made a score of expeditions to the Arctic Ocean, both guiding parties of clients and undertaking two unsuccessful solo attempts on the Pole, but, in all that time, I had never had such an inauspicious beginning.

I could feel the aircraft being thrown around by the wind as we came in to land. Snow was swirling and gusting around us and visibility near ground level was no more than 200 metres; only a very skilful and experienced pilot could have identified a safe landing strip and then put the aircraft down on it. Troy taxied to a halt and, as the co-pilot pushed the door slightly ajar, it was all that he could do to hang on to it with both hands to stop it from being torn from his grasp and smashed backwards into the side of the fuselage. Wearing all my gear, I clumsily climbed down the portable ladder and stood on the ice, feeling about as out of tune with this environment as it was possible to be. I had to remind myself that this was how it always felt when transferring from the controlled space of an aircraft into the high Arctic wilderness.

It took four of us to transfer the fully loaded sledge from the fuselage floor, at shoulder-height, down to the ground. Although the sledge was built to withstand impacts out on the ice, one careless movement while working it out of the confined space of the fuselage could easily have ripped off a runner or punctured a hole in the Kevlar and glass-fibre body. Everyone wanted to be helpful, but a split-second's inattention could have jeopardised the whole expedition, so it's fair to say that I micro-managed its short journey to the ground. I also had to ensure that every single piece of equipment made it out of the aircraft. If I left anything behind, whether it was a rucksack full of technical gear or a single battery for a tracking beacon, it was going to cost a fortune to have it couriered back to me by the same Twin Otter.

Whenever I caught the eye of Ian, Martin or Ginny, I intercepted a look that contained a mixture of their own instinctive response to this extraordinary landscape, partially overridden by a desire to convey a message of 'You can do it' to me. I suspected that their private thoughts might have been the opposite. Ginny was putting on her bravest face, but she looked on the verge of tears, and Ian and Martin soon had a strong reason for wavering in their previously unshakeable belief in me. They immediately offered to drag the sledge the 100 metres to the doorway of the hut. Martin grabbed the trace rope, Ian slung the harness over his shoulder and they took up the weight of the sledge and pulled. It did not move an inch, as if in those few seconds its runners had become forever frozen to the ground. They both lunged forwards again, straining every sinew, and it grudgingly moved about six inches, then stopped again. This was the first time they had ever had the chance to feel what it was like to pull a sledge weighing 275 pounds – more than 19 stone – over hard-frozen, flat snow and ice. Nothing was said and this time they didn't meet my eye, but I could tell that, in that moment, the full enormity of what I was about to undertake had hit them. They coordinated their next combined lunge and before the sledge's slight momentum was lost they were hauling hard towards the hut.

I didn't offer to help them. That wasn't just laziness on my part; I made it a policy never to try to pull a fully laden sledge in front of any members of my base team, let alone a journalist, because you have to exert so much energy just to move it at all, even on the flat, and you go so painfully slowly that I knew if they saw me struggling with it they'd think 'He's never going to do it.' If I encountered problems later on and was on the phone to them, they'd be thinking to themselves, 'Well, of course, it looked bloody hard when I saw you pulling it. I'm not surprised you're struggling.' If anything went wrong, I needed their support and encouragement, not negativity, so I preferred to keep them in blissful ignorance while I exuded an air of confidence and omnipotence, as if the sledge would be no more troublesome to me than a trolley full of groceries in a supermarket car park. It would also have been depressing for me to be trying to drag the sledge around when I wasn't even hauling it closer to the Pole. It would just fill my head with negative thoughts – 'God, this is heavy. Have I really got to drag this over 400 miles?' – when I needed above all else to stay positive. I'd got the sledge as light as I could, and that was remarkably light by the standards of previous unsupported expeditions.

A team can travel with a lighter load per person because they can share some of the items between them; you only need one gun, one radio and one tent whether you're one man or three. Being part of a team also helps if someone is injured or in poor health, because his sledge-load can then be shared among the others; if there is a technical problem or strategic issue to be resolved, there is a bigger pool of brains to solve the problem and more pairs of hands to fix it; and they can also share the routine work. When you're on your own, you have to multi-task, and it would be hard to overstate the physical and psychological impact of the additional workload and all the extra kilos that you have to carry. It's not just some little thought nagging at you – 'Oh, I'm just carrying a little bit of extra weight' – it's making its presence felt every step of the journey. Another downside of being solo rather than in a team is that, throughout the rest of your life, there will never be anyone with whom you can share the memories of that experience. No one's ever going to know. The only people who can even get close to understanding are people who've been out there and done something similar.

However, there were benefits to making a solo expedition which, for me at least, far outweighed the problems and pitfalls. The experience was all the purer for not having anybody else there, and what I put in, I got out, whether it was in terms of planning and customising equipment, or sledge-hauling and covering the distance. And even though I was on my own, I was hauling less weight towards the Pole than any solo expedition had ever done before – not that other polar travellers took inessentials with them, but I was using all the experience and knowledge I had built up over fifteen years to trim even the basic necessities to the bone.

I was taking an educated gamble, if you like, on how fast I could reach the Pole, but that also meant that I had less margin for error on food and fuel, and every day that I was not travelling north, I was consuming scarce and vital supplies. I also knew that once I set off on the ice, I would go up a couple of gears. All the extraneous thoughts and pressures would melt away and I would be completely and utterly 'in the zone', as athletes call it. My whole focus, the only reason I was alive, would be to haul that sledge north, and on nothing more than pure will and adrenalin I knew that I could achieve feats of strength and endurance out on the ice that would be beyond me in any other circumstances.

Ian and Martin gratefully laid down the harness and traces outside the hut and I dragged open the part-frozen door and peered into the gloomy interior of the hut. I had landed on Ward Hunt Island on numerous occasions on previous expeditions, but each time I had set off for the north at once. This was the first time I had ever entered the hut. The temperature inside its single room was almost exactly the same as outside (−33 °C) and the ceiling was thick with hoar-frost, but the hut was a refuge from the wind-chill and for that alone I was grateful; I'd be fine in here till the gale abated. The whole team, together with the two pilots, shuffled in behind me and we pulled up chairs around the formica-topped central table. I found myself instantly switching into host-mode, dusting ice particles from the seats, lighting a couple of candles for the table, offering tea from my flask and some biscuits that I'd trousered at Eureka. Everyone else seemed in shock. They simply could not believe the desolation of this hut, the severity of the weather and the horrors that lay ahead for me on the Arctic Ocean; and all this was somehow being made even more unsettling for them because here I was trying to make them feel more at home. It's fair to say that the conversation was stilted.

Troy kept casting an eye towards the fading light outside and at last he said, 'Well, Pen, I guess we may as well head off and leave you to it.' There were muffled grunts of agreement, the chairs were pushed back and they rose to leave. I shook hands with the two pilots first and as they made their way back to the plane, I kissed Ginny, whose eyes were now brimming with tears. Martin made a gallant attempt at humour and then turned for the door leaving Ian and me alone. Ian simply said: 'I know I couldn't do this, Pen, but if anyone can, knowing you as I do, it will be you. Good luck, mate.' And then he too was gone.

The plane was only partially visible between gusts of swirling snow. I stood in the hut doorway, catching glimpses of the misted figures behind the aircraft's tiny windows. I heard the engines start up and a few seconds later it lurched forward, wing-tips rocking violently in the wind as it taxied back to the downwind end of the strip. Now invisible in the white-out, I waited to see it one last time. Suddenly and silently, the noise of the engines snatched away in the wind, it swept upwards, thrown around by the gales as it banked to begin the long journey south. I knew that they would be looking down at me, and were probably thinking that I cut a rather forlorn figure, alone at the heart of this maelstrom of wind and snow. I remained standing in the doorway, a hand raised in farewell, but almost at once the clouds obscured the plane from view.

I was now completely alone, the only human being not just on Ward Hunt Island, but on the whole of the western polar ice-cap as well, for no other expeditions were being mounted from the North American side that year. I had thousands of square miles – 10 per cent of the earth's surface – entirely to myself. I turned and went inside the hut. As I shut the door, ice-shards fell from the eaves with a noise like shattering glass. The first thing I did was to lay my shotgun, fully loaded, on the table. I was only a handful of miles from open water and, as at Resolute Bay, where there was open water, there would be seals, polar bears preying on them and Arctic foxes scavenging on the seal carcasses. From now until the moment I was airlifted off the ice-cap, the shotgun would always remain loaded and within easy reach. That done, I paused to look around my tiny kingdom. The wooden walls of the hut shielded me from the force of the wind, though they creaked and groaned under its relentless impact, seeming to breathe asthmatically in response to the lulls and gusts, with each creak of the straining wooden structure followed by a momentary eerie silence. But

I was far from unnerved. Like a monk's retreat, the hut had everything needed for a quiet and contemplative existence without the intrusion of the outer world; and in my eyes at least, it had, in spades, the property-hunter's most important attraction: location, location, location.

The hut was your basic model: a single small window at the back and a reinforced glass panel in the door allowing in a modicum of natural light. The bare wood floor was scuffed and scarred by the boots of countless polar travellers and the planking gave off the faintest hint of pine resin. I found that familiar smell hanging in the cold, still air oddly welcoming and reassuring. A couple of chain-sprung beds with thick foam mattresses stood against one wall, there was a table and six chairs, and a kitchen area lined with wooden shelves on which stood a collection of tinned foods and dehydrated rations of all nations, left by previous visitors, some dating back at least thirty years. They would probably still have been perfectly edible, but I left them all – even the Fortnum & Mason's Gentleman's Relish – for some more needy future visitor and confined myself to the spare rations I had brought with me: some sandwiches, an orange and an apple, and a carton of fruit juice. A visitors' book lay on the table, signed by every traveller who had paused at this hut over the decades, but I decided to save the pleasure of reading it until I had eaten and had a night's sleep.

There was a cast-iron, pot-bellied stove at one end of the room, but as I was not in an emergency situation, I did not waste the fuel stored in a drum behind the hut, and left the stove unlit as I set about tidying my temporary home. I swept the broken ice, the patterned snow from the tread of boots and the accumulated spindrift of the long winter into a pile and took it out on the resident shovel. I rummaged in the sledge for my sleeping-bag and filled a couple of plastic builders' rubble sacks with fresh snow to melt for drinking water and cooking, then took them inside and closed and barred the door. I wasn't expecting any visitors to come calling.

The light was fading fast now and the temperature falling even lower as night came on. I lit my camping stove, and even though it only took the edge off the bitter cold in its immediate vicinity, the glow of its flickering, brilliant red and blue flames transformed the hut from abandoned building to friendly refuge. I let the stove roar away as I ate my re-hydrated chicken curry supper and drank a cup of tea. By now a circle of frost directly above the stove was melting but everywhere else was still deep-frozen, and at floor-level the temperature was still −30° – cold enough to put my booted feet at risk of frostbite. I had no fuel to waste and as soon as I had finished eating, I extinguished the stove, stripped down to my thermal base-layer, and climbed into my sleeping-bag on the bed. I lay there thinking back over what should have been my first day on the ice. There was nothing I could do until the weather broke but I tried to make a positive out of a negative: I was in a place, the Arctic, that I loved above all others, and after the stress of the months of preparation and the last-minute crises that always arise, no matter how carefully you prepare, it was something of a relief to have this period of enforced inactivity to rest and reflect, and what I needed most of all at this moment was the former. I closed my eyes and was asleep in seconds.

I woke twenty-two hours later. It was four in the afternoon. The frosted synthetic fabric of my sleeping-bag crackled as I turned over, stretched and yawned. My nose was numb, and the air felt very cold around my face – the only unprotected part of my body. I drifted back to sleep to the sound of the walls of the hut, still flexing in the rhythmic pounding of the gale-force blasts, and woke up again at six. It was pitch dark – outside and inside. I had a torch for in-tent use but its stark, blue, short-range light only added to the feeling of deep cold, and instead I reached for the head-torch that gave a softer, warmer, yellow-tinged light that was much more likely to entice me out of my sleeping-bag.

As soon as I got up, I cooked my breakfast porridge on the stove, made a cup of tea and then sat down at the table and began to read the visitors' book, my breath fogging in the freezing air. The first entry dated from over twenty years earlier, the last was as recent as the previous summer. Not every traveller who had passed through Ward Hunt had stopped to record his thoughts – like myself in previous years, many set straight off over the ice without even entering the hut – and, frustratingly, virtually none of those who had outlined their hopes, dreams and fears on those pages had ever returned to record their triumphs or disappointments. Lifted out by air, they had flown over the top of Ward Hunt Island with no more than a passing glance. And some had never come back from the ice-cap at all; the Arctic is a graveyard for more than men's dreams.

Men have been voyaging to the Arctic since Tudor times, when the search for the North-West Passage sent Frobisher, Davis and other explorers to the region. Frobisher alone made three voyages there, all remembered in perfect detail centuries later in the Inuit oral traditions, but he and his peers were obsessed with the search for gold and a feasible trade route to the Pacific, and, since the Pole offered neither of these, the idea of reaching it just to be able to say that they were the first men to have done so would have struck such practical, piratical men as the greatest possible folly.

Only one man, Henry Hudson in 1607, set off with the specific intention of sailing to the North Pole, believing that he would find there a pillar of black basalt rising from the warm, calm waters of a temperate sea. He did not achieve his goal and over the following centuries the polar regions were largely left to their traditional inhabitants. National and imperial rivalries centred on trade and territories, not on wastelands of ice and snow, and there was little serious exploration of the Pole until Admiral Sir John Franklin's expedition to the North-West Passage in 1845, almost 370 years after Frobisher's last voyage there.

Franklin, accompanied by the cream of the British fleet's officers and men, was extraordinarily well prepared, with seven years' food supplies and even 1,000 bound volumes of *Punch* to read during the long polar night, but his expedition was a disaster. Franklin, his ships, the *Erebus* and the *Terror*, and the 136 crewmen all disappeared without trace, and their fate remained one of the great mysteries of the nineteenth century. But by his disappearance Franklin had reawakened interest in polar exploration and a series of expeditions were launched in the succeeding years, ostensibly to solve the mystery of Franklin's fate, though many were far more focused on the exploration of the frozen north and the conquest of the Pole.

Over the rest of that century and into the next, a succession of explorers – Kane, Parry, Koldewey, Hayes, Hall, Nares, De Long, Greely, Nansen, Cagni, Peary and Cook – driven more by patriotic fervour than the scientific aims that all publicly espoused, steadily pushed back the polar frontier: to 82°N by the 1870s, 83°N in the 1880s and 86°N in the 1890s. Imperial rivalries were subsumed into the quest, and national prestige and fortunes were staked on the outcome. Some expeditions, like that of the Briton George Nares, were on a grand scale and conducted with military discipline, others, like that of the American Charles Francis Hall, drew on the knowledge and fieldcraft of the native Inuit, but still none succeeded in planting a flag at the North Geographic Pole. The tracks of those who tried were often marked with the graves of men killed by hypothermia, scurvy, gangrene or even poisoning after eating the livers of polar bears, which contain toxic levels of vitamin A, or their flesh which, since over half of all polar bears are infected, often leads to trichinosis.

Some men believed reaching the Pole to be impossible. Others condemned it as a pointless folly, a journey to nowhere with nothing to be gained, and, in the face of the widespread ignorance of what would actually be found there, still others concocted bizarre theories to fill this gap in human knowledge.

Some claimed that the Pole was marked by Henry Hudson's pillar of black basalt, others that it lay unmarked in the middle of an open and temperate polar sea and still others posited the incredible but widely supported theory that there was a huge hole at the Pole connecting the outer earth with a series of seven inner earths in which a range of pallid subterranean beings laboured in permanent Stygian gloom.

Against this background of ill-informed theorising and wild speculation, a handful of men set out to discover the true facts for themselves. There was a time when giants roamed the earth, and one such was Fridtjof Nansen. I have never had heroes in my life, but I have looked up to a few special men like Jacques Cousteau, Francis Chichester and, above all others, Fridtjof Nansen. His life embraced everything that a great explorer's should. He was one of the first Europeans to land on the east coast of Greenland – and that was as late as 1888 – and make contact with the indigenous Inuit in the Tasiilaq region. Against all manner of obstacles, mainly put before him by the 'experts' of the time, he made the first crossing of the Greenland ice-cap – the largest in the northern hemisphere and second only to the Antarctic ice-cap. He then devised an even more audacious plan, to be the first to reach the North Pole, exploiting the few known threads of information about the workings of the Arctic Ocean.

His plan involved designing and commissioning an 'ice-proof' boat, the *Fram*, designed to 'slip like an eel out of the embrace of the ice'. The *Fram* was braced internally with crossbeams and clad in South American greenheart timber – as strong and flexible as any found on earth. It had prows at both bow and stern and a curved hull that gave the ice nothing on which to gain purchase. As it closed around the ship, the *Fram* rode upwards until it was virtually resting on the ice. The living quarters were triple-skinned and insulated with a mixture of sawdust, felt, cork and reindeer hair.

Having built his ideal boat, Nansen then deliberately steered into the sea-ice off the New Siberian Islands on 25 September 1893 and allowed the *Fram* to become icebound. Over the next three years it was carried in an epic drift right across the polar ice-cap, but on 14 March 1895, Nansen's restless spirit and his growing certainty that however long the *Fram* remained sealed in the ice, the drift would never take his ship directly to the Pole, persuaded him to set off on skis with one companion, Hjalmar Johanssen, leaving the captain of the *Fram* to complete the odyssey across the ice-cap and bring the ship home. Carrying 100 days' supplies, Nansen and Johanssen would meanwhile attempt to reach as far north as possible, perhaps even to the Pole itself. Their early progress was rapid but, as they went further north, ice conditions deteriorated and the southward drift of the ice negated much of their advance. As their supplies ran low, they were forced to call a halt at 86°13'N – three degrees further than any man had ever gone before – and make their way south.

Nansen's only plan was to make for Franz Josef Land on the edge of the Arctic Ocean and either travel down the coast in the kayaks they were carrying, or find a ship to take them to safety. The fact that no more than one or two ships a year passed by that remote and empty island group deterred him not at all. After an epic, 146-day trek over the ice, Nansen and Johanssen reached the edge of the polar pack-ice and saw land beyond a few miles of open ocean. They crossed the water in their kayaks but were then forced to pass the winter of 1895–6 in a crude hut they christened 'The Hole', living off seal, walrus and polar bear meat. In the spring they resumed their southward journey and, by sheer luck, on 17 June 1896 they encountered Frederick Jackson near Cape Flora on Franz Josef Land. He was a member of an English Arctic expedition, the only other living souls for hundreds of miles around. When Nansen and Johannssen reached home, they discovered that the *Fram* had also emerged unharmed from its three-year sojourn in the ice. Witnesses reported that the men of the ship had returned from that frozen world like men who had made a voyage to the moon. They played like children with pebbles on a beach, their eyes full of wonder at the world to which they had returned.

Nansen's sixteen-month journey on foot across the ice is one of the greater feats of human endurance ever recorded – he even survived a prolonged swim in the Arctic Ocean to rescue their kayaks after they were washed away. He had an iron determination to succeed, but also a fatalism that allowed him to look with equanimity on the possibility of failure or even his own death. Failure would bring 'only disappointed human hopes, nothing more. And even if we perish, what will it matter in the endless cycles of eternity?'

A decade after Nansen's incredible journey, two rival American teams, led by Robert Peary and Frederick Cook, appeared to have resolved the issue of what lay at the North Pole. Both led expeditions to the Arctic between 1907 and 1909 and each returned claiming to have reached the Pole and dismissing his rival's claims. In turn both were then feted by some and derided by others. Peary, who had devoted his life to the conquest of the Pole, was far more widely believed at the time, but the arguments continue even to this day. Peary's supporters still claim that their man reached the Pole, while the members of the Frederick A. Cook Society continue to try and resurrect the damaged reputation of their almost certainly mendacious hero.

Roald Amundsen had been planning his own expedition to the North Pole, but having apparently been beaten to his goal by Peary, he switched his attention to the South Pole and reached it in 1911, ahead of the rival, doomed expedition of Robert Falcon Scott. In the 1920s, with renewed doubts cast on the claims of Peary and Cook, Amundsen set out to reach the North Pole using the newest technology of the age. His attempt to fly there in 1925 with Lincoln Ellsworth ended with their aircraft suffering engine failure at 88°N. Undaunted, they made a remarkable trek south to safety and, in company with the Italian aviator Umberto Nobile, they then made a successful flight by airship right across the polar ice-cap the following year. Along the way they became the first men to prove beyond dispute that they had laid eyes on the North Pole and were able to describe its geographical features: sea-ice, snow and open water.

The Russians Otto Schmidt and Ivan Papanin overflew the Pole in 1937 and landed at 89°26'N to set up the first polar scientific station. Over the following 274 days, they drifted with the ice for over 1,400 nautical miles. The US nuclear submarine *Nautilus* passed under the Pole in 1958, and in 1959 the US submarine *Skate* surfaced through the ice there; but, for the most part, interest in surface travel in the polar regions had waned after Scott and Amundsen's epic race to the South Pole and there were very few expeditions. No one reached the South Pole again until 1954, and there is a similar gap in the history of exploration of the North Pole, between Peary and Cook before the First World War and the new era of exploration that began in the late 1960s. A generation of exploration didn't happen and, perhaps as a result, I tend to feel disconnected from the polar pioneers.

The Briton Wally Herbert was the first man to reach the North Geographic Pole on foot while crossing the entire Arctic Ocean (although an American team led by Ralph Plaisted had reached the Pole on motorised snowmobiles in 1968). With three team-mates and using dog teams and a series of planned resupplies by aircraft, Wally Herbert set off in February 1968 from Point Barrow on the north coast of Alaska, one of the longest routes to the North Pole. He and his companions duly reached the Pole on 5 April 1969 and then continued the incredible journey to reach the far side of the Arctic Ocean on 29 May, before being picked up by a ship on the edge of the ice-cap off northern Spitsbergen. Yet this incredible expedition was virtually ignored by the media and therefore remained unknown to the broader public because Wally had the misfortune to reunite with his support vessel and return home while the world's attention was focused on man's first landing on the moon. The dubious claims of Peary and Cook still have their adherents, but Wally Herbert is the first man indisputably to have reached the Pole on foot, a feat for which he was recently – and very belatedly – knighted.

The frequency of polar expeditions has increased markedly since the mid-1980s and in the 1990s not a year went by without at least one expedition, and often several. Some border on the bizarre, like that of the Japanese Shinji Kazamas, who reached the Pole by motorbike in 1987 aided by resupplies and a large support team. Others are run by guides for adventurers seeking to experience the world's ultimate destinations; yet others, ticking off the Poles and the great mountain summits like package tourists scurrying from Buckingham Palace to Windsor Castle, attract the description 'explorer', which is perhaps over-stating the case. More often than not, such people seem to actively dislike the polar experience, enduring the privations, then hurrying on to their next target without a backward glance; but there are other polar expeditioners, like the Norwegian Borge Ousland, the Belgian Alain Hubert and the Russian Misha Malakhov – and I count myself among them – who love and are committed to the Arctic for itself. They travel there not with the purpose of repeating what others have already done, but of expanding our awareness and understanding of the polar environment and of the nature and extent of human physical and psychological endurance . . . and the Arctic still tests human beings to their absolute limits.

Much is often made of the differences between the clothing, equipment and rations of the early explorers and those of today. Every modern item, from the rations we eat to the clothes we wear and the equipment we use, is undoubtedly better than those available to our predecessors, and all those cumulative gains certainly make life less tough and dangerous than it was for them, but modern polar travellers have also used those advantages to push ever onward in the only way man has ever done – to the brink. Explorers of all generations have always sought to employ the most up-to-date, state-of-the-art clothing, equipment and supplies that their researches and funding have allowed. If satellite-driven facilities had been available a century ago, Nansen, Scott, Amundsen and the rest would have been using them.

It is easy to conclude that the two biggest advantages we have over, say, the Golden Age of Exploration around the turn of the twentieth century – communications and aircraft support – have reduced the level of risk to the point where travels in the polar regions seem almost too comfortable and safe to be worthy of the title 'expedition', but that is to ignore two potent factors. On the Arctic Ocean, most of the things that are going to kill you will do so in minutes, like falling through thin ice and drowning, being mauled to death by a polar bear or poisoned by carbon monoxide from the unavoidable use of a stove in the tent, suffering a serious medical condition like peritonitis, a stroke or heart attack, or experiencing a major crush injury as a heavy sledge descends, out of control, down a pressure ridge. Regardless of the urgency of the situation, no amount of satellite phones, high-frequency radios, tracking beacons or emergency transmitters will enable a support plane, based many hundreds of miles away, to reach your position in minutes, and probably not even hours. A delay of twelve to forty-eight hours is more realistic and, if poor weather occurs, its arrival could be delayed by a week or more.

I'm very aware of those who have gone before me and in whose footsteps I tread – not just the giants of earlier times, but those in my own lifetime like Sir Wally Herbert and Sir Ranulph Fiennes, Britain's foremost polar traveller following the epic circumpolar navigation by snowmobile, achieved by his Transglobe Expedition from 1979 to 1982. Fiennes was one of the instigators of the concept of an unsupported journey to the North Pole and it was his repeated attempts to prove its viability, and his reports of the horrendous conditions he encountered on the sea-ice, that helped to inspire me and a generation of other unsupported expeditioners in the 1990s right through to the present day. Sir Ranulph's example sparked the thought in my head: could it actually be done on foot, pulling everything you needed behind you – a 'purer', more challenging version of what had already been achieved? There would be no resupplies, no outside interventions, no other people that I could rely on or blame, and just one question to be answered: could I do it?

After Wally Herbert and Ranulph Fiennes, the next person I became aware of was Naomi Uemura, a Japanese mountaineer and polar explorer who made a wonderful journey with a dog team in 1978 from Ward Hunt Island to the North Geographic Pole, employing seven resupplies on the way. The next solo success was by the Frenchman Dr Jean-Louis Etienne in 1986. He also started from Ward Hunt Island, this time without dogs and pulling the sledge himself, and he had five resupplies. Most recently, in 2001, the Japanese traveller Hyoichi Kono made it from Canada to the Pole with just one resupply. In 1994, Borge Ousland made the first unsupported expedition to the Pole, travelling solo from the Siberian side of the Arctic Ocean. But despite many other attempts, including two by myself, at least one classic North Pole challenge remained: a solo, unsupported trek from the Canadian coast to the North Pole.

Within the polar community, the terms 'unsupported' or 'unaided', 'without resupply' and 'without aircraft support' all have slightly different connotations. The most all encompassing is 'without aircraft support' – the style of expedition that I was undertaking. Like every other polar traveller, you are going to be put down by an aircraft at your starting point and picked up by one from the Pole, but you are not going to have aircraft support for any reason between those two points. If you have some big problem and have to be picked up, fine, but to retain unsupported status, you must then start the whole journey all over again.

If you are going to be resupplied, there is no limit to your intake of calories – you eat as much as you need and your body is not going to take the pummelling it suffers when you're carrying all your food for the entire expedition and making a trade-off between food required and weight to be hauled. Inevitably you take less food than you would in other circumstances and suffer as a result, and you have to take greater care of yourself and your kit if you have no recourse to any back-up. Those both lead to slower progress, but the main thing is the weight of your sledge. People often have a very light sledge for the first fifteen to twenty days so they can rattle over those big pressure ridges north of Ward Hunt Island and then get a resupply, and that makes the whole scale of the undertaking dramatically different.

'Without resupply' requires that you do not have any food or fuel or equipment brought in to you, but it leaves open the question of whether anything from video tapes and redundant equipment to injured or exhausted team members can be taken out by aircraft. Amateur polar travellers or adventurers don't necessarily appreciate or even care about such distinctions, but there is a serious point underlying them. If someone is seriously injured then obviously no one would argue against flying them out, but in my view the expedition cannot be considered unsupported unless the remaining team members return to the starting point and begin again.

The reason is obvious; a team member may have suffered a genuine injury, but equally he might merely have fallen out with the team leader, or been used in the same way as a pacemaker in a long-distance race, or a Sherpa on Everest – someone to do the donkey-work and then step aside to let others reach the goal. There is no way of proving that it wasn't the plan all along to lose that spare person once he'd done his job of carrying your supplies for you. Taking it to its logical extreme, once the principle is breached there is nothing to stop someone from using human mules to sledge-haul his supplies almost all the way to the Pole, while he walks alongside unencumbered like a man going for a Sunday stroll. It is patently ludicrous to put that expedition in the same category as someone who drags his own supplies every step of the way, without help from any other person.

That challenge had dominated my adult life, but I knew that, even when it had finally been achieved, whether by myself or someone else, the story would not end. Progress is part of the human condition, and team and individual expeditions will continue to push back the limits of human experience. The incremental advances may be smaller and, as time goes on, they will probably become harder and harder to achieve as the human frame is pushed towards its limits, but they will go on.

Although I realise that the wider public are unlikely to be troubled by such nice distinctions, I have always been extremely uncomfortable at being described as 'an explorer' rather than a polar traveller. My efforts are not in the same league as those of Sir Wally Herbert on the Arctic Ocean, Henry 'Gino' Watkins in Greenland, and Captain Robert Scott in Antarctica, who mapped huge tracts of our planet – and Watkins and Scott both paid the ultimate price for their explorations of the earth's wild places. How I wish, like those great past explorers, that I could have stood on the shores of the Arctic Ocean looking north, wondering what lands and what phenomena I might find. But I know that the earth is round – or, more precisely, an oblate spheroid – and that no bizarre beings lurk at the North Pole; therefore that feeling of profound anticipation about what might lie over the horizon can never be recaptured.

So it's fatuous even to think about making comparisons between present-day polar expeditioners and men like Scott, Amundsen, Shackleton and Nansen. They are the gods of polar exploration and I see them as being almost in a different geological era from mine. There was no plane waiting to air-drop them supplies or lift them out if they got into difficulties, and I adore their sublimely gracious and eloquent accounts, packed with detailed and valuable observations, and can only look with awe upon what they achieved.

The only real point of contact between those men and modern polar travellers is that, in however modest a way, we are working in the same continuum. Our modern expeditions are ever more extreme and they have the potential to advance public awareness of the polar environment and its vital role within the complex and interdependent natural systems of our planet. To make any greater claims for them would be ridiculous, but the process will go on. I certainly don't want to be the last in the line and I would gladly offer my assistance to others, if they wanted my help in developing the concept of 'Alpine strikes' or other ideas. The one certainty is that someone else will push the boundary back further. The next generation will perhaps be reaching the Pole in thirty days rather than sixty-four, and one day someone will do it in as little as twenty days or even ten.

As I turned the frost-stiffened, brittle and yellowing pages of the visitors' book at Ward Hunt, I found myself brooding about what had happened to all those other expeditioners whose names were recorded in this book left in one of the most remote habitations on earth. These were kindred spirits, perhaps drawn by the same forces and impulses that had led me here, but though some of the names were familiar, many were unknown. I didn't know if they had succeeded in their aims or failed, or even whether they had lived or died.

I read and re-read the entries. Some said they were doing it for their country, others for themselves alone; some sounded full of themselves, some more nervous, trying to appease the gods or anticipate the dangers that might await them out on the ice. Some of the entries were dispassionate or utterly prosaic – a brief note of date, time, weather and ice conditions – and others were emotional, even lyrical, as the men, and a handful of women, struggled to convey what had brought them to this place and what was driving them on into the void beyond.

I began to wonder what I should write; how I would explain the chain of events that had also led me to this lonely, icebound island at the edge of a frozen sea.

PART ONE

I

Why?

That's the question everyone always asks me. Perhaps it all goes back to Enid Wigley. In 1912 Captain Robert Falcon Scott – Scott of the Antarctic – froze to death in his tent along with his companions on their heartbroken trek back across the ice, having been beaten to the South Pole by Roald Amundsen. Scott left a wife, Kathleen, and a son, Peter, who was two years old when his father set out on his final, fateful journey. Kathleen Scott had links with the Bloomsbury set, and was a sculptor and an intellectual, free-thinking and very remarkable woman – the list of her admirers and suitors reads like a roll-call of the great and the good of that era. Tormented by the belief that tales of his father's exploits would inevitably inspire her son to follow in Scott's footsteps, she was determined that, if so, he was going to be tough enough to survive the exposure to extreme cold that had claimed her husband's life.

As a result, she hired a young nanny, Enid Wigley, and gave her strict instructions: Peter was to be inured to the cold by exposing him to the elements, summer and winter, for progressively longer and longer periods, wearing less and less clothing. As a result, he rarely wore shoes throughout his childhood and was encouraged and even compelled to play outside, even in the snows and frosts of winter. This harsh conditioning regime was followed for five years, between the ages of two and seven, and though it may have shocked many onlookers, it certainly appears to have had the desired effect.

Rather than a polar explorer, Peter (later Sir Peter) Scott became a celebrated conservationist, wildfowl expert and a founder of the Worldwide Fund for Nature. His passion was for the wildfowl of the Arctic tundra and he only went to the Antarctic once in his life, but my father showed me several pictures of Peter Scott: on the deck of a ship ploughing through the Barents Sea, binoculars raised to watch a migrating skein of whooper swans, at his easel sketching red-breasted geese on the Siberian tundra and bracing a camera to his body by the foot of a cliff to film nesting barnacle geese in Greenland. In every case he was wearing only a short-sleeved, Aertex shirt, while those around him were huddled in layers of warm clothing, scarves and mufflers.

When her charge had grown up, Nanny Wigley sought fresh employment and in time was hired to look after a young boy named Nigel Hadow – my father. She never had to apply her tried and tested hardship regime to him but did fill his head with Scott and Amundsen's race to the South Pole and tales of the other great explorers. When he grew up, my father in turn decided that when he had a son, he was going to toughen him up by the same process and, as my father's first-born, I had the dubious fortune to be the beneficiary of that decision.

I was born on 26 February 1962. A numerologist once told me that palindromic dates like 26.2.62 are highly portentous . . . though of what, she didn't say. My Dad was a pig farmer at the time at a place called Bog Hall in the Scottish Highlands, but we lived nearby in an old manse set in a beautiful, very quiet valley near Gleneagles. The house had the curious distinction of being the largest rectory, of the smallest church, in Scotland. The old family retainer Nanny Wigley, by then well into her seventies, was recruited to supervise my early upbringing and under her critical eye, my father applied her spartan, 'patents pending' programme for the first few years of my life. I had the added misfortune of being born in an area where the winters were ferocious and even the summers were often cold enough to send southern visitors scurrying for cover, but it made no difference to the conditioning regime. I was out in all weathers, barefoot and dressed as if it was a balmy summer's day.

I was entered in a bonny baby competition at the local Highland Games and won first prize simply because, thanks to my regular, almost indecent exposure to the elements, I had such rosy-red apple-cheeks that any greengrocer would have been proud to display them. However the Wigley experiment came to an abrupt end not long afterwards when a friend of my Mum's dropped in unannounced one day and saw me crawling around in the snow. She pointed out that my cheeks were actually frost-nipped and Mum was so mortified that she called an immediate halt to the programme, leaving me only half-conditioned, or half-baked, as Nanny Wigley insisted on pointing out.

Dad's pig-farming wasn't a complete success either. One of his more intractable problems was a sow named Goliath, a.k.a. 'The Brute', and she and Dad just did not see eye to eye. Her strength was prodigious, matched only by her foul temper, and eventually Dad decided that she had to go. After much cursing and straining, Dad and his swineherd managed the dreaded task of loading Goliath into an old farm trailer and she was left there while they retired in triumph for a spot of lunch. They returned to discover that the trailer's side door had been smashed open – an inside job – and Goliath was now loose in the adjoining churchyard.

While digesting these already troubling facts, Dad was horrified to see six dark-suited men emerge from the church, bearing the coffin of a recently deceased parishioner to a freshly dug grave. By now Goliath had disappeared around the back of the church and Dad didn't know whether to shout a warning, shattering the reverential silence, or keep quiet and hope for the best. He was still pondering his options when Goliath reappeared, moving at top speed and clearly intent on exacting revenge on someone for her temporary incarceration in the trailer. The next moment, she rammed the back of the pall-bearers' legs, splaying bodies in all directions – including the one in the coffin. The coffin was parked on a convenient gravestone while the culprit was recaptured and then the interment was resumed. Before long, Goliath was also on her way to meet her Maker.

Not long afterwards the bottom fell out of the pig market as a whole and Dad decided to move us to the gentler climes of East Sussex in England. We emigrated down the old A1 in convoy with the removal lorry, and with all our menagerie of dogs, cats, doves, chickens, bantams, guinea pigs and even a miniature Shetland pony cooped up in the shooting brake with us. I can still remember the disembarkation process at our new house in Barcombe Mills near Lewes; it was like Noah's Ark washing up on dry land.

Despite the abrupt and permanent termination of her conditioning regime, Nanny Wigley remained very much a friend of the family. She stayed with us regularly and later Dad brought her back to live with us until the last days of her life. She was always immaculate, her snow-white hair scraped into a neat bun, and if her methods were strict, she was also a warm and kindly soul, endlessly patient and always willing to stop and lay aside her work to inspire her young charge with tales of the ways of the polar world and the feats of Scott and his peers. Some of my earliest memories are of those enthralling stories of snow- and icebound lands that alternated between everlasting daylight and eternal night, and of men strong enough in mind and body to venture into those fearsome regions and wrest knowledge and glory from the unyielding ice. They always fired my imagination in a way that tales of jungle or desert adventures, or soldiers or mountaineers, never did.

My father also played a big part in stirring my imagination, holding me spellbound with tales of our ancestors on both sides of the family. He was one of the best and funniest raconteurs I have ever heard – every time I heard the late Peter Ustinov, I was reminded of him – and he enlivened many a bedtime with his stories of our ancestors' great deeds. Curiously, my childhood experiences seem to have parallels with those of earlier polar explorers. The imagination of Robert Peary was stirred by reading the accounts of Nordenskjold's explorations in Greenland and, like my father, Peary's mother filled his head with tales of his distinguished ancestors, 'holding them up as traditional examples of splendid men'.

My mother's family, the Pendrills – my middle name – could trace their descent back to Stuart times. During the English Civil War, five Pendrill brothers saved the future King Charles II's life during his flight from the Battle of Worcester in 1651, by hiding him, first in a cheese cellar to avoid tracker-dogs and then in an oak tree on their land while Cromwell's Roundheads scoured the area for him – an incident still commemorated in the scores of English pubs named the Royal Oak. They then disguised him with labourer's clothes, tanned his pale skin with walnut oil and introduced a weary stoop into his otherwise regal gait, and he made his escape. Every generation of the Pendrill family since 1651 has retained the name in memory of this event. The Hadows were similarly proud of their heritage, and a strong streak of adventure ran through them. Among the ranks of prosperous landowners and businessmen were footloose travellers, sportsmen and soldiers of the Empire travelling to the furthest reaches of the globe.

My father would often talk about his great-grandfather, who for forty years was chairman of one of the Empire's great corporations, P&O, at the height of its power and influence. I still have a photograph of one of his eight sons, P. Frank Hadow, a stern and unbending Victorian who stares out of the picture frame with a gaze of imperious certainty. On the back of the picture, my father had inscribed P.F. Hadow's curriculum vitae: 'Harrow School Cricket XI 1872 and 1873. Winner of Public School Rackets with F.D. Leyland 1873. Played cricket for Cambridge University and Middlesex. Tea Planter and Big Game Hunter in Ceylon and India. Returned to England in April 1878 and took up the "newfangled game called Tennis Rackets". Won the second-ever All-England Tennis Singles

Championship in June of the same year, 1878. He never played tennis again, dismissing it with contempt as "A sissy game, Sir, played with a soft ball".'

Two of his brothers also played county cricket, two others went to India and set up what is still one of the largest carpet manufacturers in the subcontinent, and at the age of just nineteen, the eldest brother, Douglas Hadow, joined Edward Whymper's attempt to make the first ascent of the Matterhorn in 1865. Whymper was in such a frenzied hurry to scale the mountain before a rival party led by an Italian guide that, despite Douglas's non-existent mountaineering experience, let alone on substantial peaks in the Alps, Whymper actually recruited him and his travelling companion, a clergyman and accomplished climber, at the foot of the Matterhorn just before he began the ascent. The mountain had previously been described as 'unclimbable' but, despite his inexperience, Douglas reached the summit with Whymper and the others. However, he was one of the four who fell to their deaths on the descent, when the rope holding them broke.

No one knows what really happened but the accounts of Whymper and two of his guides inferred that Douglas had probably caused the accident by losing his footing. It still frustrates me that so many commentators have been blind to the fact that this British school-leaver, with no previous mountain experience, made the greatest ascent in mountaineering history at that time, through sheer physical aptitude and mental attitude. It was all he had, and he had it in spades. Anyone doubting it should dress in the kind of gear he wore, now held in the Zermatt Museum, and without the use of the metal handrails and ladders now in place, find out for themselves the terrifying reality of clinging to the exposed rock face with the wind buffeting their body and one slip leading to death thousands of feet below. Douglas Hadow could not answer his critics for himself – his lifeless body was recovered from the mountain a few days later – but though very young and completely inexperienced, he had given of his best in the most extreme circumstances. What more can you ask of someone?

As well as being a family historian, my father was a tremendous character, good company for adults and children alike, endlessly inventive, patient, tolerant and kind, and a great innovator and organiser. When we lived in Scotland he was one of the driving forces behind setting up the first Highland Games in Auchterader, and he also organised a long-distance road race – something of a rarity in the early 1960s. The winner of the women's event stripped to her bra during the race, causing a major sensation among the crowd and presenting the journalists on the local paper with the biggest story they'd had in years.

As I grew up, I was well aware of the family pedigree and the achievements and sporting prowess of my ancestors, and my father was particularly keen that I and my younger brother Henry should fulfil the family tradition by going to Sir Winston Churchill's alma mater, Harrow School. Hadow sons had been educated there since the 1800s. We are all listed in a huge tome in Harrow's Vaughan Library and I was told that very few families had had more Harrovian family members. I was about number twenty-one on the Hadow list, Henry was number twenty-two, and there are two more Hadows there at the moment. The one omission from that long and honourable list was my father, Nigel.

My grandmother, Sylvia, was widowed in the Second World War, when my father was thirteen, and, with limited finances available, she decided that my father would not go to Harrow. It wasn't just a financial issue; the Second World War was raging, and Harrow, high on its hill, was being hit by the occasional bomb. The school had also reached an absolute nadir; numbers had dropped from over 700 boys to fewer than 300 and its reputation was at rock-bottom. For all those reasons, it made no sense for my Dad to go there, but he was desperate to do so and was devastated by the decision. Strange though it may seem, I believe that it changed the whole course of his life.

When he was sent to another school he decided that he was at the wrong place; he didn't want to be there and behaved accordingly. He'd been head boy at his prep school but was then expelled from his public school before ending up at Millfield, where he achieved some stability. The headmaster and founder of the school, Jack 'Boss' Meyer, was a great character who was passionate about sport. During the war years, when agricultural machinery was very hard to come by, he'd drive up and down the rugby or cricket pitch dragging a piece of carpet behind his prized Rolls Royce just to make the stripes on the turf.

He tended to charge those who could pay a premium rate, which went some way to subsidising impecunious boys with sporting talent, and he struck a bizarre deal with my grandmother, which included her undertaking to keep the Millfield lakes supplied with ornamental wildfowl in return for a substantial reduction in the school fees. Dad wasn't outstandingly talented at sport but he was certainly highly competent, despite smoking prodigious quantities of untipped cigarettes from a very early age – he claimed filters made him sneeze. He was happy at Millfield and finished his school career without further incidents, but the constant disruption of his earlier wild years cost him dearly, and he left school with the barest minimum of academic qualifications. It was a handicap that affected him throughout his working life.

As an adult, my Dad changed his jobs as often as he'd changed his schools. He tried a succession of different businesses but, not for the want of trying, nothing ever really paid off for him. My Mum came from a wealthy family and had a private income from trust funds. When the stock market was high or rising, there was enough money for us to live in some style; but when the markets fell, the belt had to be tightened. Mum and Dad were determined that our education should never be affected by such downturns and, unaware of the backstage dramas, we blithely went through the happiest of childhoods. I'm sure there were some rough times, but we were shielded from the day-to-day impact which was absorbed by our parents. I know it hurt my father to find himself having to depend so heavily for long spells on invested funds. He had so much to give and was brilliant in so many ways, but neither he nor anyone else seemed to be able to harness his untrained talents to a reliable career path. It was awful to watch as I got older and realised what it was doing to the man I adored, but throughout my time at school he was the most supportive and fun father of them all – by a long way. The grown-up world's loss was my gain and he gave me the things that matter in life, and which no amount of money can buy.

My mother, Anne, was altogether quieter and more reserved than my father, but the perfect foil for him for that reason, and a hugely supportive and loving wife, helping him through some grim times. Outside her family, for whom she provided a priceless, rock-like stability, and her closest friends, she was rarely happier than with the horses, ponies, donkeys, goats and various breeds of dog and fowl that she bred, tended and showed.

I have nothing but the fondest memories of an endlessly warm and loving relationship with my parents – the envy of many of my school-mates. It was all the more remarkable because my father had been pretty 'free-range' from the moment his father was killed in the war, and had less parental contact and experience to fall back on than most; though this may have been an advantage for my brother and I, as my Dad was also less encumbered by the normal motto of the age: 'Children should be seen and not heard.' He was a father ahead of his time, and my mother did well to avoid reproducing the chasm that seemed to exist between herself and her mother, Alice, known with some irony in the family as 'Rags'. A con-tinual stream of governesses and nannies, some dire in the extreme, ensured there was virtually no possibility of my mother being seen or heard in her household, so segregated were the two generations. With no support from anyone, no horsebox or trailer, nor anyone willing to drive it even if there had been, from the age of twelve she organised getting herself to pony club events, gymkhanas and hunts, hacking up to seven miles each way in all weathers. I sometimes wonder if Rags even knew that she had a pony.

By the time I knew my grandmother, she was a Miss Haversham-like figure living in an impossibly grand apartment in a Nash terrace on the east side of Regent's Park. The distinctive smell of the highly polished wood-panelling of the residents' lift will live with me forever. When my brother and I were taken there on one of our periodic 'duty' visits, Rags would be sitting in her stately drawing room, bolt upright in her high-backed chair. She'd remove her immaculate white gloves – essential for her daily reading of the newspapers – and place them menacingly on her side-table, then carry out an inspection of laser-like intensity and speed, covering our hair (length and grooming), ties (knotted correctly and firmly supporting the Adam's apple), and shoes (laced correctly and burnished black in colour). Nothing was said. You knew if you had passed or failed before you went in, but that didn't make it any less uncomfortable. She was quite a lady, and you'd have been a fool to treat her otherwise.

My brother Henry is an entirely different character from me, exuding a relaxed, assured and laid-back air I can only dream of, and, though a fine sportsman and local hero in his home town, notably in the Uckfield Rugby Club, he never seemed to exhibit my burning need to prove myself, to my father or anyone else. I know of no one more universally popular than my brother, who works hard, plays hard and yet seems to have found that elusive happy work–life balance. We were great friends as youngsters, and I have many happy memories of endless days (always summer Saturdays in my recollections), when we'd watch my favourite TV programme – *Robinson Crusoe* – and then play together outside in all weathers, fishing, animal tracking, building dams on the stream, riding our bikes, and playing cricket and table tennis or our own version of catch, involving throwing eggs over the roof of the house to each other and trying to catch them without breaking them. Although we went to the same schools, we saw much less of each other during term-time – we were two years apart, in different houses, going to different classes and playing different sports – but each holiday we would pick up exactly where we left off and we forged a bond that remains as strong today as it was then.

The day I went away to prep school – Temple Grove near Uckfield – for the first time was a watershed in my life. On the first day the headmaster and his wife gave a reception for the new boys' parents in the library. I was introduced to the Matron, a brisk, no-nonsense lady, a good deal older than my mother, and when I next turned round, my parents had gone. They couldn't bear to say goodbye and had fled before they could change their minds. I had been hugely looking forward to growing up and going to 'stay' at school but right now it was a whole new world and I was taken aback by this apparent desertion by my parents. Later that evening, I was in the dormitory with the dozen other new boys, unpacking my enormous trunk full of brand new, regulation hankies, pyjamas, teddy bear and other boarding school essentials, when I found I had a question to ask Matron. Her door was ajar and I knocked and went in looking for her. She wasn't there, but I decided to wait and as I looked around the room, I saw a big box on the end of the bed, with some tissue paper poking out of it. I began to wonder what was in there, and being an inquisitive little boy, I lifted the lid. Inside was a human hand and arm.

Day one, night one, not yet eight years old, separated from

my parents for the very first time, and alone in a strange and very daunting place, and I'd found a severed arm in the room of the one person I'd been introduced to and told I could trust. I had a complete panic attack but, as I turned to run for it, I saw Matron standing in the doorway. Back-lit by the light from the corridor, she was a truly terrifying sight. I don't remember what happened next, which suggests that I must have fainted. When I came round Matron was sitting on the edge of my bed. I made a surreptitious count of my limbs; all four were present and correct. She then explained that the severed arm was a prosthetic limb for a thalidomide boy joining my year, but that night was hardly the most promising start to my school career.

I cried myself to sleep every night for the following three weeks, but I suppose it was just part of the weaning process and eventually I grew to love that school. The building was lovely and there was about twenty acres of beautifully land-scaped grounds: expanses of lawns and playing fields, magnifi-cent herbaceous borders, topiaried yew hedges and specimen trees, stunning banks of azaleas and rhododendrons; and a wonderful system of interconnected lakes surrounded by meadows sprinkled with vetches, buttercups and scores of other wildflowers. I used to wander through them, drinking the nectar from the flowers, and I can still picture that idyllic scene in my mind's eye.

Just before I began prep school, my Dad, who had been the British Army's Middle East heavyweight boxing champion, took me aside and told me that I needed to learn how to fight. 'I want you to be able to defend yourself, son. There may come a time when you need to stand up for yourself and give someone a bit of a thumping.' As part of my crash course in the noble art, he got me to punch him repeatedly in the stomach – he had quite a paunch on him by then, so it was a large and well-padded target. I made a feeble attempt and he wasn't impressed. 'No, no, no, no! Punch me as hard as you can. Hit me like you really mean it.' He made me do it over and over, goading me until I was really belting him with every-thing I'd got. Finally he was happy and let me go. He came in to my room the next day with a huge grin on his face, lifted up his shirt and showed me his stomach. It was absolutely covered with black, blue, purple and yellowing bruises, but he pronounced himself delighted with it.

I didn't have long to wait before putting his training into effect. Within the first couple of weeks at prep school, I had a fight to the death with the head of the school, even though I was only seven and a half and he was thirteen. We were in the changing rooms getting ready for games. He wanted more room, there was some pushing and jostling and it developed into a fight. All the other boys were standing on the benches shouting and yelling, like a scene from the film *If.* I wasn't particularly strong for my age, let alone when faced with a boy six years older, and I had never fought with anyone before, but something snapped deep inside me, and a strength born of fear coursed through my veins. I was completely focused on beating this boy who'd tried to bully me. He didn't stand a chance. I got on top of him, pinned him down and was pummelling him when, alerted by the noise, a master came bursting in and pulled us apart. I was shaking like a leaf as I walked out to the games field that day, but from then on, my stock was sky-high. I was a new boy, the lowest of the low in the school hierarchy, and yet I'd fought and beaten the head boy.

I never had any problems with bullies after that, but I was a tubby little boy, not athletic at all, and my first school sports day was a nightmare. All those, including me, who hadn't qualified for a single event – high jump, long jump, sprints, hurdles, shot putt, discus, etc. – had to enter the dreaded obstacle race, a prep school version of an army assault course. One of the obstacles was a set of three bars. You had to wriggle under the first one, set about a foot off the ground, then clamber over a high one and then crawl under another low one. We'd all been shown the course the day before – 'You're all failures and this is what you've got to do' – but we weren't allowed to practise and I got it into my head that I was too fat to squeeze under the low bars.

I imagined the humiliation of getting stuck and was dreading it so much that I scarcely slept the night before. In the event I managed to get under it without too much of a struggle, but the fact that the memory is still so strong – over thirty years later I can still feel my toes curling with embarrassment – suggests that it may well have been the moment when I decided to get serious about sport. By the time I left prep school I had grown almost as big as I am now, tall and well-muscled, and had overtaken virtually all my peers in speed and strength. I was playing football, rugby and cricket, and was captain or vice captain of all of them.

It was at prep school that I met my first mentor, Andrew Keith, a modest, dynamic and intriguing new master there. He picked me out as someone with sporting potential and took me and a few other boys under his wing. He introduced us to the Amateur Athletic Association's star system and pinned a chart to the notice board. It listed about fifteen different disciplines with the points you would acquire for any particular time or distance. The times for the 100 metres, for example, ranged from as slow as seventeen seconds to as fast as ten seconds dead – an Olympic qualifying time. The faster the time, the more points you were awarded and if you were brilliant at one event you could hoover up enough points to compensate for your less impressive disciplines and still attain your bronze, silver or gold award. But what intrigued me most was that, for the first time, I could see how my current performances rated in the bigger national scene. I was measuring myself against those targets and testing how far, how fast and how hard I could push myself. Even at that early stage I was becoming aware that competition was not only about whether you could beat the opposition, because that wasn't the best you could do.

What was relevant was how well and to what level you could perform, irrespective of the quality of the opposition.

Andrew Keith also introduced me to the concept of training. Before then, I'd just turned up for games, kicked a ball around with the other boys and played in the team, but he encouraged me to work to a planned training programme. It was my choice, I didn't have to do it and he put no pressure on me, but he could see that I was receptive to the idea. It didn't even matter to him if – as was often the case – I was the only one, he'd still come out with me, supervising the session and timing me with his stopwatch. But often I would go out training alone. The longer the distance, the happier I was, though at school the longest race was 1,500 metres and that was run only on the annual sports day. So I focused my efforts on the 800 metres and trained with repetitions of 100, 200 and 400 metres.

We used a grass track with the lanes marked by creosote, and, running in plimsolls, my feet would slip outwards alarmingly on the tight bends. I knew if I went much faster I'd just fall over. I must have mentioned this to my father, because he arranged to meet me in the school courtyard on the evening of my birthday, while everyone else was doing their prep. It was a slightly clandestine arrangement because, with the exception of sports matches, Exeat Sundays and sports days, parents were not encouraged to visit their children. With a bit of a flourish he pulled a box out of the boot of his car and handed it to me. Inside was a proper pair of running shoes, brilliant white canvas with three green stripes sewn down each side, together with a mini-spanner and two sets of steel spikes, one long and one short. I didn't even know that such things existed; no one else at school had spikes. The next day I put them on for the first time and ran the 200 metres three seconds faster than I had ever done before.

The AAA system encouraged you to try all sorts of different events – they put a stress on pentathlons and decathlons as a way of familiarising you with them – and, as part of this process,

Andrew Keith taught us the basic technique of putting the shot. I then tried it out in competition with a few friends, one of whom was bigger and stronger and threw it further than me – 8.5 metres, as far as anyone had ever thrown it at the school. I wasn't going to take that lying down, so when the group dispersed I sidled up to Andrew Keith and asked if I could borrow the shot over the holidays. I marked out a crude circle in our orchard, no more than a line scratched in the turf with a sharp stick, and I practised almost every day. By the time I'd finished, the orchard looked like a First World War battlefield, but my shot-putting had improved out of all recognition. To stop a handful of boys from monopolising the trophies, no one was allowed to do more than three events at the school sports day. I chose the 400 and 800 metres and the shot-putt, and even though I wasn't allowed to wear my spikes, I was determined to break the school record in each event. The 400 metre record hadn't been broken for twenty years but I won that in record time, did the same in the 800 and then beat the competitors in the shot-putt by a clear metre.

As a result I was entered for the Sussex Preparatory Schools championship and when I won that as well, I qualified for the national championships – a real test. Spikes were the norm here and within 10 metres of the start of the 800 metres, my race inexperience had revealed itself; I was flat on my face on the cinder track, with blood leaking out of my shin. I was lying there in a shocked state, my dreams in tatters as the competitors sped away, but then something inside me said 'Damn it, I've come this far, I've put in months of hard training, I'm not going to let all that go to waste like this.' I sprang up and tore off after them. I was fifty metres behind, but began gaining on them steadily. I felt terribly self-conscious running past the cheering stands so far behind at the end of the first lap, but I couldn't help that now. I felt no pain, I was locked on to the boy at the back and reeling him in. I passed the back-marker and, coming into the home straight, I was in with a chance for a place. I edged up to third but, with fifty metres to go, my legs suddenly went. I was running through glue and was overtaken again before the line. However, despite the fall, I had improved my personal best by several seconds. It was a real lesson to me, showing how much I or anyone could raise their game if the stakes were high enough. The battle was as much in my mind as in my body. It was a lesson that I never forgot.

It was at about this time, during my last year at prep school, that I developed a strengthening belief that I should be looking to do something, or be something, out of the ordinary; my mother still remembers me telling her so. It is a difficult thing to describe, but it became such an all-pervasive obsession that it affected the quality of my life for many years. Curiously, once more it is an experience parallelled by earlier polar explorers. Frederick Cook, for example, spoke of 'a restless surge in my little bosom, a yearning for something that was vague and undefined. This was, I suppose, that nebulous desire which sometimes manifests itself in early youth and later is asserted in strivings toward some splendid, sometimes spectacular aim.' It wasn't that I felt bigger or better or cleverer than anyone else, but I did feel a need, almost an obligation, to fulfil my destiny, whatever that might be. I was also different from my peers in another way; I was relentless in pursuit of the goals I set myself. I barely knew anyone of my age who trained at all, let alone as hard, as long or as often as I did. I even did standard press-ups, press-ups with hand-claps, one-arm press-ups and all sorts of variations for about twenty minutes or so before going to bed every night. That single-minded focus on achieving a goal was perhaps the strongest hint of the direction my later life would take.

By now, my competitive instincts were running rampant. There was a wonderful walled garden at the school and any boy could have a plot there, his to do with as he wished. Some grew vegetables, some flowers and some were quite sophisticated with landscape features like little ponds. Among his many other jobs and hobbies, my father was a national rose champion and I got the gardening bug from him; I can still picture my garden and name all the roses in it to this day: Red Devil, Papa Meilland, Super Star, Iceberg, Prima Ballerina – a standard rose on a three-foot stem – and Goliath, which had huge blooms and vast quantities of petals. In the few spare minutes in my action-packed schedule, I found time to hurry off up to the walled garden. I felt that it was a matter of honour that I win the gardening competition, as I duly did in my last year . . . even gardening had become a competitive event.

During the course of that year, I also sat and passed the entrance exam for Harrow. My Dad would have done almost anything and endured almost any hardship to ensure I went there, and I can only imagine his pride and relief when I succeeded, but the family finances were strained to the limit and my parents were really scraping the barrel to keep myself and, in course of time, my younger brother Henry there. When we were home for the holidays we would have roasts with all the trimmings, but as soon as we went back to school, they would revert to a far more spartan diet. At first, I did not know that this was going on; I was only aware of the contrast between the lavish hospitality at the houses of my schoolfriends and the much more modest fare that we provided in return. With the typical blind self-absorption of a teenager, I was embarrassed and even cross about it – to my later shame, when I realised the extent of the sacrifices my parents were making. It made me very aware of what a debt I owed them and I took on much more responsibility as a result. My school reports had always been good but I increasingly felt that I should be doing more, getting the maximum out of my time there, and I pushed myself harder and harder in classes, sports and all my other activities. If my Dad was sometimes disappointed by the course that his own career had taken, I was determined that he would be able to take pride in the achievements of his son.

I had one major setback, a term spent convalescing after a

collapse from exhaustion during my penultimate year at Harrow. It was triggered by playing rugby matches twice in three days while I was running a high fever, but I believe that it also reflected the extreme pressure that I was putting myself under, and it left me so weak that I was literally unable to get out of bed for two months. However, I didn't allow it to curtail my sporting activities on my return, though I believe that it affected both my sporting and academic performance for many years.

My Dad was a real cricket lover and encouraged my abilities even to the extent of building a practice net, complete with a concrete strip covered with coconut matting, hiring a professional coach, Ivor Underhill, for a few days intensive coaching during the Easter holidays, and organising full-scale matches involving myself and all the boys of a similar age who could be rustled up from the surrounding area, but it would be a great distortion to see him as the stereotypical 'pushy parent', living out his own frustrated ambitions and dreams through his children. Like any parents, my mother and father were proud when I did well and supportive when I did badly, but I never felt compelled to do anything and though my Dad was undoubtedly disappointed when I chose athletics ahead of cricket, ending his dream of seeing me play for Harrow in the traditional match against Eton at the temple of the game, Lords cricket ground, he never tried to change my mind and encouraged and supported me just as much in that as he had in cricket and rugby.

In my first year at Harrow, my school running coach, Mike Wingfield, gave me a tough six-days-a-week training programme for the Easter holidays, including sets of ten 100, 200 and 400 metres, alternating with distance runs. The 400s were killer sessions and I'd be in a pretty bad way by the end of the last one, especially as I had to average one second faster over the ten timed 400 metre runs each week. Dad had paced out the distance down the dead-end lane to the village church – the only reasonably level and quiet 'track' we could find in the area.

Dad would always come to help with the stopwatch and more especially to give some moral support. By the last week I was really up against it. With three 400s still to go, I was already getting wobbly legs when suddenly a chance busload of American tourists turned up to look round the church. Within five minutes Dad had them all under management and strung along the grass verge to cheer me through those last three 400s and with their vocal encouragement, I beat my target.

One of the many old traditions at Harrow was a run called the 'Long Ducker', named after an open-air swimming pool at the edge of the school grounds that had originally been a duck-pond. The shorter version, Short Ducker, started from the door of your school house (there were 11 houses of 50–100 boys each) on top of Harrow-on-the-Hill, and went down and around the hill, past Ducker at the bottom and then back up. It was a three-mile run and some school and house monitors used it as a punishment for various misdemeanours, but I required no compulsion to do it; I was using it as training for the Long Ducker. That began and ended the same way, but instead of turning round at the bottom of the hill, you ran on down to the Grand Union Canal three or four miles away, then right along the towpath to Little Venice and up onto the Edgware Road to Marble Arch at the western end of London's Oxford Street, where you turned and retraced your steps, in all covering a marathon distance – twenty-six miles.

Marathon runners were a rare breed in the 1970s. The only one I had heard of was Abebe Bikila, the Ethiopian Olympic champion, though I followed distance runners like Tony Simmons and Dave Bedford (who used to train around Harrow's cricket field) avidly in the pages of *Athletes' Weekly* and at the televised championship races. But marathons were not a mass public participation sport; there was nothing like the London Marathon or the Great North Run and hardly anyone even went jogging. The Long Ducker was similarly moribund. No one at school had done it while I was there, but in my first or second year at Harrow, two senior boys in my house started going round telling everyone that they would do the Long Ducker. They then left school without even attempting it and I thought that was pretty poor; they were getting the credit by implying they'd do it, but talk is cheap and they didn't follow through.

I didn't really know what the Long Ducker was at the time, just that it was some sort of bloody long run, but inside I was already burning with curiosity – could I do it? I thought about it a lot over the next couple of years and when I was fifteen I began serious training for it. I played rugby on Saturdays but I trained on my own every Sunday doing Short Duckers, one after another. It was tough going with a serious uphill slog of about two-thirds of a mile on each circuit – not ideal for a marathon, where you want to maintain a metronomic rhythm, but it was building my strength and stamina. I trained so hard that by the time I was ready to run Long Ducker I'd worn holes in the toes of what had been a new pair of Adidas Bamba running shoes.

I didn't even tell people what I was training for, though word soon got around. It was 1977, the year of the Queen's Silver Jubilee, and I'd decided to raise money for the Jubilee Appeal by getting my school friends and anyone else I could find to sponsor me. There were 750 boys at school but as a server at the altar, I knew that if there was £10 in the collection plate after Sunday Service the chaplain thought he was doing well; it was all halfpennies, pennies, drawing pins, half-eaten sweets and all sorts of grot from boys' trouser pockets. Undeterred by this schoolboy miserliness, I spent many hours soliciting funds on street corners, in tuck shops, libraries and classrooms, brandishing an ever-lengthening sequence of lined A4 sheets, as HRHs, Viscounts, Earls, Lords and less rarefied beings committed themselves to anything from half a pence to a pound per mile. Come the day, £103.45 had been pledged.

I was completely self-motivated. None of the schoolmasters

were involved and I planned and trained for the Long Ducker alone, but when my house-master heard about it, he was sufficiently concerned about whether a fifteen-year-old should be running a marathon to insist that I see the school doctor. His opinion boiled down to 'Well, I don't know, so do it, if that's what you want to do,' and armed with this lukewarm endorsement, I felt I was ready to try. I told my Mum and Dad, who came up to Harrow at the first opportunity to check the route with me and find points for 'feeding stations' where they could supply me with water and glucose drinks.

I set off early on a Sunday morning in December, accompanied by a friend, Myles Thompson, on his bicycle, and cheered on my way by the other boys in my house. I didn't care how long I took to run it, but I was absolutely determined that I would complete the course and that I would run every step of the way. I ran down the hill, through the deserted streets to the Grand Union Canal, and set off along the towpath towards London. My parental back-up team was waiting there and they handed me the first of a string of little plastic cups of water loaded with glucose. Then they raced ahead in the car to another road-bridge over the canal that would serve as the site for the next feeding station.

After what seemed like hours pounding the towpath, I emerged into the noise and bustle of the Edgware Road, drawing curious looks from the people taking a Sunday stroll or sipping coffee in the street cafés. As I ran towards the bottom of the Edgware Road, I saw the massive iron filigree of the gates of the Marble Arch standing wide open. Knowing that I was running to raise money for the Jubilee Appeal, John Reece, a supportive master at the school and a part-time speech-writer for a member of the Royal Household, had used his influence to arrange for the gates to be opened for me. I ran through them, jogged on the spot for a few moments for photographs and set off on the return leg feeling that I still had plenty in the tank.

Two school friends, Simon Marsh and Alex Budworth, joined me at Marble Arch to run the thirteen miles back with me, and it was just as well because they and Myles really helped to keep me going when I hit 'the wall' – the sticky patch that always seems to come for novices at some point in a long-distance run. I had found the outward leg a bit of a doddle, so much so that I was absolutely flying heading in towards London, and perhaps I'd gone too fast, too soon, because I'd only just passed the twenty-mile mark on the canal towpath before beginning the long climb back up to Harrow School, when I really began to struggle. The towpath had a reasonably springy surface of earth and gravel, but now I was back pounding hard pavements and my legs seemed to have turned to stone. I was blowing hard and feeling the effort of each stride and I was growing increasingly anxious that I'd blown it and I might not make it. The thought of walking for a bit appalled me – anyone can walk – but I was having to dig deeper and deeper just to keep moving forward. I'd lost my rhythm completely and I could hear the anxiety in my friends' voices as they urged me on: 'Come on, Pen. You've done the hard part. Just a little bit further to go.'

With just over three hours of running behind me, I was absolutely shot by the time that we at last reached the bottom of Harrow Hill. The end was now almost in sight, but this was the steepest part of the whole route and I was floundering over ground that seemed to have turned to wet cement. Myles stayed with me but the other two pulled ahead to tell the boys in my house that I'd nearly made it. As I laboured up the hill, they all came pouring down the hill in their standard Sunday attire of top-hats and tails, ready to run the last few hundred yards with me. The adrenalin surge as I saw them was like a jolt of electricity through my body. One minute I was staggering up the hill, the next I seemed to be cruising effortlessly towards the finish; I didn't even notice the gradient. I still have the photograph of me leading the way up the hill with all these guys in top-hats running behind me, their tailcoats streaming in the wind. I almost collapsed after I crossed the line, but I didn't care; I'd done it, I'd run Long Ducker. When I had time to reflect about it later, I thought back to that adrenalin-fuelled surge triggered by the sight of my friends coming to meet me, and began to realise how much of any endurance event is won or lost in the mind, rather than the body.

The next morning the headmaster made an announcement in assembly. 'Some of you will know that Pen Hadow ran Long Ducker yesterday. What he doesn't know is that he was the first boy to do this for fifty years.' The standing ovation I received must have started a few other boys thinking because within a few weeks several were labouring up Harrow Hill in training for their own attempts at Long Ducker, and it is now an annual fixture in the Harrow calendar. Every boy is expected to complete half the course from Marble Arch back to the hill – and every year a dedicated few in the Upper School complete the full Long Ducker.

After my experience of the run, the psychology of endurance events had started to intrigue me and, aged sixteen, I entered and won the school's annual Churchill Essay Prize with an exploration of the mindset of record-breaking runners, quoting athletes like Ron Clarke and Ron Hill from researched press-cuttings. I still have the original hand-written copy and some of my sentiments then clearly indicate a developing mindset. It opened: 'Races produce winners. However a winner is not necessarily the first person to pass the tape. There is an alternative, and more realistic definition; a winner is a person who works to exploit his potential. Even if he loses every race, if he has done the best he possibly can, he has won.'

I also quoted Sir Arthur Conan Doyle's description of one of the most enduring images in sport, that of Dorando Pietri entering the home straight of the track to complete the first marathon of the modern Olympic Games in 1908: 'It is a horrible yet fascinating sight, this strange struggle between a set purpose and an utterly exhausted frame. He was practically delirious, staggering along the cinder path like a man in a dream.' I found that level of performance utterly fascinating and, if I knew one thing about the destiny I had long believed in, it was that I would be going through that struggle myself one day.

2

As the time for leaving Harrow approached, I went to see my house-master and said, 'Hello sir, I think I'd like to go to university.' He almost fell off his chair with surprise. I was a bright boy but it obviously hadn't occurred to anybody that I could or should go to university, or even that I might want to. Perhaps back in those days, they expected all Harrovians to join the Guards or the family business, or do estate management at Cirencester.

When he'd regained his composure, he told me to read two books that would tell me how to apply and what A-level grades I needed for different courses and universities. I wanted to read Geography and having read the two books from cover to cover, I filled in my application form and sent it off without showing it to anyone at school. University College, London, was my first choice because it had one of the best geography departments in the country, followed by Leicester, King's College, London, Swansea – great for surfing and the outdoor life – and Queen Mary's College, London.

Not long afterwards another master intercepted me. He told me he doubled as the careers master – I didn't even know Harrow possessed one – and asked me where I had applied. I showed him a copy of my application form. He studied it for a moment and then told me, 'You haven't a hope of getting to University College. Leicester will never accept you because they don't like being put second to UCL – Oxford or Cambridge is one thing, but University College is quite another. King's won't like being put behind UCL either because they're great rivals and as for the other two, Queen Mary's certainly won't want to be put fifth, and Swansea, well, who cares about Swansea anyway?'

After I'd finished thinking, 'What a charming man', my next thought was, 'Oh hell, I made a real mess of that form', and the next was, 'Why didn't anyone tell me any of this before?' In the event I had the last laugh. I was offered a place by all five colleges and went to my first choice, UCL.

Most of my peer group had left at the start of my final term at Harrow – perhaps no one bothered to tell them how to apply to university either and they just assumed it was time to leave – and I became the Captain of Rugby by default, one of only two people with previous first team experience, and it all went rapidly pear-shaped for me. In my year in the Colts we had won every match and were an exceptional side with some very talented players, but unfortunately most of them had left Harrow through natural wastage and a few strange and quirky incidents – one was expelled, another's parents ran out of money for fees, another decided to go and throw the hammer for England – so what should have been a very strong First XV became a very weak one.

The school normally had a policy that the front five forwards always played a season after Colts level before they were put in the first team, because a rugby scrum is a dangerous place, particularly when you're pitting schoolboys against adults, but in our case the whole front five, and seven of the eight forwards in all, came straight in from the Colts; they had to, there was no one else. The outcome was predictable, we lost every single one of our games, but I have never worked or played as part of a team that put more of themselves on the line. They gave everything in the cause and it was inspiring and moving to be a part of it. I was really, really proud of them and when a master came up to me and demanded to know 'What the hell do you think you're doing losing so many matches?' I was so furious that I burst out, 'You've no idea what those boys are putting themselves through. How dare you speak to me or any of my team like that?' But the fact remains that I was captain of probably the first Harrow team ever to go through the entire season without winning a single match, and that has stuck with me ever since. I didn't find it easy to get over it, but it was a serious learning experience for me: whatever the outcome, you can only do your best yourself and encourage others to do the same.

I decided to take a gap year before going up to university, to give myself a chance to see a little of the real world and I applied for a Short Service Limited Commission with the Scots Guards, by whom Hadows had been known to be engaged in the past. At regimental HQ the recruitment officer assured me that the Regular Commissions Board was a no-brainer for someone like me. I wasn't so sure, but I had no choice, everyone has to go through RCB to become a British army officer. When I turned up with my suitcase on the station platform at Westbury I saw lots of similarly accompanied young men and I got the sinking feeling that I was heading straight from one institution to another, and in that moment I realised that it was going to have to be a pretty unusual organisation if I was going to be happy in it for long.

I went through the motions of academic and IQ tests, fitness and physical courses, social skills and confidence assessments and then came the command and leaderless tasks. The scenarios we were set were so artificial – 'the yellow oil drums are man-eating crocodiles' – or so ludicrously complicated – 'all circular objects are mines, all green-painted wood can only be touched twice by any two of your team in your allotted ten minutes' – that it drained the last vestiges of enthusiasm from me. Twice the commanding officer ordered me into his presence and urged me to get stuck in, but I just couldn't muster any enthusiasm for bossing the group about just to prove that I wasn't so embarrassed by the whole ridiculous charade that I couldn't command the attention of my fellow hopefuls.

I just could not bring myself to play these games, whatever the rewards, and for me they would have been considerable: two months on exercise in Kenya, three months on Household Duties changing the guard at Buckingham Palace, and two months on urban warfare training. Then, when the Second Battalion of the Scots Guards were due to be sent off for their tour of duty in Northern Ireland, I would be heading off to university on the full pay of a second lieutenant in the Guards. Potential officers receive one of four notifications after the RCB course: 'Delighted to have you aboard'; 'If you stick out a few weeks on a toughening up course we'll take you'; 'Come back in a year or more's time when you've matured or thought things through more'; and the one that I received, 'It's been awfully nice meeting you, but we have no need of your services here.'

Instead I took a job cleaning cars in a showroom to earn some money for a trip to Australia and returned just in time for my first term at University College. I had expected to carry on playing rugby but my experiences in my last year at Harrow had scarred me a little and I was dubious about whether I was good enough. I could run forever – I was described as 'perpetual motion Hadow' in a school report – and I could tackle till the cows came home, but I didn't have the explosive speed and powerful physique that really good flankers need. As I was wandering round the Freshers' Fair, I saw the rowing club stand and signed up for that instead. I ended up in the UCL first eight, but there was not the culture of high performance that I craved. The next step up would have been to row in the London University squad – elite rowing stuffed full of Olympic and national-level oarsmen. I adored the life of the oarsman on the water, and desperately needed to pour myself into a professional scene with an ambitious training programme; with hindsight I should have opted out of my college to one of the larger clubs on the Thames, but I couldn't see it then, and I soon began to think of rowing as another dead end.

My feelings about university as a whole were much the same.

For many people their time at college is one of the happiest periods of their life, but once more I was out of step with my peers. Despite a hectic social life as a 'Deb's Delight', I was miserable at university and became genuinely depressed. I read voraciously, but I did the minimum amount of academic work to get by. The one exception was an expedition I organised to the desert shores at the head of the Gulf of Aqaba in Jordan. One lecturer, Dr Claudio Vita-Finzi, fired my intellectual curiosity, as he has done for many before and since. I asked if he knew of any fieldwork that I could do abroad on my own. He knew six professors in as many countries around the world who had asked him to steer his students their way and I took my pick of the bunch.

I organised the whole expedition and spent six weeks collecting samples of long-dead coral from a series of raised beaches in the cliffs well above the current sea level. By radiocarbon dating the corals and recording the heights above sea level of the beaches from which they came, we could ascertain the rates of uplift of the land over the last 8,000 years. Working entirely alone and unsupervised in a supremely challenging region with interested scientists back home was a privilege which I now see as my first glimpse into the working world I now inhabit.

Sadly, when I returned to London I drifted back into my depressed and apathetic routine and finished university with only a 2:2 degree, but by that time I'd given up caring. I wasn't even doing any sport. I had a huge sense of frustration and unhappiness and felt that I was wasting my life, but was unable to get out of the black hole I'd dug for myself. I still had that feeling of destiny, of being on this earth for a purpose, but I was beginning to wonder if I would ever discover what that destiny would be. Like Captain Scott, I was unable to 'describe what comes over me, it's too indefinite. I'm obsessed with the view of life as a struggle for existence, and then forced to see how little past efforts have done to give me a place in the struggle. I seem to be marking time, grudging the flying moments, yet impotent to command circumstances. I seem to hold in reserve something that makes for success, and yet to see no working field, and so there's the consciousness of wasting and a truly deep "unrest". All these thoughts and sensations are in me, complicating simple issues and disturbing the current of daily life – and the outward signs are the black moods that come and go with such apparent disregard for the feelings of those dear to me. Have all the patience you can.'

After leaving UCL I continued to drift and, for want of anything better to do, I joined a landscape gardening company with contracts all around central London – industrial sites, commercial properties, blocks of flats and private gardens, including some tiny gardens in Kensington. At least it was work outdoors, but it was just a way of killing time for me and I hated the way that people started locking all their windows and putting anything valuable inside as soon as we arrived. In the twelve months that I stuck the job, I was never once offered a cup of coffee, not even when it was snowing, but that's city life for you.

I was still thinking endlessly about what I might want to do. I knew I didn't want to be an accountant or any of the other standard professional jobs, nor did I want to be a City slicker or a corporate animal. I was so desperate for ideas that I even ploughed through Yellow Pages from 'Abattoirs' to 'Zoos', hoping something would strike a spark. One day, with ingrained dirt in my hands and my hair stiff with the cloud of debris the mower had thrown up around me that summer's day, I was flicking through the pages of a newspaper, when an article about Mark McCormack's sports agency, International Management Group, caught my eye. Then, as now, IMG were the dominant force in the market, with a vast stable of the world's highest-profile sportsmen and women on their books as well as the representation of big events including the Olympics. I had never thought of acting as a business agent on behalf of sports events and personalities but it had instant appeal. For the first time in years, the tinder burst into flame, and I decided right then I was going to make this happen.

I phoned for the company's promotional brochure, analysed which department I thought I might work best in, and then gleaned every scrap of information I could, even scrutinising the array of executive portraits for the transatlantic dress code of smart jackets, and modern tie designs, style of haircuts and tan levels. Next I visited their European head office in central London. I went in pretending to be lost and asking for directions and even used the washroom to check the office decor. When I'd completed my research I sent a professionally prepared CV and a short covering letter. To my intense joy, I was offered an immediate interview and despite my total lack of relevant experience – I was still gardening at the time – I was then hired on the spot as their youngest-ever executive. My brief was to handle the commercial affairs of the world's most successful three-day eventer, Lucinda Green (*née* Prior-Palmer) and take responsibility for the other equestrian management rights that the agency had acquired in an ad hoc way, pulling them together to create a European equestrian division. My sole qualification for that appeared to be that I was one of the only people in the entire organisation who owned a pair of Wellingtons and knew which end of a horse to feed a sugar lump to.

Any self-respecting young man would have killed for that job. It was a dream ticket: good salary, unlimited expenses, a spacious office, a glamorous secretary and a jet-set lifestyle, flying around the world whenever I wanted, as often as I wanted, staying in the finest hotels, meeting famous people; and the more entrepreneurial flair and pluck you had, the more the world was your oyster. I had virtual carte blanche to build up the department; I could have taken on a dozen top jockeys, show jumpers or polo players and no one would have batted an eyelid. My only problems were that I didn't actually know how this international operation worked – I was out of my depth and off the pace the whole time, struggling to get up to speed – and in my heart I knew that it wasn't what I wanted to do for the rest of my life.

The dream job only made me feel even more unfulfilled because I felt that I was supporting and helping to make money for people who were at the top of their particular trees and doing what they loved – playing golf or tennis, driving fast cars, riding horses – and I actually wanted to be on the other side of the fence myself. That triggered the thought that the real question in life is not what you want to be, but what you want to do. If you can identify what really does it for you, then you'll do it with a natural enthusiasm and ability and put in the extra effort all the time. There's only one thing more infectious than enthusiasm and that's a lack of it. However, if you start by wanting to be a millionaire and then decide that you have to be a merchant banker in order to get there, well . . . that's probably why some merchant bankers look so miserable.

So that was the trigger to sort myself out. Apart from pushing my physical limits since the age of eight, the one constant in my life was the distant echoing in my head of Nanny Wigley's tales of great explorers and my Dad's stories about my adventurous ancestors. They formed some of my earliest memories, and I remained fascinated by them. My shelves groaned with books about the 'gods' of polar exploration – Nordenskjold, Nansen, Amundsen, Scott, Mawson and Shackleton – and their modern all-terrain equivalents: John Ridgway, Chay Blythe, Francis Chichester, Ranulph Fiennes, Robin Hanbury-Tennison, Robin Knox-Johnston and Chris Bonnington. I'd been a Fellow of the Royal Geographical Society since university and I often went into the deathly quiet RGS reading room and leafed through the dusty old volumes on the shelves – this was long before its transformation into a vibrant and publicly accessible world-class centre of learning.

I was doing this one day when I came across the translated

diaries of Bernhard Adolph Hantzsch, a seriously obscure nineteenth-century German ornithologist who set off on an extraordinary Arctic expedition that was compromised before he had even begun when his boat sank off Baffin Island. He lost nearly all his equipment but managed to reach a remote settlement near Black Rock Island. The missionary there took in Hantzsch and his crewmen, even though their own food supplies for the winter had also gone down with his boat. They eked out the settlement's pitiful rations until the following spring when, undeterred, he set off north with hired Inuit companions. His original plan was to cross Baffin Island and then head up the west coast to the northern tip, from where he hoped to sail home on a passing resupply ship, but he got no more than halfway before starvation started to take its toll. In the end, only two Inuit remained with him. Starving, they killed and ate a polar bear but shortly afterwards Hantsch died of exhaustion and malnutrition, his death accelerated by an overdose of vitamin A after eating the polar bear's liver. It was a remarkable testament to their admiration for him that the surviving Inuit brought his diaries and all his meticulous observations of the natural environment back to their settlement, from where they were returned to his family.

As I read his book I realised that I was one of at most a handful of people – and perhaps the only one – who had ever done so. But now I'd chanced upon it, I was prepared to believe that fate had guided me to it. I didn't care that no one in Britain and precious few in his native Germany had ever heard of him. He wasn't a Scott or a Shackleton but his efforts and achievements were deserving of a better commemoration than this dusty, forgotten volume. As I stood in that deserted reading room, I decided there and then that I would retrace the steps of Bernhard Hantzsch and finish the journey that he never completed.

I began researching and planning the expedition in every spare moment outside work hours; and I even squeezed in visits

1. Fridtjof Nansen – arguably the greatest polar explorer of all time

2. Captain Robert Scott at his desk in Antarctica, overlooked by his wife, Kathleen, and son, Peter

3. British explorer Sir Wally Herbert led the first surface crossing of the entire Arctic Ocean (1968–9) – and in so doing probably became the first to reach the Pole on foot on 5 April 1969

4. A classic map produced by distinguished Scottish cartographer Keith Johnston in the late 1870s depicting tracts of the Arctic Ocean coastline and the Pole near its heart, still unexplored

5. Enid 'Nanny' Wigley – she looked after Sir Peter Scott – Scott of the Antarctic's son – my father as a boy, and then me

6. Patrick 'Frank' Hadow – after winning the Men's Singles at Wimbledon he dismissed the new-fangled game as 'a sissy game, Sir, played with a soft ball'

7. Douglas Robert Hadow (back row, centre), aged only nineteen, was in the party that made the first ascent of the Matterhorn in 1865

8. My paternal grandfather –
Philip Hadow

9. My paternal grandmother –
Sylvia (*née* Harvey)

10. My maternal grandfather –
Laurence Callingham

11. My maternal grandmother –
Alice (aka 'Rags') Pendrill
Callingham (*née* Charles)

12. Some cold-weather conditioning at Tarmangie, Scotland (attended to by family friend Muriel Anderson)

13. In my grandmother's private garden at Cumberland Terrace on Regent's Park (aged three)

14. Early signs of attitude to risk (aged seven)

15. My Dad (and me, behind) at Seaview, Isle of Wight, on a bucket-and-spade holiday

16. My Mum, Anne Pendrill Hadow, my brother, Henry (right), and me at Polzeath, Cornwall

17. Dad and me off on one of our countless fish-free fishing forays!

18. Approaching the finish line (second from left) and encouraged by my fellow 'Parkites', 1977. The first to complete the Long Ducker for exactly fifty years

19. Mary (*née* Nicholson) and me on our wedding day

20. Wydemeet – our home

21. 'Baskers' – our border collie

22. Pondering on
Combestone Tor,
Dartmoor

23. Mary competing
aboard her beloved
Philbo

to the library during my lunch-breaks. One autumn morning in that same year, 1988, I completed my research and then walked into the IMG offices and announced to my bosses, colleagues and clients that I had decided to resign in order to retrace Hantsch's steps and complete his expedition. Their reaction was predictable – they all thought I'd lost my marbles – but I didn't care; for good or ill, the die was cast. I left IMG on good terms, albeit while still receiving puzzled looks from my former colleagues. As I often quote, 'A ship is safe in harbour, but that's not what ships were built for.'

As a complete novice at Arctic exploration, I knew I needed an experienced partner to accompany me and I placed an advertisement in a now defunct magazine, *The Adventurer*. 'Wanted: Arctic experienced HF radio operator for Baffin Island expedition.' It was answered by a man called Vaughan Purvis, who appeared ideal – an experienced polar traveller and a highly qualified radio operator. However he couldn't help but observe that I had no experience of polar expeditions whatsoever, and had never even been to the Arctic. Instead of joining my putative expedition, he suggested that I join his own seventy-day sledge-hauling journey, without air support or resupplies, across the archipelago of Svalbard on the edge of the Arctic Ocean, to study and photograph polar bears in their natural habitat. He promised to train and teach me in the ways of the Arctic and we could then consider the Baffin Island expedition, if I still wanted to, on our return. It seemed like an eminently sensible suggestion and I agreed at once. We met regularly through that winter to make our preparations and set out in the early spring of the following year, 1989. We flew in to Longyearbyen, the one significant settlement on Spitsbergen, the largest island of the Svalbard group, and then set off east on our two-man trek.

My first sight of the polar ice-cap, the frozen world that had consumed my imagination since those far-off childhood stories, was an overpowering experience. It seemed so vast, so intimidating, so featureless and monochrome, and so utterly alien, that I was as much in fear as in awe of it, and grateful for the presence of my reassuringly confident companion. But within a very short time, I shed my fears and superstitions and began to see that frozen ice-scape in all its wondrous beauty and variety. It was the start of a lifelong love of the Arctic and I was fortunate to have such a knowledgeable guide and companion during that first voyage of discovery.

I soon realised that Vaughan was a very unusual man. He'd served in the merchant navy and achieved the highest pass mark in his field in the history of the service. He also had a number of arcane specialist interests like Venetian art and Japanese cuisine of the Renaissance era. Even more spectacularly, he could write an expedition proposal in the style of a Roman courtesan, a Renaissance philosopher or a London taxicab driver. In short, he was a genius, but I think he found our personal relationship difficult and there were times when I watched him cradling a rifle with a faraway look in his eyes that, ridiculous though it now seems, I found distinctly unnerving. But I had alighted upon a rarely talented individual who, just as I was planning to do, appeared to have created a life for himself that was dedicated to spending as much time as possible doing interesting things in the polar regions. Such people then were almost non-existent and finding partners who were reliably available and competent was a big issue for expedition leaders to the Arctic or Antarctic.

Over the course of our two months' sledging together, I had my baptism into the polar world and learned a lot about strategy, tactics, procedures and techniques for operating in extreme environments for long periods of time, and how to move around safely on sea-ice and glaciers, and near polar bears – we encountered around a dozen during the expedition. Vaughan thought too many bears were filmed from tundra buggies, snowmobiles and helicopters, and that it was time photographs were taken capturing a more authentic relationship with the bear and its kingdom. Once absorbed behind his lens, Vaughan was fearless in pursuit of his prey – on occasion disconcertingly so – but Scandinavian Airline Systems, who sponsored the expedition, were later suitably impressed by his daring close-up shots of bears rummaging through sledges and nanoseconds from launching a strike at our intrepid photographer from as little as six metres away.

I learned many invaluable lessons as we travelled around the islands and I also discovered the hard way what an unforgiving environment I had chosen. In the course of sledging off the coast of Barents Island one of my contact lenses froze onto the surface of my eye. I managed to warm my eye and remove the lens fairly quickly. Later that day we found a remote hut and shovelled our way through the huge snowdrift blocking the doorway. As soon as we were inside I noticed that my vision in that eye had become densely clouded.

Vaughan at once fixed a protective patch over the eye, but I was understandably concerned about my sight. That concern was exacerbated because freak ionospheric conditions caused by solar flaring on the sun were interfering with HF radio signals. Despite Vaughan's profound working knowledge of radios and antennae, we had been unable to contact the outside world for several weeks and so could not seek medical advice. Fortunately, Ranulph Fiennes was making his third attempt on the North Pole with Mike Stroud at the time, and Laurence 'Flo' Howell was acting as base manager and radio operator for them from Ward Hunt Island. For some bizarre reason he was the only person in the world that we could manage to contact – luckily Vaughan had the radio schedule for Ran's expedition. Flo relayed my problem and symptoms to Mike Stroud – a doctor in his day-job – and then passed on his diagnosis and recommended treatment to me. Within five days my eye was fine and my vision restored, and I'll always be grateful to Ran and Mike for their help, even while they were enduring their own hardships on the Arctic Ocean. It was a rare example of unaffected camaraderie between polar expeditions, but one of the hallmarks of Ran's support of me over the years.

Perhaps it was the thought of Ran and Mike struggling towards the Pole but during the first leg of the flight home, from Longyearbyen on Spitsbergen to Tromsø in northern Norway, it suddenly dawned on me that Vaughan and I had been out on the ice for seventy days. It was one of the longer unsupported sledge-hauling journeys of the time, so long that to have gone all the way to the North Pole would only have taken about the same length of time. I'd done a bit of sea-ice work, unsupported, and the way I saw it, I had taken part in exactly the sort of expedition that would be needed to have a crack at the Pole. I thought 'That's it. I'm ready to go. I've short-circuited the system by doing one huge expedition with a very experienced mentor. I think I can give it a shot.'

Although the seed was sown on that flight, it was to be quite some time before the idea became a reality. However, Vaughan and I were very soon setting off on another demanding expedition, piloting an open, rigid-hulled inflatable boat, with no protection from the elements and two enormous 200 horsepower outboard motors on the back, on a voyage from London to Greenland. We had virtually planned it on the plane back from Spitsbergen. I secured a substantial cash sponsorship from Shell Unleaded fuel, but it wasn't enough to cover our costs and so I also invested the £30,000 inheritance that I'd just received from my grandmother. Had I told them, my parents would have been aghast but it was that or face the prospect of returning to office life within six months of leaving IMG. It kept me actively engaged in the Arctic but I was fast learning that this was a cash-burning environment. It's not like running a marathon, where all you need is a good pair of trainers; you simply cannot operate in the Arctic without cash, and plenty of it, because everything you need – flights, boats, freight, specialist equipment and supplies – all comes with a heavy price-tag attached.

Within six weeks of landing back at Heathrow, we had organised the new expedition from scratch and were bucketing our way downstream from Tower Bridge in London. There were three of us this time, Vaughan and I, and a boat engineer who was travelling with us as far as Iceland. We were planning to go all the way from London to New York via the Arctic, but it was a wild scheme and not very well thought out, partly because of a shortage of time. There was only a very narrow window of opportunity because you can only navigate the coast of Greenland in a small boat in August or early September. The rest of the year it's completely locked in by sea-ice, so we had to leave at once or wait another year. In retrospect the latter would have been the better idea, but we felt that we were on a roll and should go with it.

We hammered our way north in a series of arcs of eight to forty-eight hours duration, through some of the roughest seas in the northern hemisphere. Even the relatively sheltered first leg from London to Whitby on the Yorkshire coast gave us a taste of the problems that were to dog the voyage. When moving at speed, the boat was designed to come 'up onto the plane' and skim over the waves, but almost at once we noticed that instead it was settling lower and lower. It turned out that the hull was filling with water seeping in through rotten deck fittings. It reached the point where the air intakes were becoming awash and the engines started to fail, but we carried out some emergency repairs in Whitby and then headed on to Wick on the northern tip of Scotland.

As we roared away from the harbour wall there we put on a little show for the fishermen who'd gathered to see us off, only to be yanked clear of the water, having forgotten in our exhaustion to unfasten the mooring line. We carried on to Scalloway in the Shetland Islands, then Torshavn, the capital of the Faroe Islands, making an unnerving approach in total darkness and heavy seas, and then Hofn on the south-east coast of Iceland. There, driven by a perceived need to get back on schedule for the media following us back home, we had two near-death experiences as we tried to exit the harbour in a Storm Force 10 into a swell the like of which I hope never to see again from any boat; thirty-foot monster waves were breaking right over the top of the harbour walls. We battered our way on to the volcanic Vestmann Islands and then Reykjavik where we sheered a drive-shaft in one engine and, unknown to us at the time, also ruptured the power-head of the other engine as we hit a submerged offshore reef at thirty knots.

After another stop for repairs we made for Patreksfjordur on the north-west coast of Iceland where we waited for an eternity as we summoned the courage to attempt the crossing of the notorious Denmark Straits with negligible up-to-date information on either the weather or the sea-ice. At last, driven more by desperation and blind faith than logic, we headed out across the straits towards the remote village of Tasiilaq on east Greenland. One of the most powerful memories I have of the Arctic was to see, coming up over the horizon, a forest of jagged snow-covered peaks glistening in the orange light of the setting sun. We were so nearly there, just 20 miles or so left of the 350-mile crossing, when the damaged power-head packed up, leaving us with only one engine in an increasingly heavy following sea. The waves began to break over the low-level transom, and soon we were swamped, with our second engine's air intake fatally disappearing below the waterline. We were now adrift, with five miles of fragmented sea-ice separating us from the village on the shore. We spent a dire night secured by ratchet straps to the deck to avoid being washed overboard, but were eventually towed to the sanctuary of the harbour by a local boat.

It was a deservedly unceremonious end to an ill-prepared

venture. We had made it to Greenland, but had failed to carry on to New York and our dreams of a triumphant entry into the Hudson River and a tickertape parade down Broadway had to be put on hold. I'm not proud of failing to achieve our objective but it was a hell of an experience and I learned a lot from it, though in truth it was more how not to do things in future than how to do them. But from a standing start, by the end of that year, 1989, I had already completed two big Arctic expeditions, and could begin to think of myself as a tried and tested Arctic traveller. My only problem was that I was now flat broke and my polar ambitions had to be put on hold while I set about raising some money.

I decided to set up an adventure travel company offering guided tours to the Arctic. My client list could be counted on the fingers of one hand, but one of them, Robert Owen, was to prove central to my future in the polar regions. Now the godfather to my son, Wilf, he'd been referred to me by an adventure travel consultancy. He wanted a tough four-week expedition in the jungle, the mountains or the polar regions, and the best proposal put to him would get the contract. He visited my spartan home/office, a small, converted, wooden summerhouse in Wiltshire, and instantly felt he was dealing with someone who was more about gnarly expeditions than wasting money on deluxe office space. I duly won the contract with a proposal for a crossing of Spitsbergen – a fairly standard route except that I proposed to do it during the polar night – and Rob was amazed to have found someone who was prepared to do a trek at the most forbidding time of the year in the dark. But that's what my client wanted, and with the diary blank, it seemed like an exceedingly good idea to me.

We headed off to Spitsbergen with our sledges in early February 1991, when there was a little light on the horizon during the middle of the day but it was inky black for well over twenty hours out of the twenty-four, though it grew progressively lighter over the course of the month we were out on the ice. The air temperature at night (−20 °C) was not substantially lower than by day, but for the first time I realised the full significance of the effect of the sun on a polar expeditioner. When the sun is high in the sky I can walk over the ice dressed in only my thermals and feel pleasantly warm, but when it dips below the horizon, even if the air temperature is no different, the lack of the sun's radiation makes an immediate and dramatic difference to body temperature. On this expedition, even in my full Arctic survival gear, I was often bitterly cold.

During the long hours of darkness, we navigated by compass and used the light of the moon, the stars and the occasional sighting of the Northern Lights to illuminate our way across the ice. The Northern Lights are not often seen at the highest latitudes and, like most polar travellers, I'm more usually in the Arctic during the periods of twenty-four-hour daylight when they're not visible at all, and it was an experience that I'll never forget. No matter how many times you have seen them in photographs or on television, I guarantee that, like the first time you stand on the edge of the Grand Canyon or scuba-dive off the Great Barrier Reef, the first sight of those shimmering veils of light cascading across the night sky will leave you speechless. Depending on their altitude, they are sometimes red, sometimes green, sometimes white and sometimes blue, and sometimes accompanied by ethereal *whooshing* sounds. Filling a quadrant of the northern sky at one moment, they can then fade and disappear within seconds, only to reappear in a completely different part of the heavens moments later. I would defy even the most rampant egomaniac not to feel reduced to the insignificance of a flake of snow in the face of something so vast, unknowable and otherworldly. The Greenlanders seem immune to the power and majesty of the Northern Lights, but the rest of us can only gaze in awe on that nightly celestial light show, and the memory is something that I'll always treasure.

When we arrived back in Longyearbyen after twenty-five arduous days, Rob still had three days to spare, so we went back out on snowmobiles and did the whole thing again.

3

In 1992 my father had begun to complain of severe headaches. Not long afterwards, he was diagnosed with a malignant cancer of the brain. There were no options for treatment, the disease was inoperable. There was nothing to be done and, as with so many others in that tragic position, all we could do was to try to ease his sufferings and then simply watch him die.

His headaches grew steadily worse and then his speech began to falter, a particularly cruel blow to a born raconteur whose greatest pleasure in life was to converse and tell stories. Then his balance started to go and, all too soon, his bed became his world. I felt our time together was slipping away and yet I had to keep returning to work. As often as I could, I drove cross-country from Wiltshire, where I was living and working at the time, to my parents' home to support him, my mother and brother, and to spend as much time as possible with my Dad. Each time I'd see a further deterioration. His systems were slowly shutting down as the cancer tightened its grip. As he wanted, Mum looked after him at home to the end.

The sight of this once big and powerful man, with a remarkable zest and appetite for life, reduced to little more than a husk of a human being shocked me to the core. Finally, after months of suffering in silence, he reached the end of his endurance. On Good Friday, 1993, with my arms supporting his frail body and Mum and Henry at his side, he gave his last breath.

Later that evening, I went back in to the familiar room one final time to pay my last respects and found myself making a vow over his dead body. It was not one that he would have wished me to make, but nothing could have stopped me from uttering those words. 'Before I die I'm going to reach the North Pole – alone. No resupplies. If I do nothing else with my life, I will do that.' Then I said goodbye to my father for the last time and closed the door to his room.

The very next morning I sat down and drew up a rigorous training programme that would build my strength and stamina for the task that I had set myself: a gruelling combination of weights, rowing, running, and dragging progressively heavier weights to simulate the sledge that I would have to haul behind me to the Pole. And immediately after my father's funeral, I went down to Polzeath in Cornwall, a place I'd been visiting for twenty years, in search of a few days' respite and solitude to clear my mind of the traumas of the past months and focus all my attention on the task ahead.

In the early afternoon of my first full day there, I was surfing on the western side of the beach, at the opposite end from the lifeguards' hut. It wasn't ideally sited, because there was a promontory blocking their view of part of the bay. The black and white flags were flying, marking the section allocated to surfers, and there were two or three other surfers out, two young boys with just one white polystyrene surfboard between them and an overweight man in a white tee-shirt, who didn't have a board and was just messing about in the waves.

Over no more than about ten minutes, the whole wave pattern started to change and the most beautiful set of waves started coming in. They reared up quite quickly, about ten feet from trough to crest, perfectly formed and totally surfable, but a net accumulation of water was piling up with the surf and then flooding back out to sea as a powerful undercurrent that made it impossible to stand upright. On a surfboard it was no problem – you just hung on and enjoyed the ride – but as I glanced around, I suddenly realised that the two boys and the man in the tee-shirt were in trouble.

I could see them clearly between the waves, further out to

sea. There was a sort of thrashing in the water and the man was obviously in a panic, drowning and trying to wrestle the white polystyrene board from the two children clinging to it. There was no sign of the lifeguards. My heart started hammering and I thought, 'Action Stations', but as I headed towards them, another big wave broke over them and swept them all off the board. I could no longer see the man in the white tee-shirt, but I'd have to worry about him later. I grabbed one of the boys and dragged him onto my surfboard, then screamed at the other surfers within earshot to pick up the other boy. Out of the corner of my eye I saw one of them acknowledge my shout and start to head for the boy. Then all my attention was focused on the one I was trying to rescue, who was in a complete panic, struggling and fighting against me. I was trying to pin him down on the board and look after myself, because the next wave was already rearing up and I thought, 'I don't want to lose him and me,' and we were now dangerously near the rocks.

The wave broke over us and as we rose out of the water again, I could see that the surfer had the other boy safe, but there was still no sign of the man. I shouted to the others, 'The man in the white tee-shirt! The man in the white tee-shirt!' and then concentrated on getting the child to the shore. He was quieter now, lying still on the board, and I surfed in with him and got him on to the beach. I would have gone straight back out to look for the man but the boy just wouldn't be left alone. He was crying and clinging to me and I had to wait until the other guy brought the friend in. He was a lot calmer, so I said, 'Take your friend with you and run to the lifeguards' hut. Tell them what's happened and that there's a drowning man still out there.'

I thought that they had got the message, but it turned out that they were still in shock, because they just wandered off to find their parents and didn't pass the message on. But by then I was already paddling back out through the waves to try and find the man. I joined a few others who were still looking for him, but he was nowhere to be seen. After about five minutes, there was still no sign of lifeguards, so I surfed back in and ran to the hut; it was the first they had heard of any problem. They went out and looked for him for about half an hour and by then the Padstow lifeboat had also come out to join the search, but there was no trace of him. The next morning I went to the lifeguards' hut to ask if he'd been found, though I'd already guessed the answer. The body of a man in a white tee-shirt had been found washed up a few miles along the coast. It was another vivid reminder that life is short. Let death be your guide; if you're going to make your mark, do it today because tomorrow may be too late.

I took the first opportunity to fulfil my pledge to my father in the spring of the following year, 1994. If my sole ambition had been just to get to the Pole by any means possible, I could have done so with relative ease, starting from Siberia and operating as part of a team using air-dropped resupplies, but I saw no point or merit in simply replicating what other men had done before me. It wasn't that I wanted to break records for their own sake, but I did want to break new ground and, in however small a way, push back the frontiers of knowledge of what man can endure – mentally and physically – and achieve.

I conceived it as a solo expedition almost from the start because there was something in me that would not accept second best in anything. I wanted to establish myself and be accepted as a professional operator in the polar environment and to do that I felt that I had to set myself the hardest, the most difficult, indeed the absolute test of my abilities. Everybody vaguely understands that the North Pole is a very difficult place to reach, however you travel there, but just as a mountaineer might say 'I'm going to climb Everest, by the toughest route, without oxygen and solo,' I wanted to do the same thing in the polar world; I wanted a pure, simple and extreme test of everything one has: strength, intelligence, endurance, courage, mental toughness and technical skills, the whole nine yards. But if that urge to prove myself at the highest level was a prime motivation, there was also something else that had been driving me forward from the very first moment I ever went to the Arctic. When I returned home that first time, I found that every fibre of my body was aching to be back up there, and I've never lost that feeling. The New Zealand Maori have an expression for that sense of total identification with a place; they would describe it as being 'one of the standing places of my heart' and that's exactly how I feel about the Arctic.

In the longer term I also wanted to be associated with a new way of travelling in the polar regions. In mountaineering there is a siege approach and an alpine approach – travel slow and heavy or fast and light – but few polar travellers have got beyond the siege approach: pile up a sledge with all the supplies you need and slog your way there with the aid of a back-up team or air resupplies. But I thought I could foresee a time, if global warming hadn't destroyed the Arctic ice altogether by then, when people who were fit, strong and experienced in the conditions might be capable of reaching the Pole in as little as twenty days, carrying all they needed in a backpack or on a lightweight sledge.

It's only 470 miles, after all, like walking from Edinburgh to London or from Detroit to New York. If someone kidnapped my children and held a gun to their heads, how long would it take me to walk that far? It certainly wouldn't take sixty days. I'd do it in about eight days, I'd barely stop until I got there. So why does it take so long to get to the North Pole? Even allowing for the fact that there are no ice fields, pressure ridges and open leads between Detroit and New York, it shouldn't take four times as long to reach the Pole, and the only reason that it does is because you're dragging a ruddy great sledge behind you, loaded down with everything but the kitchen sink.

However, for my first expedition to the Pole, I adopted what I thought was a conservative, safety-first approach and made sure that I was carrying every conceivable item I might need. In doing so I was already giving myself as severe a handicap as a racehorse conceding weight to its rivals. At the time I didn't really see the significance of a 30-pound difference; I thought that hauling a 330-pound sledge would be little, if any harder than a 300-pound one, but there is a profound difference and a strength-sapping, cumulative effect. The weight of that sledge showed my lack of polar experience and my cavalier attitude to preparation for the expedition. I was physically fit and had trained fanatically hard for it – I wouldn't fail for lack of strength or stamina – but, partly for financial reasons, I had given nothing like the same thought, care and attention to the equipment I was using.

My sledge was far too heavy in itself and was poorly designed for gliding across ice and snow, and for minimising snags on ice- and snow-blocks. I had not even ensured that its runners were spaced to match the width of my ski tracks. I was also carrying far too many spares, too many off-the-shelf products and too many items built with strength rather than lightness in mind. On later expeditions I would pare everything to the minimum, even trimming the margins off the one small book I allowed myself to reduce its weight by a few ounces. That attention to minor detail can add up to a significant weight saving overall, but on that first polar expedition I had neither the wisdom nor the experience to realise its crucial importance.

I was in great physical shape after putting in six months hard fitness training under the watchful gaze of Bernie Shrosbree, an ex-Royal Marine who was now a private consultant for training and fitness coaching. Together we developed a special programme tailored to the requirements of an Arctic sledge-hauling expedition. Raising the necessary finance for the expedition proved a lot harder. Sponsorship was essential; I'd already used up my inheritance from my grandmother on the previous expedition and had no hope of covering costs that I estimated would be around £60,000. I wasn't being self-indulgent or planning a polar trip in five-star luxury, far from it – the budget was pared to the absolute minimum – but you simply cannot mount any sort of expedition to the Pole without serious money behind you. Going into the polar regions involves chartering aircraft to drop you off and pick you up, and to be on standby in case of a serious incident during the expedition. The flight companies are small specialist operators and you have to use them because there's no one else. They're not interested in doing any barter or contra-deal for publicity; they just want the money and plenty of it.

I could get much of the other equipment, clothing and supplies that I needed at a discount or even free of charge, but companies obviously wanted a benefit in return, in endorsements, publicity photographs or even motivational speeches to their employees when I got back. I thought, 'Fair enough – just give me the kit,' but the time and energy spent in negotiation and in fulfilling those commitments were desperately needed for research and preparation. With the wisdom I've acquired over the years, I would now much rather just buy almost everything that I need. That way, I don't have the distractions and I'm master of my own destiny, but back then I had so little money that I had no choice.

While I was at IMG, I had raised millions of pounds of sponsorship for big names involved in big sports with big television coverage. I was now trying to use the same techniques to raise money for a polar expedition that didn't even register on most people's radars. It proved to be a very hard sell. I started the hunt for a sponsor in spring 1993, about twelve months before my intended departure, greatly helped by my girlfriend, Mary Nicholson. We trawled through radio and TV advertisements, magazines and newspapers, billboards and Yellow Pages, and noted the names of potential sponsors on little cards. We'd bring them into the office the next day and work out how to contact these companies, either through their PR or advertising agency or their marketing or sponsorship departments, or straight to the chief executive or the marketing director. We worked out a strategy for every single company – and we approached around 1,200 of them – then wrote to them, outlining the expedition and the projected media coverage and promotional benefits to them, and closing by saying that we would contact them in four days to discuss it.

Many never replied but we followed up just the same, making a point of calling as promised in four days, trying to build credibility and transmit a sense of purpose: we were efficient people with whom they could do business. We'd rarely get through to a decision-maker, but we'd leave a message that we had called and would try them again and again, until the rejection came, as it invariably did. The Nigel Dempster gossip column in the *Daily Mail* had got hold of the story from one of the companies we'd approached, giving me useful publicity for my polar attempt. However, this had an unfortunate consequence, because I hadn't yet broken the news to my then employers, ECCO, an environmental and communications consultancy. As a result, I was hauled in for a major dressing-down by my bosses, but when they'd finished chewing me out, they offered to give me time off to make the expedition and all the office resources, for which I'll always be grateful to them. The Prince's Trust were also very supportive, as were my friends and family, but commercial organisations were not exactly beating a path to my door. It was a pretty soul-destroying experience and I was just about in despair when I suddenly had a stroke of luck. I was wandering around a shopping centre when I saw a tray of Sector Sport watches. The point-of-sale publicity had some very striking images of people kayaking off waterfalls and jumping out of airplanes on surfboards – all sorts of adrenalin-fuelled extreme sports. I made a note of the name and we discovered that the company was based in Italy, in Milan.

They responded with enthusiasm. My expedition fitted perfectly with what they called 'The No Limits Team' – people from all around the world who were specialists in particular extreme sports. They had no one involved in polar exploration and were very interested in adding me to their stable, but though their interest in sponsoring me never waned, the negotiations were very protracted and increasingly stressful and depressing. The time of my departure was fast approaching and, despite months of talks, I still had no binding commitment from them, nor any definite figure. In the end, with a month to go, I flew out to see them in Milan. I pointed out to them that hardball 'I'm the biggest gorilla in the corporate jungle and I'm going to screw you to the floor' tactics might well pay dividends when negotiating with a supplier, but were counterproductive in a sponsorship deal for an endeavour such as this. If they wanted to sponsor the expedition, I said, 'Do it now, and let me use the money to give myself the best possible chance of success, or don't sponsor me at all. But you're shooting yourselves in the foot by holding out till the last minute. I can't buy the equipment I need, and every day that goes by with this unresolved is just increasing the chances that instead of the success we all want, the expedition will end in failure.'

I was so stressed that I was just about to burst into tears. It wasn't just me, by now there were an awful lot of third parties involved as well and the whole thing was in danger of collapsing like a house of cards. Maybe the sight of a stiff-upper-lipped Englishman filling up with tears did the trick, but finally they said, 'OK, we'll sponsor you.' They offered £48,000, well short of what we had originally discussed, but I was in no position to argue. I had to take the money on offer or call the whole thing off. I came out of the meeting, into the warmth of a beautiful spring morning, full of excitement and happiness that the last obstacle had been removed; but the contract then did not arrive until ten days before my departure date, and by the time the money was paid into the expedition account I had just four days to purchase the bulk of the supplies, confirm the charter flights and complete a thousand and one other administrative tasks that could have been sorted out weeks and months before if the sponsors had not been quite so fond of corporate brinkmanship. I'd been planning and training for the expedition for twelve months, but I was now setting out much less well-organised and focused than I should have been.

I had chosen Ward Hunt Island, almost the last extremity of the North American continent, as my point of departure, and on 10 March 1994, I set out alone, dragging my fully laden sledge behind me. From the moment I set foot on the ice, I did not look back. I didn't want to see the island dwindle slowly into nothingness behind me. I had no room for emotions like sadness and regret. I was focused only on what lay ahead; nervous, yes, but also excited and elated to be free at last of the months of preparation, planning and training. I was now out there alone, pitting myself against the ice.

That adrenalin surge was very necessary, because the opening miles north of Ward Hunt were a nightmare. As I burned fuel and ate my rations, my sledge would become progressively lighter and easier to haul but right now it was at its maximum weight. The climatic conditions were at their worst – dark and wintry, with the sun still barely breaking the southern horizon – and the ice conditions were even more daunting. Before I even reached the true sea-ice, I had to cross a moonscape of old ice, permanently frozen to the coast, and then the seemingly endless terrain of pressure ridges rising from the pale grey surface of the sea-ice. Seen from the air, they look rather like paddocks on Dartmoor or in the Yorkshire Dales: a quilted pattern of stone walls enclosing small fields. But the walls are jumbled blocks of ice towering as much as twenty or thirty feet above the surface of the ice and often enclosing fields of drifted snow so fine, powder-dry and completely uncompacted that my sledge sank deep into it, almost disappearing from view. I was floundering helplessly, thigh-deep in soft snow, searching for some hold or purchase for the next step and trying to drag my sledge behind me through what felt like thick porridge.

Just as you would make your way through those English fields by taking a meandering course using gates and stiles, so I had to try to find 'gateways' through the pressure ridges, gaps or lower sections in the wall of ice, the points that offered the least resistance to the path I was trying to steer with my sledge. Sometimes there were none and then I had to scramble up and over the wall of jumbled blocks of ice. And beyond that came another ridge, and another, and another. All the time, I was weaving my way in a vaguely northerly direction, but the ice rarely allows you to head due north. I could look no further than the next ridge and the next snow-field, crossing where I could, dragging my monstrously heavy sledge over each vertiginous wall of ice, and trying to slow its breakneck descent on the other side, knowing that a moment's ill-luck or inattention might see it crashing down on top of me.

Even to move that 330-pound weight on the flat required a huge effort; to drag it through deep snow and over those rough walls of ice drained every ounce of strength that I had. When I reached the foot of each pressure ridge, I first took off my skis and strapped them to the top of the sledge, then began to scale the ridge – a task made even more difficult by the fact that my boots were not climbing boots but ski-boots. Having scaled the first few feet of sheer, slippery ice, I then had to find a secure position to anchor my feet so that there was no danger of slipping as I started to take the strain and haul on the rope traces, pulling up the dead weight of the sledge. At a certain point I then had to find a means of locking the sledge in position while I climbed higher up the ridge. It was impossible to go straight to the top and pull up the sledge in one go from there because there was never a straight path. There were always patches of deep snow, projections and ice-boulders where the sledge would get snagged, and all had to be circumvented by pulling, pushing and shoving; I just had to make it happen the best way I could.

It was hugely taxing on my physical strength and I was often hypoglycaemic, faint and fuzzy by the time I got myself and my sledge to the top of the ridge, but I just had to count to twenty, let my body re-energise itself and then begin lowering the sledge down the other side. Almost invariably it would snag and I'd have to clamber down and shove and heave to free it. To do so, I usually had to wrestle with the front end of the sledge and, once I was below it on a down-slope, I was in danger. When that 330-pound monster began to move, it went like a rocket, hurtling down, banging and crashing, and breaking anything in its path. If I'd been in the way, even on a drop of only ten or twenty feet, it would have smashed my femur or my pelvis to pieces.

I kept the sledge on a very tight leash but if I thought I was about to lose control of it, I just had to get out of the way fast, hurling myself to one side as it crashed down the slope. Even taking every precaution, there were times when I couldn't move fast enough to avoid it, and then I had to rely on quick wits and luck to keep me intact. On one occasion I just managed to squeeze my leg down into a little gully – no more than a crack between two ice-blocks – as the sledge ran straight over the top of it. Had the crack been an inch or two narrower, my leg would have been pulverised. Many travellers and adventurers have been injured in that way and, inexperienced as I was, I knew enough to realise that if it happened to me, alone out on the ice, I was as good as dead.

As I laboured to move the dead weight of my sledge, I also had to make regular halts to loosen or remove my outer layers of clothing. As Nanny Wigley's conditioning experiments would suggest, native populations of the sub-polar regions do develop a greater tolerance of the cold. Darwin observed natives of Tierra del Fuego suckling their babies in open boats apparently oblivious of the snow, spray and icy winds swirling around them, and Inuit tribes can endure conditions that few

Europeans could tolerate for long, but it may be as much to do with the fact that the Inuit are careful to regulate their body temperature by covering themselves in layers of warm clothing and minimising the amount of flesh exposed to Arctic winds and sub-zero temperatures.

In temperate regions we don't normally need to take any particular measures to protect ourselves from heat loss. If we feel cold, we can warm ourselves by involuntary actions like shivering – which can increase the heat generated by our bodies as much as fivefold – or by premeditated actions such as rubbing our hands together. In an Arctic environment such actions will not be sufficient and heat loss has to be reduced to prevent frostbite and hypothermia setting in. However, polar clothing must not only be warm enough to protect you when at rest but also have the capacity to prevent excessive build-up of heat and the consequent sweating when doing strenuous work like hauling and manhandling a sledge over the ice. Sweating is much worse than feeling cold, because the sweat rapidly converts to ice in the outermost layers. It is too late to remove layers of clothing when you are already sweating, so each morning on the ice, I made frequent stops to progressively loosen or remove layers of clothing as I warmed up: I first removed my gloves, then my headgear, then opened my coat and loosened the waist and sleeves, and then began removing layers of clothing as I and the day both warmed up. As soon as evening started to draw in, I replaced my clothing. Once more, it's too late to do so when you're already cold.

To maintain the body's core temperature in an environment like the Arctic and fuel the prodigious expenditure of energy needed for hauling the sledge also requires a vast increase in the calories consumed. The normal daily requirement for an adult male is somewhere between 1,900 and 2,800 calories. On polar expeditions I consume 5,300 to 6,500 calories a day and still contrive to lose weight hand over fist – I returned from my last polar expedition thirty-five pounds lighter than when I set off.

We lose body-heat through evaporation, radiation, convection and conduction. The first two are relatively controllable in polar regions, but unregulated convection – heat being carried away by the circulation of cold air – and conduction – the direct transfer of heat through contact with a cold substance – are life-threatening if not controlled. Wind-chill is hugely significant in heat convection and there is an exponential growth in the resultant heat loss – a wind of only 10 mph will remove not twice, but four times as much heat as one of 5 mph. In addition, the colder the initial air temperature, the more dramatic the effects of wind-chill will be. A 20 mph wind will convert an air temperature of −1 °C in calm conditions into one of −16° and a temperature of −26° to one of −51°. Loss of heat through conduction is less of a problem in air, but if a polar traveller falls into Arctic waters – as most of us have done – he is in immediate peril, because water is 240 times more conductive than air, leading to extremely rapid cooling of the body with potentially fatal consequences.

Lowering of the body's temperature, whether through rapid conduction by immersion in water, or the slower, subtler effects of convection, produces a progressive physical and mental deterioration. As blood retreats to the body's core, the muscles work less efficiently, the mind becomes confused, speech slurred and a feeling of apathy and lethargy overtakes you. Sufferers from hypothermia become so confused that they often remove their clothes, hastening their demise. It is such a frequent occurrence that it even has its own name: 'paradoxical disrobing'. If untreated, the victim slips into coma and death.

However, victims of even profound hypothermia can be revived if caught in time, though the symptoms are sometimes mistaken for death itself. The victim often lies in the foetal position, his arms and legs stiffening as if in rigor mortis, his pulse and respiration so faint that they are almost undetectable, and his pupils may not contract even when exposed to bright light. Yet people in such a condition have been revived and

'No one should be considered cold and dead until he has been warm and dead.'

While hypothermia affects the entire body, the other great peril of the cold, frostbite, is a localised injury, almost always affecting the bodily extremities: toes, fingers, nose, ears, cheeks and even genitals. As the affected parts of the body become colder and colder, blood vessels constrict and blood withdraws to the body core. Frostbite may then develop as the actual tissues of the affected part freeze and ice crystals form from moisture trapped inside and between the cells. The moisture expands as it freezes, rupturing the cell-walls. Even more serious frostbite occurs when damage to the cells and capillaries blocks the blood supply, causing sludging and clotting of the blood that may prove fatal. The first warning of frostbite is a loss of sensation in the affected area and, because of the absence of blood, the tissues will appear chalky white and feel wooden to the touch. Warming the life back into the frozen tissue may avert serious damage, but if the warning is ignored, permanent damage, including gangrene and the loss of the affected extremities, will almost certainly result. Medical advice is to re-warm the area – exotically painful as the nerves come back to life – without rubbing it at all, and once re-warmed it should be cosseted and never be allowed to be frozen again, which is almost impossible to guarantee in a polar environment. So, as with all medical advice, one listens and notes it, but Arctic expeditioners aren't necessarily able to follow it, if they want to keep the show on the road.

By my crude, stop-start method, I kept bludgeoning my way northwards, dragging the sledge behind me. At the end of each day, after six to eight hours of gruelling, unremitting effort that left me bone-weary with fatigue, I read my position on the GPS – the global positioning system, a hand-held navigational unit, which by tracking the position of satellites moving over-head can compute your position to within a handful of metres, and also gives you other information useful to a navigator. Each day, I found that I had made no more than one or two miles' progress towards my goal. The sledge was so heavy that I was forced to reduce its weight. I dumped my £2,000 video camera on one of the pressure ridges and said goodbye to all the baggage associated with it, because that wasn't critical to the mission, but even then, to make a useful difference to the sledge weight, I had to throw away some of my most crucial supplies as well and left a pile of fuel bottles and some ration packs on the ice. Having done that, I could not afford any further delays, because fuel is the one thing that you cannot run out of in the Arctic. Without it, you have no heat, no hot food and, most important of all, you cannot melt water to drink.

By the twentieth day, I had travelled just thirty miles north of my starting point, but I was beginning to encounter better ice and with the weight of my sledge reduced, I had high hopes of increasing the pace; but on that day I came to the first really big lead I had encountered. A long cloud of black 'frost-smoke' wreathing the open water had alerted me to the lead well before I reached its edge. It lay at right angles to my track, a stretch of open water, black as jet against the blue-whiteness of the ice, up to 200 yards wide and stretching away into the distance as far as I could see. I was a virtual novice on sea-ice. I'd travelled over it, but I'd never had to cross a single lead on any of my previous expeditions. I didn't have an immersion suit and my sledge wasn't watertight, so I couldn't swim across it; either I had to find a way round or wait for it to freeze over.

At the point where I hit the lead, there were terrific fields of ice-blocks and rubble to either side of me and I decided that, rather than spend days battling to the west or east in search of a place where the lead closed up again, I'd simply pitch my tent and wait for it to freeze over, allowing me to cross. It wasn't that cold – no more than −30 °C – but over a period of twelve hours at a temperature of −30°, sea-water will freeze to a point where it's about two inches thick – marginal as to whether it would take my weight if I tried to cross it. However, within twenty-four hours it would definitely have been strong enough to bear not only my own weight, but that of my mammoth sledge as well ... always providing that nothing else had changed in the meantime.

I woke up the next morning to find that the original lead had indeed frozen over, but the ice-pans had also been torn further apart by the wind and tides, exposing a fresh stretch of open water in the middle. There was nothing I could do except wait a further day and night. The following morning it was the same story: more newly frozen ice, but beyond it another fresh expanse of open water. And every morning for the next five days I made the same disheartening discovery. The lead never closed completely, because each time it froze, it also pulled further apart.

By this time I was burning up with frustration and impatience. It was worse than simply marking time, for every day I was consuming more scarce rations and fuel and wasting yet more of those precious days of the Arctic spring and early summer when a journey to the Pole is possible. I felt enormous pressure to get across somehow and continue northwards, both out of a sense of obligation to the suppliers, sponsors and supporters who had all had faith in me and invested their time or money in my expedition, but even more because my self-respect required that I find a way past this infuriating obstacle. Somehow, I had to be able to cross that ridiculously narrow, frustrating gap that stood between me and my goal.

I was now camped on a platform of solid ice, an old pan or floe culminating in an almost sheer cliff around nine feet thick, protruding perhaps two feet above the water level and falling seven feet below it. Beyond that platform was a forty-metre expanse of progressively thinner ice-layers, with a zig-zagging line of open water in the middle, in places as little as one or two metres wide. It was narrow enough to jump across, providing that the ice didn't give way beneath me, but it wasn't as simple as walking straight out across a solid base and jumping off. The ice towards the middle of the frozen lead was thin enough to bend beneath me, and as I neared the edge my weight pushed the ice-sheet down into the water, leaving me to jump from a sloping, water-covered shelf of fragile ice.

Whatever the risks, I had waited immobile long enough. Any action was better than this endless, pointless wait. I left my sledge on the thick ice-platform and took off my skis – first mistake. Holding the sledge-traces in one hand, paid out to their fullest extent – second mistake – I began inching my way out across the newer ice. I could feel it flexing beneath me. Almost imperceptible at first, the movement grew more and more pronounced as I neared the open water, and I could also see the colour of the ice changing beneath my feet. At the southern edge of the frozen lead it was light *nilas* – thick enough to be an opaque white colour – but nearer the open water it became closer to dark *nilas* – so thin that the water beneath was clearly visible through it.

I was now moving slower and slower, my steps increasingly hesitant. I was almost on the edge of the ice-sheet, and looking down, fascinated, into the ink-black depths of the open water. I had just thought, 'Maybe I can step over this', when I felt as if I was falling through a stage trapdoor. The ice simply crumbled beneath me and I found myself floundering in the frigid waters of the Arctic.

Falling through the ice is not such a big deal if you've got team-mates with you because they should be able to get you out easily enough, but if you're on your own, it's definitely life-threatening. I didn't have a complete panic attack but I came close to it, because for the first time I was no longer in complete control of the situation. I'd often tried to imagine what it would be like to fall through the ice. I'd supposed that the shock of the icy water would be heart-stopping, but to my surprise I didn't feel instant cold. I was wearing boots, gloves, mitts and layer upon layer of clothing, trapping a lot of air, and at first the layers acted like a rather primitive and leaky wet-suit, slowing the rate at which the water came into contact with my body, but within a very short time, probably no more than thirty seconds, my clothes were saturated. As the blood retreated towards the core of my body, my limbs grew leaden and the performance of my muscles began to deteriorate rapidly.

I'd taken an involuntary breath as I went into the water. I came up coughing and spluttering and facing an immediate snap decision: should I go forwards or backwards? That was easy; I had to make for the side where my sledge, tent and supplies were, otherwise I would haul myself out onto the ice only to die from hypothermia. I was wearing a heavy underwater camera around my neck – I wasn't expecting to fall into the water, but I'd been told that it would give me better pictures than any other camera in the Arctic environment where condensation is such a problem – and I was also weighed down by my bulky, cumbersome and now waterlogged clothing and ski-boots, heavy even before they were filled with water. In addition, once I'd broken through the ice, the surface tension was gone and it continued to break as I sought enough purchase on it to haul myself out. Wearing mitts on top of gloves also made it hard to take a grip of anything, let alone the slippery surface of wet ice. I reached up onto the ice-sheet again and again, but each time it either broke as I put my weight on it, or my hands just slipped off the edge, plunging me back into the water.

It began to dawn on me that my only hope of survival was to smash my way like an icebreaker all the way back to the edge of the ice that was thick enough to support my weight, but it was a long way, perhaps ten metres, and I was unsure whether I could make it. I was feeling more and more cold and tired, and my muscles were now barely responding to the commands of my brain. I was starting to suffer from hypothermia and my life systems were beginning to shut down.

In my mind's eye I was seeing front page headlines, 'Arctic Explorer drowns in Arctic Ocean', and I suddenly thought,

'They won't even know that. No one will ever know what happened, whether I drowned, shot myself by accident, died of starvation or hypothermia or was eaten by a polar bear.' That was the call to action; not because people had to know what had happened to me – I wasn't egotistical enough to imagine that many would care one way or the other – but because the idea of disappearing without trace into the Arctic Ocean was simply not acceptable to me. From then on, I was totally focused on doing whatever was necessary to save my life. I knew I'd been in the water a long time now, but while I was wondering if I would last long enough to make it, I was also still breaking my way through the ice, bringing my numbed arms down in front of me with all the force I could muster, my only forward propulsion coming from the feeble kicks of my legs in my huge, waterlogged boots.

Eventually I reached a part where the ice was thicker and would no longer break under my weight as I thrashed at it with my leaden arms. I was too far gone even to be aware of how I did it, but somehow, like a half-drowned seal emerging from the water, I dragged myself out on to the ice. I was drowsy and incredibly weary, and felt that I just needed to rest for a minute; but that thought once more set alarm bells clanging in my head; hypothermia was becoming advanced. I'd gone up one gear to get myself out of the water, now I had to do it again to get myself moving. I still had not saved myself; I could easily die of hypothermia.

I forced myself to get up, shambled to the sledge and began putting up my tent. It was very difficult because my hands and fingers were so numb that I could barely grasp anything with them, and I made no attempt to secure it properly or weigh down the valances with snow. I just knew that I had to have shelter from the cold fast.

Once the tent was up, I crawled inside, zipped up the flap and tried to light my little portable stove. I had to try over and over again, fumbling with the controls and dropping the matches from my numbed fingers, but at last, almost weeping with relief, I saw it roar into flame. I scraped a few handfuls of snow from outside the tent and put it on to boil for hot food and a cup of tea, then tore off my wet clothing, put on some dry clothes and tried to massage warmth back into my extremities. I used up an awful lot of fuel – many precious litres – warming myself and trying to dry as much of my kit as I could, but this was a life-or-death moment and there was no question of rationing fuel. Over an hour had passed before I could be certain that I had avoided frostbite in my fingers and toes, and that I would survive the threat of hypothermia. Now, with much greater experience, if I get wet I just keep my specially designed clothing on and try to dry it with the body-heat generated from hard work; if there's a decent part of the day left I just get out there and start slogging north again. But I was inexperienced then and, in any event, there wasn't enough of the day left to make it worth carrying on, so I just stayed in the tent gathering my thoughts.

I spent five more days on the edge of that lead, looking out across it every day, but every day it had widened a little more, and there was still never a time when the ice completely closed over the black water. A more seasoned polar expeditioner would have just gritted his teeth and tried to go east or west to find a way around it. Now, after many more years of Arctic journeys, I can often tell how a lead was formed, whether to go east or west to circumvent it, and how long it's likely to take to get around it, but that only comes with experience and back then I lacked that crucial knowledge.

For the first time I made myself face the probability that I would fail to reach my goal. Having dumped some of my fuel and then wasted all those days by the 'impassable' lead, I knew in my heart that there was no point in going on, because I simply didn't have enough fuel left to reach the Pole. I didn't want to let myself down or fail the people who'd believed in me and supported me – the Prince's Trust and my sponsors and suppliers – who were all expecting, or at the least hoping that I would succeed, but after agonising for ten days on the edge of that ever expanding lead, I finally made the call for an airlift off the ice.

The sense of failure, as I watched the plane that was to lift me out circle and land, was one of the bleakest feelings I had endured in my life to that point, but I really didn't think there was anything else I could do. I even managed to convince myself that it was just one of those years when there was too much open water, but the hard truth was that I'd blown it. I'd pulled out not so much through any lack of will but from sheer lack of knowledge; I simply didn't understand enough about how the Arctic Ocean works. I'd read the few available accounts of previous travellers who had often cited unusually bad weather or ice conditions as the reason for not being able to continue and that was pretty much the limit of the research I'd done. Very few books about the Arctic Ocean have ever been published, but I should have looked elsewhere, to the papers published by scientific institutions.

I'd done a few Arctic expeditions, but sea-ice work is totally different from crossing terra firma in Greenland or Svalbard, and there are special features of the Arctic Ocean with which I was not familiar; I simply hadn't done enough research and preparation, nor gained enough prior experience. But the greatest lesson I learned from the fiasco of my first polar expedition was that the attitude of 'Whatever it takes, I'll do,' that I'd thought was all I really needed, is not enough on its own. It's a very useful attribute, but to give yourself a realistic chance of reaching the Pole, you need more than luck and determination; you also have to learn the ways of the Arctic Ocean. It's the only way to guarantee that you can make informed decisions, rather than just bludgeoning away, head down, as much in hope as expectation. The one positive thing I could take from my failure the first time was the knowledge I'd gained on what it would take to succeed the next time.

4

I had been going out with Mary Nicholson since 1992 and she'd been with me through the roller-coaster of my father's death, planning the expedition, raising the money and then staying in Britain trying to keep us afloat financially while I was trying and failing to reach the Pole. We'd originally met at a party held in the crypt of a church. The relationship could easily have been stillborn – she was the daughter of an Eton house-master and I was a product of Eton's hated rival Harrow – but we hit it off from the start. She always claims that she had been looking for a husband since she was twelve years old and had just about given up hope of ever finding one, when I appeared on the scene.

When I came back from the Pole, I took her to the Caribbean on holiday and, as I later discovered, she thought that I was finally going to ask her to marry me, so every evening at dinner there was an air of suppressed tension and expectation – was this going to be the big moment? I was unaware of all this emotional turmoil across the table from me and I didn't pop the question until a few weeks later, when we were back in England. So her woman's intuition was perfect but her timing was a bit off. She accepted, and I was delighted, but also pretty anxious about it because I felt that marriage would be a hard enough adjustment to make without the added stress of having no money coming in. I grew so dispirited at my lack of income that I thought about being a minicab driver or even a male escort; rather alarmingly, Mary thought I'd be good at that. But in the end we took the plunge and decided that, money or no money, we'd get married the following June.

I can't have been great company for the rest of that year. I'd come back from the Pole feeling very low, and knowing that I was going to have to go back, but the next time some things would have to be handled differently. I felt very strongly that the dire funding situation had impacted on my levels of stress before I set off; if you get to the starting line feeling frazzled before you've even taken a step, that is not doing your chances any good. However the first priority for now was to find a job, because, even before I took three months out to try and reach the Pole, it was obvious that my time with ECCO had reached a natural end and I left the company. I took the decision with the utmost reluctance, because I was already acutely sensitive to the fact that my life could be history repeating itself. I might be my father's son in more ways than one, drifting endlessly from one failed career to another.

I was still desperate to get to the Pole solo and unsupported, but with my economic circumstances so dire, I simply couldn't look Mary in the eye and announce that I was going off to make another attempt. She knew it was something I wanted to do, though perhaps she didn't realise how important it was to me; and I probably didn't verbalise it because, given my economic situation, I thought it would be totally inappropriate and irresponsible to do so. I knew the commitment that my previous expedition had required; just trying to raise the sort of money needed was a full-time job and I simply didn't have the resources to devote to it. Nor did I want to go into debt. I had always paid promptly for anything I ordered, and I saw that as an important part of building my reputation in the polar world. This strategy had served me well over the years because when I needed things specially modified or delivered in a hurry, people knew that they could trust me.

So, even though the thought of someone else completing the solo, unsupported expedition to the Pole that I had pledged I would do for my father made me feel almost physically sick, I had to sort myself out financially before I could even contemplate another attempt. My only asset was my house, an old workman's cottage in a wonderful hamlet called Honeystreet, on the Kennet and Avon canal in Wiltshire. It was a gorgeous location, but not exactly handy either for potential places of employment or for seeing Mary, and I spent most of my time in London staying at her house. A real grafter, Mary was a very successful PR professional in high-powered media relations, but she had just gone freelance, setting up not only her own PR company but also a dress agency dealing in designer wedding dresses – only one careful previous owner – and a graphology consultancy offering personality assessment through the analysis of the subject's handwriting. The graphology involved a lot of corporate work but the media also used her to analyse some very interesting handwriting samples, including Michael Jackson and Princess Diana, as well as some serious criminals. She was the first person to throw light on the fact that Thomas Hamilton had planned his massacre in advance of his attack on the school in Dunblane.

I was soon working for a PR company myself, as deputy managing director, specialising in fashion and *haute couture*, one of only two men in a dynamic company employing eighteen women. I obviously learned something from it because I can still amaze our women friends, and their partners, by my ability to spot an Arabella Pollen or Amanda Wakeley dress at a thousand paces, but unsurprisingly it proved not to be my natural habitat. Mary suggested that I should think about making use of the contacts I'd made in exploration and adventure travel by setting up my own PR company to service the outdoor clothing and equipment industry. As if she didn't have enough work on her own plate, she duly helped me to set up The Summit Consultancy and I ran it from the spare room of her house, without notable success. It faced one crippling problem: in the early 1990s outdoor clothing and equipment was essentially a cottage industry and most of the companies involved in it simply weren't big enough to have the resources for public relations. I struggled along, hand-to-mouth, for the rest of that year but then, out of the blue, came a life-changing phone call.

In March 1995, Robert Owen, the client I'd taken on a crossing of Spitsbergen five years before, got in touch. He'd moved between jobs in the City, had a severance pay-off burning a hole in his pocket, and wondered whether I'd like to do another Arctic expedition with him? We decided on a ten-day expedition to the North Magnetic Pole, which has traced an erratic NNW path deep into the Canadian high Arctic in recent centuries. At that time it was off the coast of Ellef Ringnes Island, one of the Queen Elizabeth Islands north of Canada's North-West Passage. He gave me just four weeks' notice but I abandoned my faltering PR firm without a backward glance. Organising the expedition from scratch, I got us outfitted and equipped and booked the flights, and we set off bang on schedule. We had fine weather and a great expedition, and really had a good time together, trekking for ten days over the ice and covering about ten nautical miles a day – about 180 kilometres in all – before ending the trip at King Christian Island.

When I flew back into Heathrow with Robert, Mary was waiting to greet us. She looked me over. I was tanned, very fit and radiating an aura of happiness and satisfaction at a job well done. She'd never seen that before because I'd been desperately unhappy when I came back from the Arctic on my previous trip. Before we'd even got out of the airport, she'd sat me down with a coffee and said, 'Well, it's obvious what you should be doing, Pen. You should stop messing about with PR and get on with what you love and are really good at. This is what you were born to do: you've got to become a polar guide. Everyone knows you're passionate about the polar regions, you're good with people and a great leader. You're not destined for a desk job, get out there and do your stuff.'

I didn't need much convincing that she was right. This was the way to fulfil the destiny of which I'd been aware for most of my life. Just like my former clients at IMG, I'd now be earning my living doing the thing I loved most. There was just one minor question: could I make it pay? But the only way to answer that was to try. The Polar Travel Company was born there and then. Robert had been the catalyst, the first spark, but Mary was the one who instilled in me the confidence to do it. She gave me her wholehearted backing and support, and she worked as hard as I did to make it happen.

I did some serious thinking about what I wanted the company to be, and we spent many hours firing ideas to and fro across the kitchen table. One thing on which we both agreed was that The Polar Travel Company had to be radically inclusive. I felt that men and women, young and old, of all races, shapes and sizes, experienced or inexperienced, able-bodied or disabled, should all have the opportunity, if they so wished, to accept the challenge of a polar expedition at one level of difficulty or another, and experience something of the beauty and allure of the pristine wilderness areas of the Arctic and Antarctic. To some it might have seemed foolish or dangerous to take people with no experience into one of the most extreme environments on earth, but then, as now, I was a firm believer that if you give people the right encouragement, advice and technical support, and let them develop skills and confidence through a stepped progression rather than throwing them in to sink or swim from Day One, they have the potential to achieve the most amazing things. My fundamental principle in taking inexperienced people of varying strengths, ages and capabilities to the polar regions was that the safety of the client overrode all other considerations. What you do with yourself is your own affair but if you can't ensure the near absolute safety of your clients in the Arctic, you shouldn't be taking them there. There are dangers and extremes of weather and remoteness to deal with, but my years of experience there made me confident that whatever danger might threaten, I could protect my clients and ensure their safety and survival;

and, indeed, enable them to extract the most value from the experience.

In between compiling guest lists and writing invitations for our wedding, I planned a series of Arctic and Antarctic expeditions of varying degrees of difficulty, ranging all the way from a chance to gauge their entry level on a Polar Preparation Course for less than £400 on Dartmoor, right up to an 'All the Way' expedition to the North Pole at over £35,000. Once I'd sorted out those, I designed and typed up a brochure and had it printed at Prontaprint in London's Fulham Road. All we had to do then was let the world know that we existed.

Mary and I were married in June 1995 and after an idyllic honeymoon, we buckled down to preparing for the August launch of The Polar Travel Company. We had no money for advertising, so we had to rely entirely on our wits, promoting the company through editorial coverage in newspapers, magazines, radio and TV. Fortunately, my in-house PR person was one of the best in the business. She hired the Explorers' Room in the Carlton Towers Hotel in Knightsbridge, rounded up the media and laid on a splendid stunt for a baking hot day in August during the media's traditional silly season: we borrowed the only snowmobile in Britain and parked it in the road outside. An ITN camera crew and battalions of national press photographers turned out for the photo-call and I was just about to do my big launch speech when a report came through that Alison Hargreaves, one of Britain's leading mountaineers, was missing, presumed dead, on K2. With a genuine tragedy involving a British adventurer to cover, the media instantly lost its appetite for self-serving publicity stunts by another one. By the end of my talk fifteen minutes later, the camera crews and virtually all the photographers had gone. Instead of the blanket coverage we'd been hoping for, all we got was a paragraph on an inside page of the *Daily Mail*, and even that was wasted because the *Mail* didn't print our phone number and, due to a great British cock-up, when people phoned up Directory Enquiries they were told that there was no number listed for The Polar Travel Company. The first I knew of this was when someone called having got our number by a roundabout route, and said, 'You're bloody hard to find. Why aren't you in the phone book?'

Mary was furious; we'd worked damned hard trying to get the company up and running, and we were now facing a disaster. But when she's firing on all cylinders, Mary can be a very scary woman. She worked her way up the British Telecom hierarchy and within an hour was talking to the deputy chairman. It transpired that they had a system for situations like this; each operator had a scribble board in front of them and the number was hand-written on to these. By the time she'd sorted that one out, Mary was heaving big sobs in the back garden. We couldn't get press coverage, we couldn't even get Directory Enquiries; the company was sunk before it had even been launched. We couldn't relaunch it with another story because there wasn't another one to do. 'Actually, there is another story,' I said.

One of the first polar projects I'd become involved in was an expedition to the North Pole for someone who has since become one of our greatest friends, Caroline Hamilton. I met her at a drinks party and we had a conversation about how she had been to the Arctic Circle on Midsummer's Day to see the sun go all the way round the horizon. Now Caroline wanted to go further, to the North Pole itself, and I said 'Fine, I can organise whatever style of trip you like. When do you want to go and how do you want to do it?' There were a couple of minor problems: She wouldn't be able to devote months to training and building up Arctic experience because of work commitments; she would have to limit her expedition experience to three weeks' holiday leave; and she only had £1,500 readily available – a drop in the ocean compared to the cost of that sort of expedition. With the best will in the world, you're not going to go all the way to the North Pole in three weeks on £1,500 but I really wanted to make it happen for her because here was my first real client and I felt that I shouldn't be turning any customers away.

I was talking to Mary about the problem when I hit on the solution: an all-women relay format. We would have five teams of four women and Caroline, the leader of the expedition, would be in the last team that would do the final leg to the Pole. She and all her team mates would be part of the first historic all-women North Pole expedition, but no individual would have to put in too much time, effort or money. In order for it to be a truly all-women expedition, I couldn't be the one to act as guide. In the whole world there were only five women qualified to act as Arctic guides at the time and as only two were available, they pretty much chose themselves.

The point of an all-women expedition was partly to showcase the inclusive nature of The Polar Travel Company; these were ordinary women, with normal, run-of-the-mill jobs, who were working together to achieve something extraordinary. It was also a concept that was sure to appeal to the media and, in turn, that would help to attract the sponsors needed to underwrite the substantial cost of mounting the expedition. I asked Caroline if she would mind if we did another press conference to launch both the company and her expedition. She said that was fine, so we hired a room at the Institute of Directors and invited the press to another launch. Once again they all turned up and this time we were lucky to hit a slow news day. We had a good spread of coverage and a classic 'page three' shot – albeit in the *Daily Telegraph*, so they kept their clothes on – of Mary, Caroline and assorted girlfriends, all kitted out in full Arctic gear and sitting in line on a huge sledge like birds on a branch. The theme was that these women were going to the Pole and if you wanted to join the fun, get in touch. Within a week we had had 300 enquiries.

Mary and I had been looking for a house deep in the country

since we got married. I couldn't be happy for long living in a town or city and Mary wanted somewhere with stabling for her horse and open country in which to ride it. In December of that year we found our dream home and took on another lifetime project: Wydemeet, a derelict wreck of a house in a narrow valley surrounded by the moors and tors of Dartmoor. A fast-flowing salmon river, the Swincombe, ran through the valley, draining the marshes of Fox Tor Mire, a setting appropriated by Sir Arthur Conan Doyle as the 'Grimpen Mire' of *The Hound of the Baskervilles*. The house was a large stone fishing lodge with wisteria-clad walls and honeysuckle twining around the door, reached by a twisting drive through gardens full of ash, beech and rowan trees and rich with spring flowers. The wood-panelled rooms didn't seem to have been decorated or cleaned since the year it was built – 1914 – and even to my inexpert eye, there were signs of woodworm and dry rot in the timbers, and a number of slates missing from the roof, but the beauty, peace and isolation of the surroundings and the light streaming through the windows must have blinded us to these minor blemishes, because before we drove back down the road we'd made up our minds to buy it.

We moved into Wydemeet on 21 December 1995 and three weeks later we held the first selection call and introductory weekend for the seventy-five women on the long-list for the expedition to the Pole. The final selection course was in September 1996, when we reduced the list to the final twenty, plus one reserve. They then had six months both to prepare themselves and raise their contribution to the expedition, beginning in March 1997. The actual cost of the expedition was going to be £325,000; divided between the twenty women, it worked out at about £16,000 each. Since the aim was to enable women to take part no matter what their personal circumstances, we set the individual contributions at £1,500: enough to demonstrate a serious commitment to the project but not enough to break the bank for anyone who was in paid work.

While this was a seriously good deal for the women, it was dependent on the participants raising the additional money through sponsorship. That is hard work even for professional fundraisers and for enthusiastic amateurs it was next to imposs- ible. Caroline and I found that we were progressively increasing the hours that we were spending on the project to the exclusion of almost everything else, not least because we really wanted to make it happen. I'd gone public about it at the launch, my polar reputation was on the line and I wanted it to be done right. Just like Long Ducker all those years before, it's no good just saying you're going to do it – you have to follow through; but there was a major cash shortfall to overcome. Even the most successful fundraisers among the chosen twenty women – a mother and daughter combination who raised something like £10,000 each, one largely from her employer, the other through the Damart thermal clothing company – were well short of the target figure of over £16,000 each, and the rest, except for Caroline and two or three others, raised nothing like that amount.

To cover the yawning, £250,000 gap, Mary and I had to become completely immersed in working with the team to raise the money ourselves. Mary sometimes joked that we had set up the world's first polar social services department, and there were times when I paused to wonder how many tour operators would have gone to those lengths – usually the clients pay you, rather than you raising the money for them to go on holiday. The company was so strapped for cash that I couldn't even draw any wages. The women thought that I was doing it all for the publicity, and of course that was my prime commercial purpose, but by far the biggest motivation was a personal one in wanting to make it happen, full stop, and I was taking an enormous personal and financial risk to do so. Everything was in the melting pot, including my company, my house and my marriage. I didn't tell the expedition members that, of course. I kept up a well-organised, professional front, and I think a lot of them would be quite shocked to know what was going on.

The stresses of launching a business, renovating a house and chasing sponsorship money as I struggled to pull together a massively expensive expedition probably contributed to me becoming seriously ill with pneumonia that winter, and, after further personal contributions from the team members and some substantial financial risk-taking by me as the organising company, it was Mary who eventually secured the clinching sponsorship deal, bringing the biscuit manufacturer McVitie's aboard. The fact that no penguins had yet reached the North Pole inspired them to link the expedition with their Penguin brand and the injection of cash they contributed to purchase the title rights tipped the balance.

By March 1997, when the first team of six women began moving north from Ward Hunt Island on the first leg of the McVitie's Penguin Polar Relay, The Polar Travel Company was also up and running. At the same time I was taking a party to the North Magnetic Pole using snowmobiles and sledges. And within what seemed like about five minutes of coming back from organising and leading that expedition, I was off with another, leading a group – all of whom, apart from one rock musician who'd somehow been added to the mix, were ex-military men and now chief executives of substantial companies – on the first of what became our most popular expeditions: 'The Last Degree', flying in to 89°N and then sledge-hauling the last sixty miles to the North Geographic Pole.

In that year alone, we organised three expeditions to the North Pole in the ninety-day window in spring and early summer when it is possible to trek in the high Arctic, and had set up one to the South Pole earlier in the year. All the time I was out on the ice, I was learning my craft and improving my skills – often through trial and error – but the logistics and the fundraising placed huge demands on my time and energy, and I had started recruiting people ahead of the season to spread the load. Mike Ewart Smith was first on board. He had been doing some work for Operation Raleigh in Uganda, and when he joined us, he hit the ground running. He was really competent; seriously into administration and spreadsheets, and just the man to introduce some sense of order into my often chaotic paperwork. A friend of his, Peter Noble-Jones, then joined us and, as the workload continued to mushroom, we took on another friend, Serena Chance. But even with four of us working flat out on the project, plus Mary handling the PR side, we were still overloaded with work; we could have had a team of ten and it still wouldn't have been enough. We were all squashed into our attic office at Wydemeet with the phones going the whole time and people talking to media and customers, chasing sponsors and doing deals with equipment suppliers; the pressure was simply horrendous. But because we put so much into the McVitie's Penguin Polar Relay, which reached the Pole successfully on 27 May, and all the other expeditions that we were running in 1997, we rather took our eye off the ball as far as marketing for the next year was concerned, and as 1998 was about to dawn, I found that we had only a handful of clients booked and none at all in the spring months. I was already feeling that, despite all my Arctic knowledge and experience, a gap was opening up between what I had actually achieved and what I thought I could do, and I was even feeling a bit of a fraud, uncomfortable with the esteem in which I was being held by my clients, when I didn't feel I'd really achieved enough to earn their respect. I was enabling people to do things that they wanted to do, and the all-women relay was an extreme case of that, but part of me was thinking 'If only you could have applied all the effort to your own expedition.' So the opportunity afforded by the lack of clients was too good to miss.

I took a deep breath and then announced to Mary that rather than sit at home twiddling my thumbs, I was planning to do something constructive and seize the chance to make another solo, unsupported expedition to the Pole that, if successful, would also act as a PR and marketing flagship for The Polar

Travel Company. It turned out that Mary had an announcement of her own to make: she had just discovered that she was pregnant with our first child. That fantastic news could have changed everything, but Mary was insistent that I would be back a good four months before the birth and that I should go ahead with the expedition. She has always had very definite opinions and has never been afraid to voice them. If she had not wanted me to go, she would have said so loud and clear, but she knew what had attracted her to me in the first place – that I was a maverick sort of character with whom life was obviously going to be a bit of a roller-coaster ride – and she strongly felt that it would be a mistake to try to change me and harness me into a steady nine-to-five job. She'd shown the courage of her convictions through some very tough financial times and saw no reason to change them now. Provided that I wasn't burning money that could have been better channelled into the business, she was happy that I was doing something constructive. It was a good opportunity – so I should go for it. Nonetheless, it was still a tough decision to take, and I could not have even contemplated going to the Pole without Mary's unequivocal blessing.

5

I'd taken a conservative approach to my first solo polar expedition, reasoning that it was not the occasion to take big risks but rather to make small improvements on previous expeditions. But the biggest lesson I'd learned was that by far the largest cause of slow progress across the ice was the weight in the sledge and this led me to an interesting thought: if I'd only taken half the rations, I'd have moved faster and travelled further. And the way to make my next attempt seemed to be to move away from crossing the ice at a snail's pace, dragging a massively loaded sledge behind me. Instead I wanted to take an 'Alpine approach' in mountaineering terminology. If I was going to move much faster over the ice, I'd need a lot less time en route and therefore much less food and fuel – the two biggest weight components – and therefore I could put all my supplies in a rucksack and a small sledge. It would be an all-or-nothing process, predicated on my ability to move over the ice at unprecedented speeds – almost twice as fast as a normal expedition – but if I succeeded, I would have demonstrated a radically new way of tackling shorter and mid-length polar expeditions where speed across the ground was key.

My first problem was the shortage of time; it was now the end of December and I would have to be ready to go in four months maximum. I also had some serious work to do to build up my fitness levels, because I had been doing no specific training, just the general strength and aerobic work needed for guiding clients during the two- to three-month Arctic season, and I needed sponsorship money fast. I decided that it was pointless to waste time writing to hundreds of companies as I'd done before the first expedition. Instead I made an ultra-focused approach to ten companies that, for various different reasons, I'd identified either as possible title sponsors for the expedition in their own right, or as bridges to organisations that might be. The first person I spoke to was Julian Hanson-Smith, another client who had become a good friend of The Polar Travel Company, and who ran a public relations company in the City called Financial Dynamics. In turn, he put me in touch with Phil White, the chief executive of the coach company National Express. In late February, just over a month before I was due to leave for the Arctic, I met Phil at his company's headquarters in a beautiful Georgian house near Winchester. I drove up the sweeping drive, past orangeries and colonnades, walked into the reception area and was shown into a huge old dining room where Phil and a public relations executive were waiting.

The first thing I did was to spread a map of the Arctic on the table; I always like to take one of my favourite, really attractive maps with me. Lots of people love maps and they're a great icebreaker, because they draw everyone in, you don't have to have eye contact, you can all just be looking at this beautiful map in the middle of the table. As you trace your route with your finger while explaining the environment and challenges, you've virtually done the journey in your and their mind's eye: 'I'm going from here to here, job done.' As I showed him the map, I gave him my background and Arctic experience and explained my belief in an Alpine, lightning-strike approach. My passion must have communicated itself to him, because he said, 'Just stay here a moment, I'm going to have a chat with some colleagues.' He came back a few moments later and told me they'd pay £50,000 in return for my titling the expedition 'The National Polar Express'. That was it – bang. I had gone from spending twelve months approaching 1,200 companies and getting virtually nowhere to talking to one company and doing a deal on a handshake with the chief executive after a twenty-minute conversation.

It was a fantastic feeling but it also made me very aware that having talked the talk, I now had to walk the walk. I had to deliver results, and I had barely a month to pull it all together. I already had some equipment from my general Arctic guiding work but there were several vital pieces of kit, including clothing and a rucksack, that I had to have custom-made. My notional target was to reach the Pole in forty days instead of the normal sixty to seventy, but I was hoping to do it in thirty-five, and I had deliberately set an unusually late departure date, 14 April. As the temperatures then were much higher than in March, I would need fewer calories per day – I took 25 per cent less food per day by weight than on my first expedition – a lighter sleeping-bag, less fuel, less spare clothing – less everything. The savings in food and fuel alone – always the heaviest items – were huge. Instead of a 330-pound sledge, I would set off with a sledge-load of 140 pounds and a rucksack weighing 60 pounds. As I consumed fuel and food, the weight I was hauling would decrease at the rate of around two pounds per day. The warmer ice also offered less friction and resistance to my sledge, and I could see no reason why I should not travel much faster. The only downside I could see was that I would be encountering more open water than normal, because the season would be so much more advanced.

I completed my preparations in some haste and set off from Wydemeet at the start of April 1998. I had guilt pangs about leaving Mary in the throes of pregnancy with a half-finished house and a business to run, but she brushed my worries aside; she and the baby would be fine without me and she was looking forward to some peace and quiet. She stood at the gate and waved until I passed out of sight around the corner of the hill. It would be the last time that I would see her until I got back, and I would have no direct contact with her at all while I was out on the ice. I had no satellite phone in those days and my high-frequency radio and Argos beacon could only be used to talk to my Canadian base manager, Gary Guy, in Resolute Bay.

Mary also had to make a quick trip to see my Mum, who was in a terrible state, imagining all sorts of dire fates were about to befall me. Mary did her best to reassure her, saying 'It's all right, Pen's a big boy now. He's strong, well-equipped and he knows exactly what he's doing.'

'I know,' Mum said. 'But what you don't understand is that when you think of Pen you see a man. When I think of him, I still see a little boy of five years old in short trousers with his socks round his ankles, lost and all alone and crying for his mother.' Now aged thirty-six, I hoped it wouldn't come to that this time. Throughout my childhood and, to my excruciating embarrassment, even into my teens, my Mum had always stopped me as I was about to go out of the door and said, 'Have you got your woolly jumper? You don't want to get cold.' I thought of it as I put the phone down after calling her from the airport to say goodbye. Where I was heading this time, it would take a bit more than a woolly jumper to keep me warm.

Although some people regard the Arctic Ocean as the final frontier, the last refuge from bureaucracy and government interference, I had some paperwork to complete when I reached Resolute Bay: a wilderness permit obtained from the Royal Canadian Mounted Police station there. It covers who you are, the dates of your departure and planned return, your approximate route, contact details of your base and home, the frequency of your high-frequency radio, your distinguishing features: height, hair and eye colour, and the colour of your sledge, tent and clothing – everything that they might need to locate you from the air in an emergency . . . or to identify your body if you are found dead. Technically it doesn't have any binding legal force; it's not a permit, it's just a courtesy, but it's a compulsory courtesy nonetheless and you'd have to be pretty intellectually challenged to set off without completing it.

My form-filling wasn't quite complete, because I also needed a licence to carry arms. If you are travelling through polar bear territory you need the right sort of firearm and the right sort of ammunition, and you've got to be competent in their use. Neither the weapon nor the ammunition I was taking was standard issue and my firearm licence had to reflect that. I was carrying a single-barrelled, 12-gauge Magnum shotgun, but the fact that the barrel was rifled made it a 'rifle-shotgun', and that required a Section One licence rather than the normal firearm or shotgun licence, and my ammunition was also subject to special restrictions. The police wanted to know exactly what I was up to, because they're not going to let just any old person go wandering around with those, but if you're travelling solo in polar bear country, there is not much option. The baton rounds might be enough to scare off a marauding polar bear without doing it significant damage, but you have to have the killing ammunition as well, because it might be the only way to stop a charging polar bear in its tracks.

The danger of a polar bear attack can be overstated but it is not insignificant. They're predators in a region where prey is never abundant and sometimes almost non-existent and any living creatures there – including Arctic travellers – are potential targets for a hungry bear. You have to assume that you may be put in a position where you have to kill a bear to save your own life. That makes a firearm essential. If you're lucky, you will never need to use it, or may only have to fire it to scare off a bear, but you have to be a good enough shot to kill if necessary, which requires not only practice on the ranges before you set off on your expedition, but also the calmness and confidence to be sure of hitting the target in the much more demanding environment of the Arctic, with an aggressive bear charging head-on, presenting a small target in your sights.

The noise of a gun being fired is not necessarily much of a deterrent. The pressure-wave from a bullet going right past a bear's head might do the trick but the sound of a shot is far from guaranteed to strike terror into its heart because, although humans and their noisy machines are great rarities in the Arctic, it is a far from silent environment. The noises that the ice makes as it moves under the pressure of wind, tides and currents, pulling apart into leads or piling up into pressure ridges, is simply unbelievable. It is like being in a foundry or a scrap metal yard, with all kinds of terrible metallic rending, hammering, pounding, screaming and crashing sounds filling the air. If you've never heard it, you'd be forgiven for wondering how ice – mere frozen water – can possibly generate such a cacophony, but I can assure you that it does.

For solo endeavours I always take two sorts of ammunition with me: a few solid rounds the size of my thumb, big enough to stop a bear in its tracks, and a few more plastic baton rounds so as not to injure the bear, in the hope that a severe bruising may be enough to drive it away. It's not very nice knowing that there's a bear around or being followed for a couple of days but, as with most things, knowledge, experience – and quick thinking in a crisis – are often enough to avoid or defuse a potentially dangerous situation. Although I've prob-ably encountered thirty to forty polar bears in my polar career, I've never had to fire directly at one, let alone kill one. It would be heartbreaking for me if I did, because I've never shot such a big animal in my life and I feel very strongly that we don't have to be there; it's the polar bears' territory more than it's ours.

I have been warned by professional hunters to be prepared to be shocked by the bestial desperation of such a large wounded animal, and the bloody carnage of a close-range emergency shooting. The thought of seeing a bear staggering around, with blood spurting everywhere and it voiding its bowels and bladder from shock, while it draws on every ounce of its ebbing strength and wits to try to overcome its foe, fills me with absolute horror.

Having completed the formalities, my chartered aircraft dropped me off at Ward Hunt Island on 14 April 1998, exactly as planned. I barely glanced at the weathered wooden hut there, as I checked my sledge and stowed my supplies, and began heading north straight away. I'd been apprehensive about the extent of open water I would encounter after setting out this late in the season, but, in the event, it didn't give me any real problems, because the weather proved to be very kind to me. The sky was overcast much of the time and, in those conditions, you can actually see stretches of open water reflected in what's known as 'a water sky'. Because sunlight can't penetrate the sea-ice that covers most of the Arctic Ocean's surface, open water appears jet black in colour. In overcast conditions, that inky blackness is reflected on to the undersurface of the cloud. It often gives a gunmetal black-blue hue to the cloud, distinctly different from the look of normal dark clouds; you can tell that it's a water sky from up to five miles away. By studying the clouds, I was able to weave a course around the open waters simply by tracking the grey-white clouds between the swathes of water skies; and for most of the time, I never even saw the water.

However, perhaps partly as a result of the weight of the rucksack and the speed that I was travelling over the ice, I was beset by a series of incidents from the start. Even before I left the permanent ice-shelf locked to the coast of Ward Hunt Island, I fell through the ice into a crevasse. My skis would normally have spread the load sufficiently to prevent such a fall, but I had not been expecting to encounter crevasses on the ice-shelf and the accumulated snow of the winter, hardened by the winds, had made walking a better option until I reached the sea-ice. The snow on the surface had rendered the crevasse invisible; my first inkling of danger was when the snow gave way beneath my feet and I found myself free-falling downwards. The sledge would inevitably have plummeted down on top of me if the crevasse had been any wider, but luckily it became wedged across the top, leaving me swinging below it, dangling from the straps of my harness. Having eased myself out of my harness and my rucksack, I climbed a few feet further down the crevasse and took a photograph looking back up past my dangling rucksack to the sledge at the top, framed against a thin strip of sky. Then, by bracing my arms and legs against the opposite sides of the crevasse, I worked my way back up to the surface, rehitched my sledge and rucksack and carried on to the north.

That incident was a shock, but cost me no more than a few minutes of lost time. The next one was potentially much more serious. Within a couple of days the bindings began to pull away from my skis, something that had never happened before. I knew the brand of skis well and had used them on several previous expeditions, but what I didn't know was that, although the ski looked the same, weighed the same and appeared to be exactly the same in all respects, the manufacturer had recently changed the method of construction. As a matter of routine, I had always drilled through the upper surface of the skis to fix the bindings to the skis with five substantial screws but, instead of the traditional multiple bonded layers – like a piece of plywood – the skis now had a cellular structure, like a honeycomb sandwiched between the upper and lower surfaces. This increased the structural strength of the skis but it meant that some of the screws were not biting into solid wood. The bindings had seemed to be well secured but, as always, they were subject to extreme shear and lifting forces as I skied across the rough ice, and these continuous stresses gradually worked the screws loose.

I didn't have any spare skis or bindings, so I now had the choice of either drilling new holes with the risk of creating a line of weakness across the middle of the skis or to try and plug and re-use the original holes. I didn't have an Acme ski mending kit so I had to improvise a field repair using the emergency Swan Vestas non-safety matches I always carry with me on expeditions. I completely filled each hole with broken bits of match, ramming and hammering them home with the butt of the handle of my Leatherman multi-tool penknife until they formed a dense, immovable plug. I then shaved off the projecting match-stubs with a sharp blade, and screwed the binding into these filled holes. It was the best I could do, but it was a very 'gash' repair and it was demoralising to know that, however well I mended the ski, it was not going to last more than a few days and, on occasion, only a few hours, before it had to be repaired again. It wasted a lot of time and I was dreading even worse damage to the skis and practically tiptoeing my way north on them, a horrid way to go on when I just wanted to be travelling to the Pole at top speed. After a while, the original holes became too mashed and mangled to refill any more, and I had to drill fresh holes with the spike on the Leatherman, further weakening the ski.

The next incident was even more serious. On the tenth day, I was climbing over one of many pressure ridges when I slipped and fell awkwardly. My right knee got trapped between two ice-blocks under a loose covering of snow. The weight of my rucksack stopped me from regaining my balance and, as I continued to fall sideways, the knee took the full combined weight of myself and the rucksack. I felt a stab of blinding pain and stars flashed in front of my eyes. Then I passed out. When I came to, snow had already started to settle on me. I took a look at the damage straight away, unzipping and rolling up the trouser leg. I knew it would be bad but had not envisaged how bad; when I saw the huge, grotesque swelling around my knee, the sight and the delayed shock caused me to pass out again. It may have been for a few seconds or a few minutes, but when I came round I was seriously cold and my first thought was that, even though the April temperatures were reasonably mild, no lower than −25 °C, I could die there if I didn't get down off the ridge and put the tent up.

Fighting waves of pain at each movement, I dragged my leg out from between the ice-blocks, and crawled down the pressure ridge with the rucksack on my back. I pitched the tent on a patch of roughly level ice about ten metres from the ridge in case it became active while I was tent-bound. It took about two hours instead of the usual fifteen minutes. I didn't dare take the strongest painkillers I was carrying – Pethidine, usually given to women during childbirth – because I was nervous that if I took them, I might drift off into some drug-fuelled fantasy world and die of exposure out on the ice. The ones I did take barely took the edge off the excruciating pain from my knee. When I had at last managed to erect the tent, I dragged my sleeping-bag and supplies inside, got the stove going and things started to calm down.

I made a snow pack in a nylon bag, strapped that around my knee and elevated my leg to help reduce the swelling. I stayed resting it in my tent for thirty-six hours – all the rest of that day and the next. Then, though my knee was still swollen like a balloon, I set off again. I suppose it's an indication of my attitude that I went on for another thirty days with my knee in a complete mess, much longer than I should have. The fear of failure was definitely a motivation. When it rears its head you can tap into it as a force to drive yourself forward and I definitely didn't want to be going home having failed to reach the Pole for the second time. With the aid of the drugs, the pain became a bit more bearable – the nerve endings probably got bored with sending the same message and eventually shut down – but I could feel the mechanical grinding of cartilage against bone and I knew I was doing my leg no good whatso-ever. I was still making slow progress north, but I was now well behind schedule and getting alarmingly low on food and fuel. I had reached 86°15'N when I was hit by a triple-whammy: my skis were on the point of complete disintegration and I had been travelling so slowly because of that and the handicap of my injured knee, that, even on the most optimistic projection, I was going to run out of food and fuel well before I could reach the Pole. I had also run out of painkillers. I was faced with the choice of either pulling out completely or radioing for a resupply – if my sponsors, National Express, were willing to meet the cost of one. If not, I'd simply have to pull out, because that extra flight would cost another £25,000 and I had no way of raising that money myself while out on the ice. I asked Gary Guy to contact them and see what their thoughts were and they very generously agreed to fund the flight. Once you have to resupply you may as well be supplied with everything so I was air-dropped more food, fuel, a fresh pair of skis and painkillers two days later.

I had already gone further than any previous solo expedition on the North American side, so in a very small way I had achieved something, but it was a feeble consolation for the bitter knowledge that my hopes of an unsupported trek all the way to the Pole had now evaporated. To be the first Briton to have achieved this or that was of zero interest to me, it had to be something that pushed back the boundaries – period. But I also understood that my responsibilities went beyond my own personal goals. I was representing National Express and carried the hopes of many other third parties for whom reaching the Pole would be a good, if not a great result, regardless of the number of resupplies.

So I kept plodding on to the north and by the thirty-eighth day on the ice I had reached 87°20'N – as little as twelve days' journey from the Pole – and was skiing over a flat ice-pan when the final incident occurred. It was an overcast day, with bright but flat light, and the going was exceptionally good – large pans of first-year ice around a kilometre in diameter, that were drifting slowly over the Pole from the Siberian coast where they had formed that spring. These pans often have cracks running across them, clean fractures of the ice, ranging upwards from a few centimetres in width. There was just such a crack on this pan, in line with the course I was taking, but hidden beneath a layer of frozen snow. I had no warning of it. One minute I was skiing along normally, the next my right ski dropped into a broad, straight crack. Once more I toppled over to that side, and my full body weight was transferred through my knee as my leg became trapped. I felt another blinding flash of pain.

I lay motionless on the ice for ten minutes or so, not even attempting to extricate my leg from the crack, just gathering my thoughts and weighing up the wisdom of continuing or pulling out. I even drifted off for a short while, then woke up as the sun broke through the cloud, warming my back as I lay on the ice. It was an indication of how tired I was that I was completely unconcerned by this impromptu rest. By the time I had hauled myself upright, there was not an ounce of adrenalin left in me, and I realised that this was an incident too far. I'd been worn down by almost thirty days of constantly having to shut out the pain and wondering how prudent it was to continue, and this fall had knocked the last bit of stuffing out of me. I had the supplies to reach the Pole, and my body might have been able to make it, but at what cost? If pushing my injured knee beyond yet another pain barrier meant that I could never run again, or even walk comfortably, was that a price worth paying? In the days, months and years leading up to this attempt, I had thought about such an eventuality and I had always imagined that the answer would have been an unequivocal 'Yes', but faced with the reality, I realised that the prize, already tarnished by the forced resupply, was simply not worth the risk. There was no more internal debate. I was going home. My attempt on the Pole was over. I made the radio call asking for a flight out.

I agonised then – and I did so for years afterwards – was I just a quitter when things got too tough? And I was desperately low when I got back home. I tried to shrug my shoulders and smile about it, but deep down I knew that this wretched thing was going to haunt me. Was I ever going to get to the Pole solo and unsupported, the goal I'd dreamed of for so many years and pledged on my father's deathbed that I would achieve? But I also became concerned about the impact that my obsessive pursuit of this goal was having on Mary, my children and a lot of other people around me. I always seemed to be exhausted and, after particularly demanding phases of work or seasons in the Arctic, I'd collapse in bed with a high fever, with symptoms similar to malaria. It would last for days and leave me so drained that, for weeks afterwards, I'd barely be able to move from room to room around the house, and it would take several more months before my strength was fully restored. For years there had also been a creeping gloom, like the imperceptible darkening of the autumn skies at dusk, in my demeanour at home. Even my closest friends were completely unaware of this darker side. In the presence of others, whether it was Dave the Post on his morning rounds, family and friends visiting, or a business meeting, I'd be firing on all cylinders and appearing relaxed, engaged and good-humoured. But when the last person had walked out of the door, I would instantly revert to my introverted, intense and self-absorbed self, and Mary had always had to bear the brunt of that.

My doctor, friend and ally, Peter Edwards, always gave me his full support in any way that would keep me upright and moving forward, but on this occasion he was away on leave and a locum doctor showed up. As I lay in bed, fever-wracked and drenched in sweat, barely able to think or speak coherently, the second doctor gave his prognosis. 'If he doesn't give up his business and his expeditioning, and create a less demanding lifestyle, this is only going to get worse.' He swept out of the room never to be seen again. I knew he was right, but that did not necessarily mean that I should give up now. Now could be the very moment to push on, complete my self-imposed mission and win through to the sunshine on the other side. In the months that followed, both Mary and I grew to accept that the best course for us all in the long term was to press on and win through together.

I hoped that if I could get through this exhausting obsession, I would then be able to relax and be a less driven human being and, most especially, a better husband. I was very aware that I owed so much to Mary and couldn't have been doing this without her support; above all, I didn't want to get to the point where I'd say, 'Right, I'm ready for you now, I can give you some quality attention' but find that it was too late. So, I sat down, did some hard thinking and told myself that I had to sort out the company and start making some money before I could even contemplate another solo attempt on the Pole. The company was still very much a hand-to-mouth affair. We had no financial resources, no advertising budget and no personnel, our seasonal temporary staff having come to the end of their contracts. What we really needed was a cash injection from someone prepared to put in the money to make it work, but there was neither a hard-nosed investor nor a fairy godfather on the horizon. It remained an unending struggle and every now and then Mary and I would have a painful discussion that ended with me saying that if we hadn't cracked it by the end of the next season, I'd call it a day. But when that time came, there were always just enough bookings and reasons to believe that the following season would be the turning-point. I was working all hours to make it happen. In 2002, my annual leave consisted of one day: a day-trip with Mary and the children down the River Dart from Totnes to Dartmouth.

Within five weeks of returning from my second failed attempt on the Pole, our first child, Wilf, was born. Unlike his father, the Nanny Wigley formula would not be applied, but with Dartmoor as his adventure playground, Wilf's already showing the spirit of an explorer. If he ends up becoming one, though, I think I will have failed as a father to open his eyes to all the other options available. There's no greater pleasure for me than walking over the moors or along the riverbank with him, sharing his pleasure and excitement at the world around him. However, though my new responsibilities changed many things for me forever, and all for the good, I have to admit – rather uncomfortably – that though I did review my polar ambitions thoroughly in the context of our new-found family status, this did not affect my commitment to a further solo polar expedition. I was still absolutely committed to fulfilling the vow I had made to my father. Above all other things, even the birth of my son, it seemed to be absolutely central to my being.

In the year 2000, I guided one Last Degree team led by Howard Marshall from Resolute Bay up to the North Pole at the spring equinox, to see the dawn of the new millennium as the sun rose above the horizon for the first time that year – the last place on earth to experience the millennial sunrise, eighty days after the first; and then came back, via Resolute, to Dartmoor. I had five days back home and then led another Last Degree expedition to the Pole from the Siberian side, immediately followed by a 'Last Half Degree' with a client who was desperate to reach the Pole at the end of that season.

In 2001, I dedicated my whole Arctic Ocean season to guiding a single unsupported polar expedition from Cape Arkticheskiy, the northernmost land on the Siberian side of the ocean, leading a young private client with no previous polar experience. It was to be unsupported simply because funds were not forthcoming to provide a resupply, so an already ambitious undertaking now became a truly formidable challenge but, undeterred, my client was determined to give it his best shot that season rather than wait another year. Predictably, the strain of hauling a fully laden sledge in such extreme conditions took their toll on my young charge and, despite his best efforts, it proved to be too much, too soon. We got just past halfway before being forced to withdraw. That unexpectedly early end to the expedition allowed me to take a few weeks off, relaxing with Mary . . . which may help to explain why we discovered shortly afterwards that she was expecting our second child.

I organised and led two Arctic survival courses on Spitsbergen in late February and early March 2002, giving me a four-week leeway before the birth of our daughter, Freya, on 12 April, so that I was back at home to look after Mary if there were any problems. It was the first time that I had spent Easter in England for five years, and I revelled in all the things that I'd been missing out on: spring sunrises over the moor, the succession of wildflowers in our garden – snowdrops, crocuses, wild daffodils, bluebells, wild geraniums, poppies and foxgloves – the trees coming into leaf, and Easter egg hunts and long walks with Wilf. He and I have sometimes felt more like brothers than father and son, messing about on the moors, wading across river beds, turning stones over to see what's there, and scrambling about on the wind-blasted tors. That spring was when the special bond with my son was really cemented; we spent many early mornings and late evenings wandering the valleys and moors, Wilf walking alongside me or riding on my shoulders as he chattered about birds and fish and butterflies that he'd seen, or the shapes of clouds drifting overhead as we lay on our backs on the grass, the air filled with birdsong and the sound of the river.

It was a brief, wonderful interlude for me, before resuming the relentless round of preparations and expeditions, but the next one was something very special. Each expeditioner to the North Pole has defined their own challenge, for their own reasons. For some it is to walk solo without resupply from the coast, for others it's to be guided from the last degree of latitude about 100 kilometres out from the Pole, and for others still, who may barely be able to walk, it is to cover the last 100 metres, with or without support. The previous year I had been approached by a client who was planning to raise awareness and funds for muscular dystrophy through a Last Degree expedition. Word of this plan soon reached the ears of a remarkable man, Michael McGrath, who had the condition and he asked me if I could set up a separate expedition for him and his support team, arriving at the Pole on the same day as our Last Degree expedition to create an even more powerful message to the public back home. Michael required the support of his professional guide and friends for much of his journey, but he reached his Pole, on his knees but triumphant.

6

Guiding numerous clients of The Polar Travel Company on Arctic Ocean and high Arctic expeditions was undoubtedly helping me to improve my own skills and techniques. All the time I was becoming more professional in the way I operated and slowly mastering my chosen craft, but guiding others on their expeditions also kept fuelling my burning desire to make another solo expedition of my own. Over a period of time, the thought began to crystallise in my mind that I had to make one final attempt at the Pole and then call it a day. To carry on beyond that wasn't fair on Mary or the children and it wasn't making me happy either, and I made a conscious attempt to maximise the likelihood of success by learning all the lessons from my first two solo expeditions.

On the first expedition in 1994, I had thrown myself into it, but to some extent I had lacked the local knowledge and, more crucially, the specialist field experience to achieve success. On the second in 1998 I was simply too ambitious, wanting to break new ground and demonstrate a radically new way of doing things by going really fast and light. I should have taken a more progressive view: first reach the Pole and then go on to develop and demonstrate the low-weight 'Alpine strike' technique after that. To try and do both things at once was a big error of judgement.

I still felt that the Alpine approach was perfectly feasible, but it introduced an element of risk that wasn't strictly necessary and might jeopardise my chances of reaching the Pole, and that was already going to be tough, challenging and interesting enough. Only when I had achieved that would it be appropriate for me, or someone else, to take it to the next stage, a lightning strike. For the 2003 expedition, I would confine my ambitions to reaching the Pole solo and unsupported from the North American side, a feat that had never before been achieved. If I succeeded, my dreams and my pledge to my father would at last be fulfilled. If I failed . . . well, I'd cope with that one if I had to.

This time I was going to roll with the punches that I knew were bound to come my way, and my attitude was no longer a brittle and unrealistic 'I'll do whatever it takes.' Friends used to be surprised to hear me say 'If I reach the Pole . . .' and would be quick to point out this was not the attitude that built the Empire; I should be saying 'When I reach the Pole . . .'. I thought about this and modified my phraseology to 'If and when I reach the Pole . . .'. 'If' reflected a genuine humility about taking on the challenge, but it also emphasised my non-aggressive approach. I was not out there to 'fight' my way through a 'hostile' environment and eventually 'conquer' the Pole. It was a privilege to be able to undertake this journey into such a pristine and spectacular wilderness and if, despite my failings, I made it to the Pole, it would have been worth the years of effort.

I had every intention of making it if I could, but I accepted that I might be found wanting – again – and I also knew that unforeseen events like a serious crush injury or a family bereavement might occur, bringing an end to the expedition. But barring acts of God or *force majeure*, I felt confident that my competence in the polar regions, developed over fifteen years, would help me to make the right decisions as I went along. If that led to success, it would be deserved, and if it did not, that was just the way it was going to be.

As I was drawing up my preliminary plans in the early summer of 2002, I had a moment of pure serendipity. It came in the form of a phone call from Robert Elias. I'd first met him in 1999, in Punta Arenas in Chile. I had been on my way to Antarctica to act as a forward base manager and technical consultant to the British all-women M&G ISA expedition; having successfully reached the North Pole, Caroline Hamilton and the remarkable team she'd selected from our relay squad, including Ann Daniels, Pom Oliver, Rosie Stancer and Zoë Hudson, were now switching their attentions to the opposite Pole. However, getting out of Punta Arenas soon began to seem even more difficult than the trek to the South Pole; we were stuck there for twenty-three days while we endured a succession of daily briefings from the flight operators, giving the latest reason – aircraft problems, bad weather, surface conditions, etc. – why we were unable to fly into Antarctica.

While spending yet another aimless day hanging around the hotel, I had a chance meeting with an imposing, athletic figure, wearing a white tee-shirt, blue jeans and a big peaked baseball cap. I didn't know who he was, but he looked very much his own man. We exchanged wry smiles during the briefings and got chatting afterwards. He introduced himself as Robert Elias, and it turned out that he was the president of The Omega Foundation, a Nevada-based organisation with a remit to support work of special cultural, environmental or scientific significance in high altitudes and high latitudes. He was also held up on his way into Antarctica, following one of his supported expeditions operating near Mount Vinson, the highest mountain in Antarctica.

We got to know each other pretty well over the following days. We told each other about our personal projects and discovered that we shared the belief that there is not only a role for expeditions to promote the work that professional scientists are doing but to collect raw data for them as well. Polar travellers also go to places that 99.999 per cent of the public will never see for themselves and can bring back observations and images of places that are as strange to their audiences as they are valuable in informing people about the world in which we live.

In the course of conversation, I invited Robert to meet the

24. Vaughan Purvis (left), me (right) and a representative from one of our sponsors, Stringfellows, seeing us off on our open-boat adventure

25. Vaughan Purvis (prominent) and self (less so) on our way to Greenland, August 1989

26. Rob Owen and me crossing Spitsbergen in the polar night, 1991

27. The picture that launched The Polar Travel Company's first big project – the McVitie's Penguin Polar Relay – Caroline Hamilton (far left) and Mary (far right)

28. James Heath, aged eleven, arriving at the North Pole with his father, Ron (both in yellow), to meet our Last Degree expedition team led by Charles Shaw (second from right)

29. Jack Russell (here controlling a challenging forward abseil from above) has directed every polar preparation course we've ever done on Dartmoor – the ultimate professional

30. Hauling a sledge of over nineteen-stone deadweight up such obstacles took every ounce of strength

31. The view through 'dark *nilas*' toward the seabed 4 km below, 1998

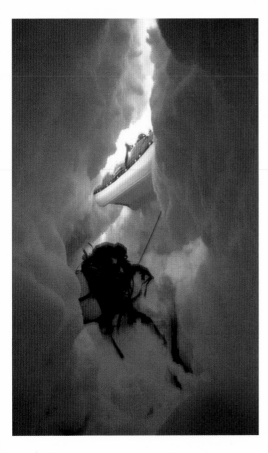

32. Lucky escape! Saved by the sledge jamming across the top of the crevasse, 1998

33. Endless refitting of the ski-bindings with my trusty Leatherman, 1998

34. 'Pressure ridges' – chaotic jumbles of ice – come in all shapes and sizes! Hundreds of these obstruct the route to the north; this is from the 1998 expedition

35. Scene of a near fatality in 1998. Snow on top, water underneath – no ice in between! I almost drowned in the snowy quagmire

36. Wilf and me off on one
of our night-time jaunts

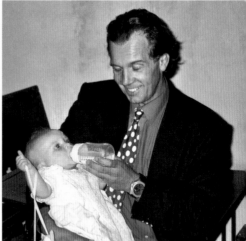

37. Topping Freya up in St Raphael
Church at Huccaby on Dartmoor
before her christening

38. Father and son sailing

39. Freya enjoying one of
the good things in life

40. The dreaded sport-specific training of tyre-pulling on Dartmoor

41. My 'Snowbirds' team in the inaugural national adventure racing championship (2002) – with my outstanding British team-mates (from the front): me, Freya Bloor, David Burckett St Laurent and Philippa Arding

five women who were about to set out for the South Pole and, as we strolled along the tree-lined boulevards, I mentioned that they now had a budget overrun as a result of the long delay in Punta Arenas. He duly met them, and, following a subsequent meeting in which the team outlined the valuable scientific work planned by the expedition, he offered to contribute towards the costs of the expedition on the proviso that The Omega Foundation would be a recipient of the scientific data, reports and findings coming out of the expedition.

I'd kept in touch with him since then – we spoke regularly by phone – and I always enjoyed our conversations and felt he was very much a kindred spirit. Now, after chatting for a few minutes, out of the blue he told me that he could really use my help in developing a new aspect of The Foundation's work in Antarctica. 'There're areas of research and organisation on the logistics that you can assist us with and, if your work commitments allow, we'd appreciate you coming with us to our base camp in Antarctica next season.' I accepted the commission with alacrity – the work would be fascinating and contribute useful income in between polar guiding seasons, and it was for a foundation that was not only dedicated to its work in Antarctica but also understood the challenges and responsibilities of operating and studying there – and had the resources required to meet them.

We talked a while longer and because it was in the forefront of my mind and we were talking about what gave us the energy to go on in life, I told him about my burning passion to make my solo, unsupported journey from the North American continent to the North Pole. Knowing my interest in undertaking scientific work on polar expeditions, he immediately asked what I had in mind. I replied that I had already been developing separate pilot studies for the oceanographical and psychological raw data I could collect en route with British scientists and explained the value of the potential findings. 'How much would that cost?' he asked. I told him that at this stage I could only give bracketed figures. 'OK,' he said, 'The Foundation will contribute the midpoint figure, if you want it.'

I was in shock. I couldn't believe it. Was he serious? 'No question. That's what this Fund is about. There are people out there, like you, Pen, who have something original and potentially valuable that they really want to do and we can help them to do it. If you can summarise and confirm on paper what you have just told me about your scientific projects, The Foundation will support you all the way.'

I ended the conversation in a stunned state. I hadn't even been looking for sponsorship, we'd just been catching up over the phone, and now The Omega Foundation was underwriting, if not quite the whole costs of the expedition, the vast bulk of them. I kept this overwhelming information to myself for the rest of the day, then sat Mary down at the kitchen table before supper and told her that, while I had not committed myself on the phone to Robert, I now had the money to do another solo expedition; I asked her what she thought.

Mary knew how much I wanted to, even needed to go, but there was an issue to be discussed. For years we'd felt that we'd been partly responsible for generating what was definitely now a growing swell of interest amongst the public in travelling to the polar regions, and we kept thinking that we were finally going to catch the resulting wave and ride it into a more profitable future; but, as each year passed, we still seemed to be paddling about in the swell, waiting for that wave to emerge. So when I told her about The Foundation's offer, I was not expecting her to jump for joy, mainly because I thought she felt that The Polar Travel Company needed me to be there to make the most of the business that we had spent so long developing. But when we had talked it through, she agreed that it was an opportunity that could not be allowed to pass. It was not pure selfishness on my part, a blind determination to fulfil my pledge to my father whatever the cost to those around me . . . or at least I don't think it was. The Polar Travel Company still had no advertising budget and, if successful, a solo expedition to the Pole offered the prospect of media coverage that would propel the company into the public consciousness in a way that no amount of paid advertising could achieve. But there was also another factor. I felt that I had found my métier – polar travelling and guiding – and I felt I had the capacity to be in the upper branches of that particular tree. This was my showcase and, while I appreciated that the media and the public at large would understandably neither know nor care about the finer points of the expedition – the technical skills, the innovations in equipment and techniques – the people that mattered most to me, my family and my professional peers in the polar community, would know what I was trying to do, and what a huge task I had set myself. Many teams and individuals, including special forces, had tried to make an unsupported trek to the Pole from the North American side, but almost all of them had either failed to reach the Pole at all or had needed at least one evacuation or resupply, and often several of them, to do so. No solo expedition had succeeded unsupported from North America.

So I went ahead, and for the first time – on my third attempt – I had most of the funding in place well before the time when I was due to depart. I could now plan confidently, start the training, obtain the supplies and source and/or design the specialist equipment so that when I finally got to the starting line, I would have the best kit and the best preparation possible to maximise the likelihood of success, rather than starting off, as I always had done in the past, compressing too much preparation into too short a time for reasons beyond my control.

The first thing to do was to draw up a budget and, when doing so, I deliberately did not include a contingency to allow for a resupply. In my eyes, even budgeting for one would have been a tacit admission that I knew I might fail, and I was determined to avoid the least trace of negativity. I would focus only on reaching the Pole, not worrying about what might happen if I fell short. I hoped to make the journey in sixty days, but planned to take rations for sixty-nine days and fuel for seventy-five, giving me a reasonable contingency to cope with accidents or unusually bad weather or ice conditions. But I was determined to pare the weight of the other equipment and supplies I was hauling down to the absolute minimum.

I would be using a state-of-the-art sledge originally designed by Alex Bierwald of Acapulka in association with Borge Ousland, and another piece of equipment, again developed by Borge with Helly Hansen Spesialprodukter: a lightweight immersion suit that would enable me to swim the kind of leads that had sabotaged my first expedition. If I could tackle the thin ice and open water – the main technical hazard – then I could take a relatively straight line to the Pole. I felt that I had finally got myself to a level of competence that meant I could deal with almost anything that came my way. I wasn't afraid of anything and I was going to roll with the punches that I knew were bound to come my way. I could keep going north over any kind of terrain, knowing that I could deal with every eventuality. No obstacle was going to stop me: a very positive and empowering thought to have in my head.

Pretty well every other part of the expedition kit had to be modified or prepared to a greater or lesser extent. It isn't like yachting where the market is so large that it is worthwhile for suppliers to make and sell every possible piece of kit in all sorts of variations. Whether it's a special sail, rope, deck fittings or navigation software, you can buy it off the shelf. In polar exploration there are only a few of us knocking around, no more than a score of professional guides. We don't constitute a worthwhile market for manufacturers and so we have to go round like magpies, picking up ideas and bits of kit from mountaineering, yachting, aviation and the military.

We either have to custom-build our own things from first principles or buy an off-the-shelf product and modify it for a different use than the one for which it was designed, and there are always several factors to consider. Everything has to be as light as possible but must also be robust enough to keep working for the duration of the trip, and lightness tends to be at odds with strength and durability. Everything must be easy to operate while wearing mitts or gloves and have minimal heat conductivity. You can take metal items or tools, but anything that you might touch, even with gloves or mitts, let alone your bare hands, must have minimal conductivity and is best insulated with low-conductivity foam to reduce the risk of frostnip or worse. And everything has to be able to endure temperatures down to −55 °C. It's a daunting set of criteria but there can be no exceptions; every single piece of kit has to meet it.

I could have organised an expedition to the North Pole for clients in no more than two weeks, using off-the-shelf kit with minimal tweaking, but on a project as ambitious and difficult as this, one of my operating principles was to maximise the likelihood of success by getting the last percentage point of performance out of every single piece of equipment. I could have done a whistlestop tour of the internet and outdoor shops and bought all my kit off the peg. It would certainly have been cheaper and I might have got away with it, but even if I could have, I didn't want to be embarking on the most crucial venture of my life on the basis of 'Well, I might get away with it.' I wanted to be setting off knowing that there was no better kit that I could procure, design, develop or modify anywhere in the world, and that knowledge would give a significant boost to my morale and confidence as I began heading north from Ward Hunt Island.

Just getting that additional performance and reliability, the extra few per cent that might make the difference between success and failure, required an unbelievable amount of research, time and effort. I wasted hours and hours just trying to source a one-litre titanium vacuum flask – titanium is lighter than the usual stainless steel ones – but every one I found was only 650 ml. Finally I thought I'd discovered the one place in the world – Minnesota – where I could get one-litre ones. But when it finally arrived, the packaging showed it to be the ubiquitous 650 ml flask. It had been a misprint on the website. So back it went, and that was the end of that particular wild goose chase. It might seem a huge amount of effort for something so minor, and in one sense it doesn't really matter whether your flask is 650 ml or 1 litre, or your GPS weighs 100 grams or 90, or you source batteries that weigh 2 grams less than the normal ones. All you've saved is a handful of grams. But all those micro percentages add up to significant savings, particularly when you know that you'll be hauling every extra gram across eight million metres of ice. You need to know when you set off that every part of every component of every thing that you are taking has been assessed for weight as well as durability and that there's nothing else that you can do to improve things. You're working on very small margins and that extra bit of research or work tends to be the difference between getting there and falling short.

Having failed to find a titanium vacuum flask, I made do with a one-litre stainless steel one, but it then had to be modified for polar use. The surface of the flask was smooth metal, with no projections from it whatsoever. And, from previous experience, I knew that when wearing gloves or mitts I simply would not be able to get enough traction on the metal to undo the screw-topped lid, particularly when, as often happened, a tiny drop of moisture on the thread would freeze solid in the sledging sessions between breaks. To make my life easier, my base manager, Ian, suggested and made a minor modification – one of the countless tasks that he and Martin performed for me without complaint and often without even being asked. He wound duct tape – a very strong woven fabric tape – around the outside of the flask to attach insulating foam to the body of the flask and, every inch or so, he taped down a wooden match stick around the mug lid. He smoothed the tape down around each match stick and then used a hairdryer to make the tape adhere to the metal as tightly as possible. I now had a vacuum flask that not only had no exposed metal that would freeze to bare skin, but one that also allowed me enough purchase to get it open without a struggle, even if it was frozen shut. It was a minor thing but such little irritations can gnaw away at you under the stress of an expedition and even at that micro-level I was looking to make my life as easy and manageable as possible.

We also modified just about every other piece of kit that I was taking. My skis were specially made for me by Arthur Asnes of Asnes Ski in Norway and Helge Hoflandsdal, who had given me much technical support with skis, skins and bindings in the past. They looked like standard Sondre skis but had been reinforced with an additional 200 grams of fibreglass and resin, giving 65 per cent extra strength for a minimal increase in weight. It was vital, given the abuse the skis would take while bridging gaps between ice-blocks or coping with sudden shock loads as the sledge careered about on pressure ridges. Several previous expeditions, including one of my own, had been blighted by skis snapping and delaminating, and I had to minimise the risk of it happening to me again.

My ski-boots, though based on an old Canadian design, had some useful new features, and were light for the protection they offered. Even so, I weighed smaller size pairs and decided to take one size down from my normal one. It was a slight risk in that a boot's warmth is partly a function of the volume of air – the great insulator – it can hold around the foot, and a smaller size might result in dangerously cold feet, but I'd worn the boots often enough to be confident of avoiding problems. I also swapped the thick wool insulating insoles for substantially lighter foam ones. Why all this concern for the weight of a boot? Because weight on the body, and particularly at the end of the limbs, has a disproportionate effect. In the military, every pound saved on your feet is reckoned to equate to four pounds on your back. I was going to be taking sixteen million footsteps and I wanted them to be as light as possible.

Similarly, I chose the lightest ski-poles that were strong enough for the task and I also made sure that they were shorter than the standard poles for downhill and cross-country skiing, which leave a sledge-hauler's hands higher than his heart, increasing the risk of frostbite because the circulation to them is impaired by the effects of gravity. Fractionally shorter ski-poles were not only lighter, but reduced the risk of dangerous cooling.

I then reduced the weight of the poles a fraction more by stripping off the paintwork The tungsten tips were replaced with larger stainless steel spikes, ideal for testing the strength and thickness of the sea-ice, the plastic ski-pole baskets were replaced by a leather crosspiece and aluminium hoop fashioned at our local saddlery, and the handles had abrasion-resistant, high-density foam tape wrapped around them to prevent heat-transfer between hand and handle.

I'd chosen a synthetic main sleeping-bag rather than down, because of the latter's propensity to lose much of its insulatory value when moisture accumulates in it – inevitable during the colder, early weeks of an expedition, whatever liners and vapour barriers were fitted. It was only rated to temperatures of −25 °C, even though I knew that I'd be encountering temperatures much lower than this in the early stages of the expedition – from −35° right down to −50°. That left a huge temperature deficit but a big saving in weight, and to save a little more I also had the bag shortened by removing a six-inch strip from the bottom end.

To counter the extreme cold I also had an outer sleeping-bag, which we trademarked as the 'Mammoth Smock', tailor-made by my most loyal, long-serving and talented supplier, Andy Woodward of 'Antarctica' in Llandrindod Wells, who also modified my tent, designed my clothing, and manufactured an array of gear including all my mitts and headwear. The smock was like an ankle-length monk's robe, with three-quarter-length arms and a generously proportioned lined hood. It was made of very light but warm synthetic fibre-pile enclosed in an outer windproof but 'breathing' fabric that I could wear when I needed extra warmth outside the tent – you tend to get very cold when making field repairs to your equipment or keeping watch on a marauding bear – but which would also pull over the sleeping-bag at night as an extra layer of insulation. As the Arctic weather grew warmer I could progressively cut it back and discard it, saving even more weight. I would say that that saved about 300 grams at the start.

By the time I left for the Pole I'd not only invested a lot of time and money in sourcing and modifying the right supplies and equipment, I'd also done a vast amount of physical training. I always keep myself fit enough to guide any length of Arctic expedition at any time, but I needed to be super-fit for a solo, coast-to-Pole expedition, and that required two or three hours training a day over a period of nine months. It was a huge commitment when I already had a full day just running the business, preparing for the expedition and making time for Mary and the children, though for many months this amounted to no more than an hour or so before the children's bed-time and a smash-and-grab supper with Mary, before going back to the office till the small hours. And my training time was non-earning time or, more accurately, business-going-backwards time.

I began specific training for the expedition in May 2002, immediately after my phone call with Robert Elias. Long-range sledge-hauling is as specific in its physical demands as it is unusual in its technical skills and technique, but like all forms of exercise it is fuelled by the four different sources of energy that we all have. Creatin is a substance that is permanently stored in the muscles and drawn upon in a 'fight-or-flight' situation – the super high-'octane' fuel for explosive energy that powers 100-metre sprinters – but I would only use it in emergency situations like the first moments after an unexpected immersion when trying to get back onto firm ice. And I did not need to train to build this energy system, it was simply there if ever I needed it. The next source of energy is glycogen, stored in the muscles and liver. It is topped up overnight by the reconstitution of consumed carbohydrates and we all have a finite amount of about 450 grams when we start the day. Also known as the anaerobic system, it is another high-octane fuel, but provides strength and power at a lower level for a longer period. When a marathon runner 'hits the wall' and finds himself forced to slow down, it is the classic symptom of having totally depleted his glycogen store. The runner is now forced to rely primarily upon the oxygen or aerobic system, and while oxygen is an unlimited source of energy brought into the body by breathing, it cannot deliver high rates of energy output. The final source of energy is the fat stored in our bodies. It cannot be converted into energy fast enough to support anything other than very low output but, along with my aerobic system, it was the key to my capacity for endurance.

So most of the time my body would be relying on energy from the latter three sources, the proportions changing in line with the effort required to move the ever lightening sledge over the ever changing ocean surface. Most of my training revolved around improving my body's ability to work at the highest energy output possible, so that I would be able to drag the heavy sledge as far as possible, while ensuring that the glycogen was burnt up slowly enough to last the full sledging day of ten to twelve hours. To do this, I had to increase the volume of oxygen I could draw into my lungs, and, more especially, the efficiency of my body's use of that oxygen; but I also had to increase my body's ability to exploit my body fat. In this way, I would not have to use up my precious, limited glycogen at such a high rate, and thus run out too early in the day.

My training involved a ten-day cycle of one to two sessions a day, six days a week. Fortunately there was nothing to be gained by replicating the duration of a sledging day during training, because all three systems could be steadily improved by sessions lasting less than two hours. I had adopted several important training rules over the years. The first was always to build up the number, duration and intensity of the sessions very gradually, allowing the first six weeks to create a basic fitness platform. The second was to do a variety of exercises throughout the programme to reduce the likelihood of injury – my standard rotation involved cycling and dragging car-tyres attached to a sledging harness on the hilly lanes, hill-walking with a weighted pack, cross-country running on the moors, and indoor rowing on my machine. These longer sessions of 45–120 minutes were supplemented by two to three strength work-outs a week in the local fitness centre and a couple of shorter, harder sessions, either on the rowing machine or cross-country running designed partly to improve my ability to remove the accumulated toxins associated with strenuous exercise, which, if allowed to build up unchecked, would drastically impede performance. Apart from the strength work, every session was geared to exercising at a predetermined heart rate that, from regular treadmill tests linked to computerised analysis of blood glucose, exhaled gases and fat burning, was known to ensure I was working the appropriate energy system.

I tended to run on the moor because my knee has never fully recovered from the damage I did to it on the second solo expedition and the shock-loading on it is not brilliant on the roads. I also did mountain biking, hill walking with a very heavy rucksack – up to ninety pounds – and used walking poles to develop the ski-poling muscles. Working on the rowing machine gets very dull after a couple of hours, but I rowed like a mad thing, because it exercised all sorts of body parts and was particularly good training for pulling a sledge. Tyre-pulling was the most sport-specific but also the most unappealing exercise. Progress is so slow and the friction so unrelentingly great. The two-gear option – dead slow and stop – was so frustrating because it gave no sense of exhilaration or ener-vation, or of having covered much distance for the effort expended as one slogged away – unlike running for example. Actually it was all too sport-specific. I drag a chain of tyres behind me along a road, simulating the frictional value you get hauling a heavy sledge across the ice. The type of surface dictated the number of tyres I needed to pull, but at the start I was usually hauling two car tyres linked by a rope in a line snaking out behind me, and that increased to five tyres in the last three months of my training programme. Friends would kerb-crawl alongside me as I dragged my tyres around the lanes, keeping me up to date with the local news, and I'm sure that the odd tourist, edging homeward on a foul and foggy night, must have thought a convict had escaped from the nearby Dartmoor Prison, dragging some new-fangled ball and chain device behind him.

To give focus and structure to my on-going fitness training I even set up an adventure racing team – the Snowbirds – with a pool of super-fit friends; we competed in a national series of events around the country throughout 2002 and qualified for the inaugural national championships where our novice team did well to be placed eleventh overall.

The other priority before the expedition was to build up my fat reserves, like a polar bear preparing for winter. When I was in the Arctic I would be consuming about 5,300 calories a day, but my work rate combined with the cold temperatures would be demanding about 7,500 calories, and those extra calories had to come from the fat I carried on my body. Since one gram of fat converts into about nine calories of energy, I would be losing about 250 grams (roughly half a pound) of fat per day. Standard weight loss regimes using a mixture of diet and exercise tend to say one can lose two to three pounds per week safely and sustainably, so the seemingly dramatic thirty-five pounds I expected to lose over the ten-week course of the expedition was not that abnormal or alarming. I actually got thinner during the intensive, fat-burning training and then put on most of the required surplus weight in the last two months, when I was so heavily involved in the final planning and preparation of the expedition that I just didn't have time for the full training programme. My usual weight is twelve and a half stone but by the time I left for the Arctic, I was up to fourteen and a half stone.

As the departure date approached, I started to develop a heightened sense of awareness. Everything was more intense: skies were bluer, flowers more scented, the colours and textures of the hills and moors around my home more vivid. A steady stream of people dropped in and though I was generally buried deep in the office, I always tried to pop through for a coffee and to say 'Hello'. I knew it was the last time I would be seeing them before I set off and they obviously wanted to wish me luck. But there was something else; often they looked at me in a way that said, 'This may be the last time I ever see you.' Those feelings and emotions had to be recognised and addressed, rather than ignored or suppressed, but, curiously, it seemed to bother other people much more than it worried me. It wasn't that I was indifferent to the prospect of never seeing my friends and family again, but I always know that, while I may die, I love being up there on the Arctic Ocean; it's my world and I know and understand it and look forward to going there, so I don't have the fear and trepidation of the great unknown. I found myself trying to put people at their ease, offering reassurance that, though it might sound dangerous, it wasn't really that bad, and I went through all the reasons why I expected to get back safely.

I didn't become particularly difficult or introspective as the day of departure approached – though Mary may have a different view about that – and in some respects I started to come alive – I was stepping up to the plate to do what I needed to do. As the time to leave approached, I had an aura around me radiating a sense of energy and urgency. I don't have a specific departure ritual but, as on my previous solo expeditions, I did find myself taking mental photographs; little scenes like Mary asleep in our bed with her hair spilling in a halo around her, Freya crawling around on the grass, holding up her finds for us to see and admire, or kissing Wilf goodnight in his bed, or standing in the kitchen doorway, watching him quietly eating his cereal. I was trying to hold and concentrate those images, scanning them into my brain so that I could summon them up when I needed them out on the polar ice-cap.

I left Wydemeet in February when the ground beneath the trees was carpeted with snowdrops and crocuses – the first signs of the coming spring. Mary was well used to my departures by now and Freya was too young to understand, but I had a few conversations with Wilf in the last few days. I could feel his eyes on my face all the time I was reading him a story. He knew I was going away and I didn't think there was any point in lying to him and pretending that it wasn't going to be for a long time. He had to accept that. I told him, 'Now you'll be the man of the house, and you've got to try and look after Mum and Freya, like Daddy does. Try to keep Mummy happy, look after your sister, and just do the best you can and I'll come back as fast as I can.' I told him that I would be away a very long time, but that I would come back, of course I would. But I also lodged in his mind that if I seemed a long way away at any time, or if for any reason I didn't come back, then he would always be able to look at the Pole Star, Polaris, and think of me.

Polaris is a yellowish star positioned almost directly over the North Pole, one hundred times the size of the sun and the only apparently motionless star in the heavens. Fourteen other stars, seven bright, seven faint, rotate around it, forming the constellation we call Ursa Major – the Great Bear. Over the preceding weeks I had shown him how to find Polaris and deliberately sown the seed in his mind: if a time came when I wasn't there any more, he could always look at the Pole Star and think, 'That's where Daddy is.'

As I packed my bags, I hesitated over a book of Winnie-the-Pooh stories. I'd taken it on my first expedition to the Pole and it had become something of a tradition with me. I'd grown up near Ashdown Forest in Sussex – the original Winnie-the-Pooh country – and I was brought up on the stories. As an adult, I came across a miniature edition with the original paintings in colour, and I took it on my 1994 expedition because it was the smallest, lightest book I could find and it was the right kind of story too. You don't want to be reading *War and Peace* in your sleeping-bag at night, you want something that will soothe you and send you to sleep happy, and the simple truths, evocative language and familiar characters of *Winnie-the-Pooh* were just right; I'd feel my eyelids drooping within seconds of starting to read. It became a habit to read Pooh stories to my clients on Polar Travel Company expeditions – bedtime stories for grown-ups. We would all be there in the tent after supper, dog-tired from our day's sledge-hauling. I'd start reading a Pooh story and before I had got to page four they would all be asleep.

However, when it came to this expedition, I decided that Pooh had to be jettisoned. I had one last run-through the kit to get the weight down and several things went, including the Bear of Very Little Brain. I felt that I had moved on and didn't need that sort of security blanket, and perhaps I was even a bit weary of those over-familiar stories – I could probably have recited them word for word from memory – but it might also have been because they were just too personal, a reminder of the family I was leaving behind. I'd read all the Pooh stories to Wilf, played Pooh sticks with him from the bridge just down-river from our home, and, just before I left, I took him down to a group of pines on the river bank that look identical to the ones on the last page of *The House at Pooh Corner*, where Christopher Robin says goodbye to Pooh before he goes to school – a place he has to go to, but where Pooh can't go with him. He explains that he'll never forget Pooh, but that he won't be seeing him so much any more. Pooh knows something important and sad is happening but doesn't really understand what. With that emotional weight, let alone the physical weight of the Pooh stories, it seemed wiser to leave them at home. However, I did take something to read – one of the James Herriot books – that was similarly lightweight in both senses. It was good-humoured, evocative of simpler, happier times, and though it was excess weight, my two previous expeditions had convinced me that morale and mental factors were as important, if not more so, than physical ones.

I could delay my departure no longer. I kissed Freya, Wilf and Mary in turn and then took the coward's way out – I hurried away before the emotions of the moment overcame me. It would be the last time I would see or even talk to any of them until I returned. I don't talk to Mary at all while I'm away on an expedition; it just doesn't work for either of us. She's got her world in Wydemeet and I've got my world in the Arctic. She can't help with my problems on the ice and I can't help her with a broken washing machine or the children's schooling, and I just can't cope with worries about what's happening back at home. I have to be absolutely clear and focused on the task in hand or I won't succeed.

As I drove away from my home and my family, I thought of the comment Fridtjof Nansen had recorded in his journal on his departure for his epic journey across the polar ice-cap: 'It was the day of leave-taking, the immutable day. The door closed. Alone one walked for the last time from the house down through the garden . . . Behind lay everything that was dear in life, but what lay ahead and how many years would pass before one might see it all again?'

PART TWO

7

I came out of my reverie with a start. I had been sitting still too long in that frozen hut on Ward Hunt Island and I was seriously cold. My chest felt as if it were in the tightening grip of a vice. My booted legs were frozen, wooden and lifeless from the knee down. The visitors' book still lay open on the table in front of me. I wrote a brief, hasty note: 'This is Pen Hadow writing my last words before setting out on a solo expedition to the Pole, without resupply. Who knows what's going to happen? But I feel I've prepared myself as well as I can.' It wasn't exactly *War and Peace*, in either length or literary quality, but it was the best I could manage. I signed and dated it, and closed the book. Perhaps tomorrow I could begin my journey to the Pole.

As I lay in my sleeping-bag that night, drowsily listening to the keening of the wind, I thought of Mary and the children back at Wydemeet. I could almost hear the rush of the wind forcing its way past the protecting stand of pines in front of the house and the distant rumble of the swollen waters of the Swincombe charging over the boulders as a spring gale swept in from the North Atlantic. Those thoughts unsettled me and I lay awake a long time before I finally fell sleep. When I woke the next morning, 16 March, a dim light was seeping through the windows, and the wind, though still shaking the hut, had lost its bullying gusts. In a burst of imprudent enthusiasm I wriggled free of the sleeping-bag and rushed outside wearing only my down-filled bed bootees and thermals. The wind was still coming from the south-west, but it had definitely quietened down. Dark clouds were now discernible, racing out to sea below a blanket of higher, grey cloud cover. All the same, I knew that the gaping leads to the north were so broad that, even at a temperature of −30 °C, it would take a further twenty-four hours of light or no winds for them to freeze enough to bear my weight. Even then, the only way to be sure was to get to the edge and start walking out onto the ice. I decided that it was wiser to spend one more day in the hut and then set off the following morning. I stood motionless for a few minutes, drinking in the scene, awe-struck as always by the endless Arctic vistas, but without my outer layers of clothing in a temperature of 30° below, I soon became seriously cold. Stiff-limbed, I tottered back inside the hut. I couldn't heat the room with my stove, so I headed for the only place that would not cool me further – my sleeping-bag, which still had some residual warmth from my body-heat – and nodded off again for a couple of hours.

After breakfast, I dressed in my full outdoor gear and went outside. I was now feeling that, after the weeks of sleep deprivation and an out-of-control workload, I was almost back on track. I looked around me. Over the years I had got to know the topographical features of Ward Hunt Island pretty well, purely from looking at my charts. My favourite, a 1:250,000 scale map produced by Canada Energy, Mines & Resources, was pinned on the wall by my desk in my office at Wydemeet, and I had visited the island in my mind almost every day since we'd moved to Dartmoor. On my two previous solo expeditions, I'd headed north within minutes of landing, but now my delayed start offered me an unexpected opportunity to explore the island. This might well be the last time I ever stood here, and I was going to make the most of it. That decision was perhaps also indicative of a less desperate attitude this time around. I was going to set off for the Pole on my terms, when I judged the time to be right, not like a hyped-up downhill racer released from the starting gate. I made up a flask of tea, slung the shotgun over my shoulder, stuffed some cartridges in my pocket and set off.

As I scanned the rising ground behind the hut to pick out my best route up Walker Hill, I saw a little flurry of snow, like a dust devil, whirling across the ice towards me. I was just thinking, how strange, I've never seen one of those before, when it came to a sudden halt on the skyline, and the 'snow-flurry' resolved itself into an Arctic hare. A moment later a second hare revealed itself. It was an inspiring moment for me. I wasn't completely alone; even in this icebound wilderness, at least two other creatures were managing to eke out an existence, nibbling on the stunted wisps of vegetation beneath the crust of ice and snow. If hares could survive here, there was nothing for man to fear, and to know that these two would be busying themselves on the island, by choice, as I trekked out to sea, was a strangely comforting thought. I stood and watched them for some minutes as they scratched at the snow, completely unafraid of me, before lolloping away out of sight, their snow-white fur camouflaging them so perfectly against the ice and snow that only their movements betrayed their presence. I felt a small pang as they disappeared; they were likely to be the last animals and perhaps the last signs of life of any sort that I would see for many weeks.

Before I began to climb the hill, I walked in a wide circle around the hut and was glad to find no tracks or traces of any larger creatures – polar wolves or polar bears. To my knowledge only one person, the highly acclaimed Japanese explorer Naomi Uemura, has actually encountered a bear on Ward Hunt Island, but anywhere that the polar pack-ice – the floating sea-ice – abuts ice that is permanently frozen to the land, like the ice-shelf surrounding Ward Hunt Island, you tend to find them, since the movement of the pack-ice against the permanent ice regularly opens shore leads where seals will emerge to breathe and, if unwary, become prey. Polar wolves have also been seen on Ward Hunt, but their reputation is far worse than their intent. They are curious about humans and their food, but acts of aggression are almost unheard of in unpopulated areas like this.

The attitude of polar bears to humans is much more complex. Not a year goes by without reports of at least one or two deaths somewhere in the Arctic, and whenever I've come across a bear or fresh tracks, my heart-rate has gone through the roof. I had been at maximum alert from the moment I stepped off the plane but, so far at least, there appeared to be none in the immediate area, though on each journey to the far north it always takes a few days to really 'get your eye in'. Your mind starts to accept that you are not going to see trees, television, lights and people, and suddenly you reacquire the ability to see the ice-cap not as a featureless frozen mass, but as a place of endless subtle differences, nuances, variations and gradations of colour and form. The ice is a myriad of blue, green, aquamarine and grey, and the sunlight refracting through it produces every colour in the spectrum.

Visual experiences, upon which our minds normally feed so avidly, are particularly dramatic because some of the other senses virtually shut down in the Arctic. There are virtually no smells because the cold suppresses them. You can only taste hot food; the cold stuff – even chocolate – tastes like lumps of wood. Your sense of touch is also greatly diminished because you're almost always wearing gloves and mitts, insulating you from contact with the external world, and in any case your finger ends are permanently numb. And though your hearing is only slightly impaired by your hats, neckovers and hoods, the only sounds are the repetitive *ssst, ssst,* of your skis, the keening of the wind and the occasional phases of creaking and groaning from the ice as it flexes and distorts.

So you are thrown back on your sight and your inner eye. Some, like me, find it rewarding and almost therapeutic; but it can be very disorientating and disturbing for others, and some feel the isolation and the lack of stimuli so acutely that they come unglued under the strain. I've heard of a couple of people in Antarctica recently who lost it so completely in the space of less than a week that they had to be sedated by the base doctor and flown out at once. And I was once driven to take my sleeping-bag outside the tent in 40° below and sleep under the stars in an attempt to reassure a nervous group of clients that they had nothing to fear.

As I've grown older and become more confident in that environment, I have come to appreciate the aesthetic experiences even more – in what I now call 'Freya moments', after my beautiful daughter, who bears the name of the Norse goddess of merriment, love and beauty. My 'Wilf moments' are like my son, more physical and vocal. They revolve around phrases we use together: 'Easy, Tiger', if I'm overdoing it and becoming too aggressive with my sledge, and 'Only joking, or no?' in a thick Devon accent, if towards the end of the day, I half-think that I might stop. A quick 'Only joking, or no?' would keep me going for another session at least.

My Freya moments included taking in the dazzling variety of colours and the bewildering complexity of sculptural forms carved in the ice. I used to resent anything that was stopping me from going north – even the two minutes that it took to stop and take a photograph of some breathtaking ice-formation – but I've came to appreciate it as a reward for good progress or compensation for poor progress, capturing something of lasting value from the day. Those subtle changes in texture, shape and colour are not just of aesthetic interest, but of operational value. They can mean the difference between life and death, like spotting the almost invisible outline of a polar bear against the ice, or knowing the differing look and texture of 'marginal good', 'marginal' and 'marginal bad' ice. The seasoned polar traveller can identify many different kinds of snow and ice, knows which is the best to use for melting for water or for building a shelter, and will often be able to tell from the lie of the ice around a lead, which way to head in order to circumvent it. He will learn to gauge the strength of the bending, shifting ice beneath his feet, what will bear his weight and what will not. He will spot a seal's breathing hole, or the tracks of an Arctic fox or polar bear, and will also develop a sense, almost an instinct, for danger, the thing out of place or the faintest unusual movement in a wind-scoured 'landscape' that is rarely completely still. Such faint clues, often the only hint that a polar bear is stalking him, may save his life.

There are certain precautions you can take to minimise the risks of an attack, but you can never eliminate them completely and you have to have your wits about you at all times. Just like wolves and sharks, bears have an unfortunate and ill-deserved reputation for being heat-seeking missiles, locking on to humans with inevitably fatal consequences. My experience is that, in nine cases out of ten, they are driven not by hunger or bloodlust but by simple curiosity, and are relatively easy to deter.

Rule One is that if you are confronted by a bear, do all you can to disabuse the bear of the notion that you're a seal. So never retreat towards a lead or open water, because then you're doing exactly what a seal does: trying to escape back to the protection of the water. Make as much noise as possible: singing, banging ski-poles or pans or whatever you have to hand – all have a remarkable deterrent effect.

Rule Two is don't try to run away – you'll never win the race and there's nowhere to hide anyway on the sea-ice, so get organised, get wrapped up, and prepare for a blisteringly cold showdown with a firearm at the ready. Rule Three is that there is one situation where you can effectively guarantee being attacked and that is if you come between a polar bear and her cubs. It can happen all too easily; you might approach from downwind over a pressure ridge and find the mother on one side of you and the cubs on the other. Young bears stay with their mother until they're about two years old and, because they are inexperienced, their behaviour is very unpredictable. They may well come running up to you in a playful way, sending the mother into protective attack mode. But even if they keep their distance, the mother will attack you without hesitation if you appear to be threatening her cubs, even if only by blocking her route to them. If that happens, you have to get the hell out of there without hesitation.

Those very basic rules apart, polar bear behaviour is essentially unpredictable. Even when you've observed them over a long period, you can never rely on a pattern of behaviour being repeated on the next occasion. They may attack in complete silence and without warning but, particularly if aggravated by humans, they will sometimes make hissing noises, growl or grind their teeth before launching an attack. On a number of occasions I've seen a bear out on the ice make a series of wide, but ever decreasing circles around me. None of these bears ever turned its head towards me, or looked me in the eye, as if they were saying, 'No, I hadn't noticed you really; I just happened to be walking in a circle around you', but the circles keep getting tighter and tighter. All the time the bear is circling, it is gathering information and gaining confidence, and eventually it will reach the point where it will either attack or decide you're neither a threat nor potential prey and turn away.

If the bear is coming upwind towards you, it is still gathering information about you through its nose and may not be sure what to do and, even if it rears up on its hind legs in what may appear to be an aggressive posture, it still may not be planning an immediate attack. If there is little or no wind, the air can be quite layered and it may be standing up to scent different levels of the air for information. It may also be trying to impose itself and see what happens if it adopts a threatening stance. But if the bear is coming towards you with the wind at its back, it is not scenting you at all, and that is a very big danger signal, because it means it is not interested in gathering any more information about you. It's made up it's mind that you're toast, and you had better be ready to deal with it.

However, another bear, another time, may simply decide to charge straight at you at top speed without any preliminaries whatsoever. They'll attack dog teams like that, charging in from 100 metres away, and either seizing a dog or just veering aside at the last possible minute when all the dogs are going berserk at the realisation that there's a bear heading for them. You can't prepare for that sort of attack, least of all if you're lying in your sleeping-bag when a polar bear decides that your tent is a big seal or a walrus. You're just going to have to deal with it the best way you can. Every few days I made myself think through the sequence of instant manoeuvres I would have to carry out to fire the gun if surprised by a bear in my tent: getting my arms and upper body out of the zipped sleeping-bag and multi-corded hoods, and firing the gun through the tent wall. That mental rehearsal might save my life. It does happen. In 1979 Naomi Uemura was on a solo expedition with a dog-team a few days out from Ward Hunt Island when his sleep was rudely interrupted by a bear that pounced on his tent. He was unharmed but the bear ran off into the distance trailing part of his tent behind him, so Uemura had to call up a plane to bring up a fresh tent. In 1990, Kagge and Ousland were forced to shoot a bear around 88°N, and in 2000, a helicopter engineer suffered appalling injuries from a bear attack at a camp at around 89°N, but lived to tell the tale when the pilot shot the bear dead as it wrestled with him. Three friends of mine were recently in camp thirty miles from the Pole, when they heard a noise. They looked out to see a bear sniffing around the tent, but fortunately it lost interest and wandered off without investigating further. They didn't even need to fire their gun to drive it away, but I think it is fair to assume that they probably didn't sleep much for the rest of that night.

The authorities all say that you should leave your sledge and especially your food supplies a good 150–200 metres away from your tent at night, because the smell of the food you are carrying will attract bears, but the body-heat and stove warmth in the tent will create organic smells that are far stronger than the super-cooled contents of your sledge. However, even more important, if a lead opens up during the night, you might find yourself on one side of it and your sledge and supplies on the other, and that is clearly a non-starter. In any case, I'd rather be protecting my sledge from a bear than waking up in the morning to find one had trashed it and ended the expedition without my knowing about it.

You're breaking lots of rules on a polar expedition anyway. Every stove manufacturer and tent manufacturer that ever lived has included in their instructions the warning that under no circumstances are you to cook in your tent. Well, OK, no one is going to go to the polar regions then. There's no choice; if you try to cook outside, you'll use twice as much fuel and probably freeze to death while melting snow for water. So you have to cook inside your tent, but you have to be very aware of the attendant risk of carbon monoxide poisoning. You're not going to open the zip of the tent more than you have to because it's so ruddy cold outside, but you have to ventilate it enough to stop a fatal build-up of gas. The same goes for the danger of polar bear attacks. You have to be wary, but the risk of losing your sledge by leaving it a long way from the tent is greater than the danger of attack by a bear through keeping it nearby.

My biggest fear was an attack when I was at my most vulnerable, and that was not when I was asleep in my tent, but when I was using my immersion suit, because in the water and slithering out onto the ice, I resembled nothing so much as a large seal. Although my shotgun was always close at hand on top of the sledge, when I was wearing the immersion suit with its integral mitts, there was no way that I would have been able even to get the gun off the top of the sledge, let alone fire it. So before putting on my suit, I always scanned the immediate area of ice and the horizon all around me to make sure there wasn't a bear in the area. I kept checking all the time I was wearing it and was never wholly relaxed until I was back in my sledge-hauling gear.

The polar bear is a massive creature, yet moves with easy, fluid grace. Emerging from the water onto an ice-floe, he makes barely a ripple, and stalking a seal, sliding across the ice hugging the surface and propelled by his rear legs, he seems to merge with the snow- and ice-scape so perfectly that the only visible trace of the bear is the black of his nose. It's said that to a basking seal scanning the perspectiveless Arctic wastes, that black dot resembles nothing more threatening than another seal seen at long distance. By the time it realises its error, the bear will be upon it. Polar bears are occasionally found swimming twenty miles and, exceptionally, over a hundred miles from the nearest shore. They roam the ice-cap from its fringes to the very Pole itself. Wherever there are seals there are polar bears, and trailing in their giant footprints come Arctic foxes, scavenging in the bears' wake.

Polar bears may stand as tall as two men when rising on their hind legs to sniff the air, their great heads swivelling from side to side, and they can weigh as much as a thousand kilos. When charging over short distances they can attain a speed of 25 mph and they are powerful enough to stun a seal or even a small whale with one blow from a forepaw, or toss a 200-kilo seal into the air. Yet they are also subtle enough to mimic a drifting ice-floe by floating motionless in the water as they close in on a target seal.

They can dive to the seabed for kelp and shell fish, travel overland in summer for up to a hundred miles to feed on berries, and roam the dark and icy vastness of the ice-cap throughout the long polar winter, never hibernating and pausing only from the relentless hunt for food when 'denning' cubs. They cover vast distances; some have been tracked over thousands of miles. Their only enemies in water are the killer whale and the walrus. On ice or land they are wary of men and the walrus's needle-sharp tusks, though they will take walrus cubs if the chance presents itself, and, if hungry, they will stalk both adult walrus and men. To venture into an abandoned polar bear den and see the deep striations made by its claws in the ice-covered walls is to realise the power of these magnificent animals.

Inuit people have claimed that polar bears even use tools,

breaking in the roofs of seal lairs with lumps of ice and pushing ice-blocks ahead of them to hide themselves from basking seals. They also say that polar bears press snow into a wound to stop bleeding and, perhaps strangest of all, that most are left-handed and that one should therefore jump to the right if trying to avoid a charging bear. Western scientists have dismissed most of these claims as Arctic myths, but the Inuit have been studying polar bears an awful lot longer than the scientists.

The bears' fur is unique, keeping them warm on the ice by the combination of a layer of soft fur overlaid with a mat of long 'guard hairs' – hollow like drinking straws and so hard and shiny they appear to be made of plastic – which prevent the Arctic wind from carrying away their body-heat. Polar bears are so well-insulated that they do not even show up on infrared photographs of the ice. The only visible warmth is in their tracks because they discharge excess heat through the skin of their paws. But the fur plays little part in keeping polar bears warm in water; like seals and whales, they rely instead on a thick layer of blubber for insulation. The fur is not white but colourless when new; the refraction of light makes it appear white, just like clouds of water vapour, and exposure to sunlight gradually gives the fur yellowish tones ranging from the palest ivory, cream and lemon to buttermilk and gold.

At the onset of winter pregnant females carve out chambers in deep snow as dens for themselves and their cubs. Just like the Inuit in their igloos, they vary the thickness of the snow walls and the size of the ventilation holes to maintain or adjust the internal temperature. They draw all their food and virtually all the water they need from their stores of body fat. They do not hibernate in the sense that other bears do, and even though they reduce their respiration and heartbeat to very low levels, they can react to any danger in seconds. Between one and three cubs are born in December or January. They are utterly helpless at birth, blind and deaf, weighing no more than half a kilo and unable to survive the cold without the warmth of their mother's body, but they grow so rapidly on their mother's milk that by March or April they weigh over ten kilos and will emerge from the den around this time, when the Arctic weather permits.

Polar bears can and do kill men, and in turn bears have been hunted and killed since the Inuit first reached the Arctic, but they are now protected. Only the Inuit are allowed to hunt them, and the numbers they can kill are carefully controlled. Others living or travelling in Arctic regions are only allowed to kill a bear in self-defence and they will then face a searching interrogation about the circumstances and will be fined and forced to pay compensation to the Inuit if their story is less than completely plausible.

However, the risk of attack by polar bears on the Arctic Ocean is growing, simply because global warming is making more and more of the ice-cap an attractive proposition to them. Over the last quarter of a century, the average thickness of the Arctic ice has reportedly shrunk by 25 per cent; it used to be twelve feet and now it is only nine. It is an enormous change in such a short time and provides some of the strongest evidence of global warming. It also has potent implications for Arctic travellers. What was once thin ice is now open water and large areas of once relatively thick ice are now dangerously thin, and the thinner the ice, the more mobile it is and the more prone to breaking up. At present rates I would be surprised if my son Wilf were able to make the Arctic journeys that I have made, simply because by the time he grows up, there's going to be too much thin ice and too much open water.

A key biological indicator of the way things are going came in April 2001, shortly after I set off from Cape Arkticheskiy in Siberia to take a client to the North Geographic Pole. I heard over the sat-phone that a mother polar bear and her cub had been spotted three miles from the Pole. That used to be a freak occurrence, a male bear doing a massive transpolar trek in the breeding season or a marginalised bear – old, diseased or immature. But a mother and cub four or five hundred miles from the nearest land is a different matter entirely. They could only have been there because there was open water near the Pole. The seals could use it to come to the surface to breathe and the polar bears and Arctic foxes inevitably followed to prey on them. So, because of global warming, even the North Pole, the most remote and inhospitable spot on the planet, is now a normal environment for polar bears and their cubs.

I began climbing Walker Hill, picking my way over the ice and the iron-hard drifts of wind-packed snow and scaling the pinnacle of black, frost-shattered rock. It took forty minutes to reach the summit, but it was worth the effort. As I looked down, I transposed the familiar features of my office chart onto the topography of the island below me: the lake, drained in summer by a small river flowing south, that separated Walker Hill from the apron of low-lying land – larger than I had imagined it – at the eastern end of the island. The ice-sheet extended northwards as far as the eye could see, but beyond the west–east corrugations of the Ward Hunt Ice Shelf, there was a distinct break in the surface texture – the beginning of the polar pack-ice. No individual features were visible from this distance, but the darker, rougher texture showed the shadowing created by the pressure ridges formed in the sea-ice under the relentless power of wind, tide and current. But to my relief, when I looked further to the north I could see no give-away black strips indicating the presence of open water. The refreezing of the leads was under way.

Raising my eyes still further towards the horizon around me, I felt as if I were standing at the edge of the known world. To the south, past the dazzlingly lit peaks of the Queen Elizabeth Islands, lay a vast land mass extending 10,000 miles, populated by billions of creatures. To the north lay a frozen ocean covering five million square miles, populated by no more than a handful of highly adapted mammals: the occasional surfacing ringed seal, a few polar bears making forays beyond the coastal margins, and an odd Arctic fox hoovering up the remains of some unwary seal. And tomorrow, one human being would be taking his chances out there too.

It was not the hardest ascent I'd ever done, but the view north was so loaded with memories of past sadness and expectation of better times, that I knew that no future climb would ever be able to match this moment. I now felt ready for life on the frozen ocean. Tomorrow I would be on my way. I scrambled down the flank of the hillside, and went back to the hut for the last time.

Following John Ridgway's maxim: 'Always try to leave people and things better than you found them', I spent the rest of the day spring-cleaning the hut ready for the next occupant, and then checking and rechecking my equipment. My biggest fear is always that I'll forget something small but absolutely crucial like matches and will then have to fly some in at a cost of thousands of pounds – the most expensive matches in history. I needn't have worried, for I had left nothing behind, but I did have a brief panic because when I put in a short call to Ian, now safely back at base in England, he reported that the operators of my satellite tracking transmitter had received no data at all from my Argos tracking beacon.

I had a satellite phone as well, but it was not possible to 'ruggedise' it for polar use, and contemplating setting out without my primary means of communication – my most important piece of equipment – gave me serious pause for thought. I had used an Argos beacon on every previous visit to the Arctic Ocean, but I was now trialling a newer, lighter model, previously unused in polar environments. It could compute my position to within one metre, offering both greater safety and valuable scientific data on sea-ice-movements while I slept each night. Its cleverest innovation was its ability to predict the arrival of individual satellites arcing over my position from one horizon to another, switch itself on to download or upload to them, and then switch itself off again to save battery power.

But none of these technological wonders was of the slightest interest if it didn't work.

If the satellite phone failed or the batteries went flat, I'd be out on the ice with no means of communicating with my base, left only with the option of setting off my emergency locator beacon to report an emergency – the ultimate humiliation for any explorer. If I'd only had myself to worry about, I'd have considered taking the gamble, but there were my responsibilities to Mary and the children to think about too. I decided that if I couldn't get it to work, I would have to wait in the hut while Ian found another beacon – the manufacturers were in Toulouse – shipped it to Resolute Bay and then summoned another aircraft, at a further cost of £15,000, to bring it up to Ward Hunt Island. The delay could hardly be less than a week and it would seriously jeopardise my chances of reaching the Pole.

On the off-chance, I began disassembling and reassembling the Argos, more in hope than expectation that it would solve the problem. There were only half a dozen moveable components, so my hopes weren't high, but, to my inexpressible relief, I discovered the problem almost at once. During my final preparations back at Resolute I'd been overzealous in tightening the screw on the battery cover. Once I'd loosened it a little, the beacon's self-check lights pulsated happily and it functioned perfectly. I breathed a huge sigh of relief and settled down to my last night in the hut before beginning the expedition.

I woke early the next morning, 17 March 2003, in bright daylight. When I went outside, the temperature was cold, −33°C, but the sun was shining, though its low, flat arc above the horizon would keep it hidden behind the Challenger Peaks and Walker Hill for the next few days. The sky was mid-blue overhead, fading to an off-white on the northern horizon. And there was something else . . . or rather an absence of something. There was total silence. The absence of wind gave me confidence that no further new leads would open and that the existing ones would not widen any further. I felt well rested and ready for the challenges to come. I ate my breakfast, packed away my gear and reloaded it onto the sledge, leaving the shotgun on top for easy access if needed. I put my 'sledger's nosebags' – the nuts, salami, shortbread and chocolate that I ate in the breaks between sledging sessions – into my rucksack and hitched it onto my back then took a last look around the hut and closed the door.

I put on my harness and attached the traces of the sledge, then put on my skis and picked up my ski-poles. This was the moment, the first step on the long haul to the Pole. There was a slight feeling of dread as I took the strain; I knew, after all, exactly how heavy the sledge would be, like trying to drag a twenty-stone, comatose man behind me, and I wasn't hauling that dead weight across a flat, shiny surface like an ice-rink. The Arctic ice is rough, cracked, pitted and pocked with holes, lumps, bumps, projections and cracks where your burden be-comes wedged or threatens to topple over, spilling its load. The low temperature is not just uncomfortable, it also makes the sledge travel slower. When the ice 'warms up' to around −25 °C the runners flow much more easily over the surface. At −40° it is like trying to drag it across a gravel path.

However, the first short stretch from the hut was slightly downhill and that, and the adrenalin surge from the knowledge that I was finally on my way, helped to get the sledge moving. I had soon passed the last physical sign of man's presence, a metal pole buried deep in the ice, presumably left by some scientist to measure the movement of the ice-shelf. Although there was no visible sign of the transition, within a few minutes I knew that I had left the last land behind and was now dragging the sledge across the ice-shelf extending out over the sea. I didn't even glance behind me. The hut and Ward Hunt Island were already consigned to the past; the only direction I was interested in lay ahead to the north.

The process of skiing over the ice was far from silent, especially in these temperatures of −30 to −45 °C. Each movement of my ski-poles in, through and out of the ice was accompanied by a squeaking, wrenching, mechanical sound, while the skis made a repetitive rasping *whoosh, whoosh,* as they slid over the snow. Rougher bumpy ground – and there was plenty of that – created a terrific ski-noise, a rattling and banging like a public address system to all polar bears in the vicinity: 'Free meal. Roll up, roll up.'

On that first day out on the ice, the noise seemed so loud that I found myself cringing and trying to go more quietly, almost tiptoeing along on my skis, but, within a few hours, I had tuned the noise out of my hearing so much that I was barely even aware of it. I would listen closely each morning as I set off, however, because the noise the ski-poles made was a sure indicator of the air temperature. As any child making snowballs knows, as snow warms up it becomes more pliable and mushy, and as a result the noise of ski-poles working through it becomes much softer. I could tell to within a few degrees how cold it was, just by putting a ski-pole in and skiing a few paces. My other senses also provided clues. The extent and texture of the icy rime of hoar frost on the inside of my tent in the mornings changed with the temperature, and even the amount of flavour from the chocolate in my sledging rations was an indicator. If it tasted like wood and was so hard I could barely bite into it, it was probably −40 °C or worse; if it was still tasteless but I could bite through it with a bit of an effort, it was a few degrees warmer, maybe −25 to −30°, and if it had a genuine chocolate taste and my teeth could sink into it fairly easily, it was probably −15° or warmer.

The permanent ice-shelf is not flat but gently undulating like a scaled-down version of the rolling countryside of the English Downs, and the uniform colour of the ice and the brightness of the light made it difficult to discern the contours. Heading north on Day 1, I just knew that I was travelling on a gentle down-slope for a while and then the horizon began to rise and the effort of hauling the sledge increased as I started to climb towards the next crest. This continued for a few miles until I reached the junction between the permanent ice-shelf and the ridge of fresh ice-blocks that marked the transition to the polar pack-ice, forever in motion, prey to the ocean currents, the tides and, in particular, the winds.

There would be no more gently rolling curves, this was a fractured, fissured, vertiginous and boulder-strewn ice-scape, that had to be climbed as much as crossed. And lying beyond it were the three vast leads that had already caused me three days' delay. When I reached them, would they have closed or frozen over, allowing me to head on to the north, or would they still be black water or perilous thin ice – dark *nilas*? If so, it would force me into yet more delays or strength- and morale-sapping detours to east or west when the only direction I wanted to be heading was north. These were troubling thoughts to carry with me as I entered this forbidding region and found a site to make my first camp.

I pitched my tent, filled my plastic builders' rubble sack with snow to melt for drinking water for the night and the next day, piled my in-tent kit and my rations onto my sleeping-bag and dragged it through the tunnel entrance into the tent. I closed the drawstring and busied myself with the nightly tasks, arranging everything within reach of my sleeping-bag and then lighting the stove, heating water and preparing supper. As I worked, 'snow' continued to fall even inside my sealed tent as my exhaled breath froze to the canvas and then drifted back down as the fabric was shaken by the wind. It made me think of an account I'd once read by an Austrian member of a nineteenth-century polar expedition. As he trudged across the ice in an air temperature of −59 °F, he apparently noticed a tinkling sound and claimed that it was the sound of his exhaled breath falling to the ground as ice crystals.

I followed my housekeeping rituals with fanatical care, using the small plastic brush that I had already christened 'Mavis' to sweep the ice, snow, frost and condensation from my headgear, clothes and boot-liners, careful to leave not the smallest scrap behind. I regarded some of the inanimate objects I used as neutral; I thought some were malevolent and didn't trust them at all, but I grew very fond of others. It had become my habit on expeditions to anthropomorphise these favoured objects, assigning names and personalities to them – even the humble sweeping brush – and holding regular conferences with them on the nature of the terrain, the right route to follow and the speed of our progress over the ice. Anyone seeing me in earnest conversation with a small plastic brush would have harboured fears for my sanity, but as well as allowing me to hear the sound of a human voice – even if only my own – in the midst of that great Arctic void, these one-sided 'discussions' also helped me to clarify my thoughts and ensured that the decisions I took had been thought through first.

While sledging outside, my ski-poles were my constant companions and advisers, testing ice strength, keeping me balanced on awkward traverses and so on, but inside the tent, Mavis was queen. She made her customary excellent job of sweeping the loose snow from my sleeping-bag, but I knew that, even with this precaution, my exuded body vapours would freeze onto the fibres inside the filling of the bag during the night, forming blocks of solid ice that would slowly increase in size and weight with each passing night, adding several extra pounds to the load I was already hauling, and reducing the thermal efficiency of the sleeping-bag to vanishing point. Only when the sun rose high enough above the horizon to radiate appreciable heat, could I start draping the sleeping-bag over my sledge during the day and begin to reduce the ice in it by evaporation. Until then, the loss of warmth and the uncomfortable lumps inside my sleeping-bag just had to be accepted, though both impacted on the quality and quantity of my sleep.

The first five days were 'the survival phase'. The mission

was simply to get through them and keep in the game – keep moving the sledge north and establish a pattern both during the sledging day and in the camp at night, to get the systems up and running. Over the next five days I would aim to fine-tune everything, ensuring that I was doing each task in the most quick and efficient way possible and spending the minimum time on all the 'domestic duties' in my tent. This wasn't aimless nit-picking; I felt very strongly that, in attempting something in which the likelihood of success was already relatively slim, if I didn't do even the most trivial things – right down to tying the knot on the guy-ropes – in the most efficient way I could, then I probably wasn't going to get there at all. Even in the best-case scenario, the amount of resting time was insufficient to allow my body to repair itself and I had to do all I could to minimise the gradual erosion of my strength, both now and in the 'high-performance' phase of the expedition, from Day 11 onwards, when I would need every ounce of energy and every minute of rest and sleep to sustain the prodigious effort of dragging the sledge over progressively greater and greater daily distances towards the Pole.

For the first five days I was aiming to do no more than five to six hours sledge-hauling a day. On the next five I would pick that up to six to seven hours, from Day 10–15 it would be eight to nine hours, and from Day 15 onwards I'd be aiming for a minimum of nine hours, equating to six full sledging sessions including breaks. It may not sound a particularly long day – lots of people do eight-hour days at work – but they aren't operating in temperatures of −40 °C, carrying out a task that requires them to expend every ounce of their physical strength just to keep the show on the road, while also maintaining relentless concentration on macro- and micro-navigation, and 100 per cent awareness of the surrounding environment. Even on those short, five- to six-hour days, I ended every one close to exhaustion, wanting nothing more than to eat and sleep.

The shorter days at the start reflected the more difficult terrain, the greater weight of the sledge and the colder conditions, but I was also concerned to take a calm, measured approach, and not throw myself into it madly as I used to do on my early expeditions, desperate to cover plenty of miles but risking injury, hypoglycaemia and the possibility of burning out, mentally or physically, before reaching my destination. My friend Caroline Hamilton, who I'd helped to reach the Pole with her all-women expedition, had given me some advice before I set out. 'Treat yourself as a guide, Pen, and don't do anything that you wouldn't do with a client.' It was excellent advice; if I wouldn't risk a client going through thin ice instead of finding a way round it, why would I risk my own life and limb – especially as I was alone?

It always seemed to take a few days to get into my routine and, on this first night, the tent seemed very cluttered and the things I needed weren't always ready or to hand. As a result, every job took a little longer than necessary. But within a couple of days, I was arranging my equipment inside my tent with the precision of an anally retentive filing clerk tidying his desk. The matches, mug, saucepans, food, tea bags, sugar, satellite phone, batteries and my other kit all went in exactly the same place every night, and it made things much easier and less stressful and the tent seem a lot less cluttered and claustrophobic. I also mentally divided the tent into separate areas: the dining-room (complete with butler), kitchen, study and bedroom, and imagined myself moving between them – not easy in a tent measuring little more than two metres by one, but another way of attempting to impose some domestic normality in a thoroughly undomesticated environment.

As I boiled the water for my food and my cup of tea, I checked my position on the GPS which recorded my latitude and longitude in degrees, minutes and seconds, with an accuracy of about three yards. (As the names suggest, a minute is a sixtieth of a degree and a second is a sixtieth of a minute. A degree of latitude equates to sixty nautical miles; a minute is therefore equivalent to one mile and a second to just under thirty yards.) I also completed the first of my daily logs of distance travelled – exactly three miles north of Ward Hunt Island – ice and weather conditions. I was too tired to add much personal detail and, within a few minutes of finishing my meal, I had given up the struggle and extinguished my head-torch. Despite my fatigue, I slept poorly this first night out on the ice, partly because I had not yet reaccustomed myself to sleeping under canvas, but much more because of the cold.

The next morning and every subsequent morning, I checked my GPS before setting out (though I did not expect any significant overnight drift until two degrees or so further north), and updated the magnetic bearing to the Pole, offset over 80° to the west from the true North bearing because the North Magnetic Pole was located not far away in the Arctic Ocean. Most of the time I was using solar navigation to keep me on track, by computing my local noon using my longitude and Greenwich Mean Time, but, if the sun disappeared behind the clouds, I could use the compass to keep my bearings. I preferred solar navigation only because it was quicker; I didn't have to fumble for my compass, take the bearing and then find distinctive ice-shapes in the right direction that I could use as reference points. Even finding those was not easy when the flat light and monochrome icescape created by the lack of direct sunlight, and the complete absence of other objects by which we normally establish scale, would sometimes have me heading for an apparently huge ice 'boulder' 200 metres away, that turned out to be no more than a small projection from the ice at a tenth of that distance from me.

The highlight of my day was to check my progress on my GPS. It showed not only my position, but the distance I'd travelled that day, and it was such a treat that I always saved it and looked forward to it as I pitched my tent and did my evening jobs. Only when I'd got my outer clothes off and was settled in my sleeping-bag for the night with a cup of tea in my hand, did I allow myself to turn on the GPS. The figures I read would elicit either a groan or a cheer depending on how bad or good my progress had been. Before setting off the next morning, I'd check it again, because beyond 86°N on the ice-cap, the ice-drift really begins to kick in, and you want to know how far away from or towards the Pole you've drifted during the night and what magnetic offset will be required to track true North. And when you get very close to the Pole, your longitude can change significantly if the winds are driving the ice east or west. As all the lines of longitude converge on the Pole, one kilometre to the right or left can put you onto a different line of longitude, and therefore a different time zone, which is relevant for solar navigation.

On the following two days – Day 2 and Day 3 out on the ice – I crossed the first and second of the three leads which, as expected, had frozen over to produce 'light *nilas*' – perfectly strong enough for my purposes. I'd again slept badly, not helped by the zip on my sleeping-bag having broken already. I made a gash repair with a drawstring. I was also starting to daydream about food, especially butter, a sure sign that the workload was beginning to have its effect. They were particularly gruelling days with a number of rubble-fields to traverse as well as the leads.

Every sense was on maximum alert as I approached each lead. There were other, subtler hazards to beware, as well as the possibility of black, open water. Some cracks in the ice and edges of leads are covered with a layer of snow and are very hard to distinguish from the snow-covered ice surrounding them. Even the most experienced and wary traveller can be caught out, especially in very overcast, flat light conditions. I'd stopped at the edge of one such lead as much from instinct as any visible difference in the terrain and, probing the snow with a ski-stick, I broke through the apparently solid, snow-covered ice, revealing the black water swirling beneath. And there are other, even more hazardous leads, filled with '*shuga*' – water so saturated with snow, slush and ice crystals that it resembles quicksand on land – impossible to swim through or escape from.

Fortunately, the only hazard from the first lead was that it was still marginal ice – grey *nilas* – with traces of the dark colour of the water below showing through. I tested it thoroughly, then inched my way on to it before speeding across, feeling it flexing beneath me as I moved. There were a few unsettling creaks and one unnerving cracking sound from the ice, but I made it safely across. After another night's savage frost, the second lead had frozen solid and the flat, new ice provided the easiest going of another exhausting day.

I was now in a region of ice as scarred and littered with obstructions as a First World War battlefield, and navigating north through the pressure ridges and boulder-fields in the most efficient way was a constant drain on my mental resources as well as my physical strength. The ice-fields were like a giant's maze and there was no guarantee that there was any correct solution to the puzzles it set. I just had to get north the best way I could and that inevitably required a good deal of moving west and east to circumvent obstacles or to search for a relatively easy way through the ice-barriers confronting me.

Often there was no easy way and if the route was too awkward for the sledge or the gradient was so severe that I really couldn't move it fully laden, I had to break the load into two or even three parts. I'd unhitch the sledge, take off my skis and then move ahead on foot to reconnoitre the best route. It was tempting to just put down the traces and go – I was never planning to go more than fifty yards away from the sledge – but each time I left it, I made myself stop, unstrap the shotgun from the top of the sledge and take it with me, repeating a mantra to myself: 'Think of your family. You promised to come back to them. Don't take unnecessary risks. Take the gun with you.'

It was important to use this mantra because the effects of the severe cold make the brain function more slowly and less efficiently in the high Arctic, leading to losses of concentration and symptoms that are like being drunk. From studies at the South Pole, the US National Science Foundation has found that thought and reaction times are almost three times as slow in extremely cold environments, and I found that those little mantras were necessary to keep me focused on important things. It was all too easy to be tempted into an unnecessary risk, through inattention, lack of concentration or even just sheer cold-induced laziness. It was easier not to bother unpacking the gun from the sledge and 99 times out of 100, maybe 999 times out of 1,000, I'd get away with it, but there were enough dangers to be faced without adding stupid, avoidable risks to them.

Having found the best route, I dumped the thirty-five-pound rucksack, came back, took the much heavier – eighty-five pounds or so – webbing bag containing more of my food supplies off the sledge and staggered with that to where I'd left the rucksack. As I walked there and back again, I was preparing the route, stamping down or kicking away any projections from the ice that I thought might snag the sledge. Finally, I picked up the traces and pulled the sledge through. I hadn't lightened it that much, but it was almost invariably enough to get it over the obstacle I was facing, even though it sometimes took every ounce of strength I had. Sometimes I'd have to repeat that three-stage shuttle a few times, but I never had to make more than five three-stage shuttles in sequence to traverse a difficult stretch, and at other times I'd do it once or twice and then be able to reload the sledge, put my skis back on and plod on to the north.

Over the years I'd become a pretty good navigator through

pressure ridges and rubble-fields, and I was usually confident that I'd found the best way through or round each set of obstacles. It makes a huge psychological difference because there is nothing more dispiriting and damaging to your morale than knowing that you're expending this huge amount of effort to make progress that is only intermittently in the desired direction, and that a better route may exist nearby. The furthest one can normally see from the top of a pressure ridge is perhaps two kilometres ahead. That might include as few as two, or as many as twenty ice-pans separated by ice-rubble at their edges; and I was continually keeping in mind the big picture – the optimum overall direction I wanted to take – while also constantly scanning the ice closer in front of me, looking not just for ways through the large obstructions like the pressure ridges, but for all the minor imperfections and undulations on the surface of even the flattest ice-pan. Once the sledge was moving it was important to keep that momentum, and even a small bump could slow it down dramatically, so I was constantly taking a weaving course around even the smallest obstacles, trying to find the smoothest path for the sledge. It became almost intuitive after a while – I often wasn't even conscious of having chosen a particular route – but it paid off and whatever extra distance I had to travel as a result was more than compensated for by the energy saved by keeping the sledge in motion rather than repeatedly putting in the gut-wrenching effort to move it from a standing start. It's the same principle as marathon running – you don't hop up onto a kerb to cut off a corner, you go the longer distance on the level, because rhythm is everything. I found a high point, scanned the ice ahead and then chose a route that I could then navigate by using the distinctive colours and shapes among the jumbles of ice. They were often geometric or architectural shapes – pyramids, cubes, cathedrals, blocks of flats, houses, thatched cottages – and sometimes animals – dolphins and sharks, camels and hippopotami. I then rehearsed my route by going over it with my 'team' – the collection of crucial pieces of equipment like my sledge and ski-poles upon which, like Mavis the sweeping brush, I had already bestowed names that suited their characteristics. The sledge was 'Baskers', because in its inertia and reluctance to move, it reminded me of my collie dog, Baskerville, or 'Baskers' for short. He loves more than anything else going on long runs with Mary's horse, but doesn't like training runs with me and, as it slowly dawns on him that the horse will not be joining us, I'm always having to turn round and shout for him, and I invariably find him hiding behind rocks and tufts of grass, hoping he can slope off back home for a lie down. My sledge often didn't want to come with me either, and was always getting caught between blocks of ice, out of which it then had to be coaxed, cajoled, threatened or manhandled.

My ski-poles were named 'Curves' and 'Swerves'. The former had acquired her eponymous shape after taking my full weight when I slipped, almost fell, and bent my left ski-pole over a block of ice. Luckily I let go of it at the critical moment and it didn't snap, but it was irretrievably bent out of shape. Two minutes later, I did the same thing again, and as I slipped in three different directions, my weight sent the other ski-pole swerving between three different blocks of ice. Somehow she emerged unscathed, so she became Swerves. On past expeditions I've ended up hating my sledge as if it were my most mortal enemy, but there had been a sea-change on this expedition since I started calling him 'Baskers' and now he was a fully fledged member of my inner circle: The Team. I'd return from each reconnaissance and then announce, 'Right, Team, it's looking hard, easy, hard, easy. We're going left of the large blue diamond, heading for the white ball, on to the three-humped camel and then left of the cathedral spire.' There was some method in this apparent madness, because the repetition of my planned route during the conversation with my ski-poles and sledge, as I rehitched to the sledge, was a way of fixing it in my mind, and breaking down the difficult section into manageable challenges. It was never, 'Oh my God, another ten weeks of grinding out the miles.' It was only, 'Get to the cathedral spire and you've done the hard bit of this section.'

I was now feeling that I was well 'in the zone', as utterly and unswervingly focused on my goal as any medieval pilgrim and, like a pilgrimage, one of the wonderful things about the North Pole for me is that there's no correct route, there's no map, and when you arrive it's a completely conceptual experience. It's just yet more ice, with no defining point to say that you've arrived, and it's only exciting or important because of the intellectual and emotional value that you have invested in it. It never mattered to me that there was nothing at the Pole, in fact I loved the idea. When I first began travelling and exploring in the polar regions I had the clichéd idea that it was 'me against the Arctic', and all that macho-man kind of stuff, and I thought of it primarily in terms of the 'challenge': 'Am I man enough?' But though the physical rigour and difficulty is still what generates the sponsorship and the media interest, to me, the inner mental journey is now equally, if not even more important.

I trust my competence in looking after myself in Arctic environments. I know that things are going to go wrong – equipment will break, my health may fail and I am often going to have to think on my feet – but it's a real bonus for me that I have to sort it all out myself. I want to be entirely responsible, to operate in a vacuum, cut off from the outside world. If I fail, it's my fault. If I succeed, that's also down to me being able to deal with everything – physical and mental – that the journey throws in my face. But I'm not trying to win the title of 'The Planet's Toughest Man'; my journey to the Pole is a mental, psychological and spiritual journey as much as a physical one – a sort of Grail quest, if you like – and it has a purity about it, an otherworldliness, that is almost in the realms of the mystical.

On a spiritual pilgrimage, you live a simple life on the road, wearing functional clothing, staying in basic accommodation and eating plain food. It's a great thing to do once in your life – or even more often – very humbling, self-effacing and hard, hard work. A polar journey is similar, and almost monastic in its simplicity; you take nothing with you that is not essential to your journey. You have a hood like a monk's cowl, closing out the wider world and forcing you to focus on a narrow field of vision: the path you must follow. You look like a monk, you feel like a monk, and you move at a steady, measured metronomic pace; I try to keep my heart-rate at around 130 beats per minute, and I can keep moving for twelve hours a day at that rate. That hypnotic rhythm, plodding north on automatic pilot, frees your mind to think and reflect, and towards the end of the day I get to an almost transcendental stage, where suddenly I find I've travelled two or three hours without being aware of it at all. I've just been weaving past the obstructions like a bird flying through the branches of a tree.

When you finally reach your destination, you stand in a world turned upside down. There is no east or west or north at the Pole; whichever way you face, the only direction you can take is south. There is no time – you stand in all twenty-four of the earth's time zones simultaneously – and no familiar, reassuring succession of day and night. The world seems as frozen as the ice beneath your feet: perpetual day, perpetual twilight, or perpetual night.

The North Geographic Pole is also a part of the Celestial North Pole, the end-point of an axis that is used for astro-navigation and extends into space 'to infinity and beyond', as Buzz Lightyear would say, and it speaks volumes to me about the inner journey and the process of journeying rather than the purely physical experience that you have to go through – an important part of it but nowhere near the whole story. If you stand at the Pole on the winter solstice, the stars circle above you all night and not one of them sets. From Polaris, the hub, almost directly overhead, to the last visible star scraping the southern horizon, all travel in perfect, concentric circles across the sky. For the only time in your life, the earth and the heavens really do seem to revolve around you.

I at last slept well that third night on the ice, for fourteen hours in all, and I was glad to catch up on the lost sleep even at the price of a late start the next day, Day 4, when I crossed the last of the three leads during the afternoon. The fierce temperatures of the previous days had done their work and the lead was now completely frozen over with a thick layer of opaque ice, but, as a result of my late start, I managed only 1.9 nautical miles northwards through an endless minefield of huge pressure ridges and boulder-fields. My target distance at that stage of the expedition was three nautical miles, but I didn't allow the lost mile to faze me; I knew that I didn't have to achieve the individual target every single day, providing my overall rate of progress was satisfactory.

The next day, Day 5, even though the temperature remained around −40 °C and the sun barely climbed above the horizon, there was just enough heat in it to evaporate the rime from my sledge-top for the first time. It was a great psychological boost because it showed me that it wouldn't be long before I could put my sleeping-bag on top of the sledge during the day and begin using the sun to remove the accumulated ice inside the bag by the process of sublimation that, even in deeply sub-zero temperatures, converts solid ice directly into vapour.

I was also starting to find a few larger ice-pans among the ridges and boulder-fields, making for easier going. It gave me increasing hope that the very worst of the ice conditions were now behind me and that I could begin to pick up the pace a little. Each ice-pan was like a little enclosed field, surrounded by a wall of ice, but there was always a point where the ice wall was lower or easier to cross, making a gateway into the next pan beyond.

On Day 6, I made another 3.5 nautical miles, stringing ice-pans like pearls, finding gateways between them with relative ease. In the course of the entire day, I only had to take my skis off three times to manhandle the sledge over really steep pressure ridges. That night I wrote in my journal 'Good ice as far as ridging is concerned. PLEASE let it continue.'

Snowdrifts tapering down to the ice-surface form in the lee of every pressure ridge. Once hardened by wind-action and thermal cycling, they form ramps and, since the prevailing Arctic wind is from the north-west, that would normally have helped me to scale each ridge. However, I couldn't see any signs that there had been any sustained winds from the north-west at any time since the previous autumn and, with the winds blowing instead from the south-west, the drifts had formed on the northward-facing sides of the ridges. That meant there were no ramps for me to use to help me up the pressure ridges, but that really didn't trouble me at all, for the other implication of that unusual, but consistent pattern of south-westerly winds was very beneficial for me. If the ice-cap had not been pushed towards the North American land mass by the winds that winter, it would not have been under its usual degree of compression and throwing up pressure ridges, suggesting that I could expect unusually flat ice conditions as I travelled further north. It was early days, and the winds there may not have been the same further north, so I could not allow myself to hope for too much, but it was a very significant development with potentially huge implications.

The Arctic winter was almost at an end but the endless daylight of the polar summer had not yet begun and for those first few days I had had a full day and a full night. Even when there was no moon, the nights weren't inky black, but more of a dark grey twilight born of the dim phosphorescence of the sunlight leaking from below the horizon and the starlight reflecting from the snow. Travellers dread the long polar night – man perhaps fears the absence of light above all other things

– but even in the depths of the Arctic winter, the night is not the blackness of a mine-shaft deep underground. Starlight, even when diffused through clouds, is gathered and reflected by the ice, diminishing the polar darkness a little, and moonrise brings an opalescent, milky-blue light. Reflected and refracted by the ice, it creates an eerie, softly glowing landscape, devoid of form or shadow, as if seen through water. At a full or near full moon, there is enough light to cross the ice almost as well as by daylight.

As the sun begins to approach, the darkness of midwinter slowly gives way to a diffuse, grey twilight, then to daylight and finally to full sunlight when the disc of the sun at last appears above the horizon. It rises and sets at almost the same point, 'like a whale rolling over' as Barry Lopez described it in *Arctic Dreams*. Another reassuring pillar of the familiar world has been removed: this far north, the sun at first does not rise in the east and set in the west; it rises and sets in the south and then, for weeks on end, it does not set at all.

I have seen nothing anywhere on this earth to equal the beauty of the March polar sunrises and sunsets, when the sun is still low on the horizon. After months of unbroken polar night to be there for the first sunrise of a new year, let alone the first of a new millennium, is an inspiring, life-affirming experience. There is a long period of false dawn, with the sky gradually lightening, but the sun is still hidden by the curve of the earth and then at last the first ray of sunlight reaches across the ice, setting it sparkling like a vast veil sprinkled with diamonds. The air is so cold, arid and clear that the colours of the sky shine with a depth and radiance seen nowhere else on earth, and in colours that make rainbows seem pallid in comparison. Crimsons, violets, golds, azures and aquamarines wash the morning sky, fading only slowly into the familiar deep blue of the Arctic sky as the sun climbs higher above the horizon. The sunsets are if anything even more magnificent and, even when the sun has gone down below the horizon, it leaves a halo of light behind, refracted into an arc of jewelled colour through the prism of the ice particles suspended in the air.

Equally extraordinary are the Novaya Zemlya images, named after the region where Barents and his men first saw them in 1597. They are mirages caused by the refraction of the sun's rays by the atmosphere, making the sun appear to have risen in the sky when it is actually still below the horizon. On such occasions there is the bizarre sight of the sun rising twice in one day.

At the latitude of Ward Hunt Island, the first sunrise of the year occurs in early March, but at the North Pole the sun doesn't appear above the horizon until the spring equinox – 21 March. It makes a complete circuit around the horizon without ever dipping below it, and, at the end of that day, it has risen a fraction higher in the sky. So it goes on throughout the summer, spiralling ever higher in the sky until Midsummer's Day, when it reaches its highest elevation and describes its tightest circle. It then unwinds the spiral until it disappears below the horizon on 21 September – the autumn equinox – not to reappear above it for a further six months.

Seen from a few miles north of Ward Hunt, the sun's trajectory included an element of dip – it rose above the horizon in the morning and described a low arc through the sky before setting again in the late afternoon; but it neither rose high above the horizon nor sank much below it, and there was soon some dim daylight even at midnight. Late in the afternoon, as the sun began to set, the light cast cream, gold, orange and russet tints over the ice, and then, as it disappeared below the horizon, the colours shifted further and further towards cold, lunar tones of blues and greys, deepening and darkening as the evening advanced. The lower the light, the more it seemed to bring the frozen world around me into sharper and sharper relief, sculpting the ice and snow – almost featureless in hard daylight – into scarps, cliffs and screes, mounds and monoliths, and shapes that mimicked every conceivable natural form. I was so fascinated by this twilight world that I regularly walked on much later into the evening than common sense and my prior planning dictated, and, as a result, I missed some of the early light and heat from the morning sun. The best practice was to stop, set up camp and cook my evening meal while a little of the relative warmth of the day remained, then sleep through the coldest hours of the night. In practice I often found myself setting up my tent with the cold of night already advancing. It was inefficient because it meant that I burned more fuel, but it was a price worth paying for the morale boost that walking through the twilight 'lunar' landscape gave me. I was already struck by how calm and relaxed I was in the face of difficulties like leads and horrendous terrain that on previous expeditions would have seen me turning the air blue with the colour of my language and being much more aggressive with my sledge and equipment, with the inevitable consequence that things tended to break. This time I was being much more philosophical. Mentally, I had prepared myself for the worst circumstances imaginable and so wasn't so shocked or upset when I encountered them.

When I woke on the morning of Day 7, I at once heard the wind blasting over the ice-cap and battering the tent fabric. A gale had blown up during the night and with the temperature at −40 °C and dropping even lower during the day, the wind-chill of around −90° made it well-nigh impossible to move north. I did not want to be taking a rest day at this stage – after the enforced idleness in the hut at Ward Hunt Island, I wanted only to be out and moving north, but conditions seemed close to impossible. To make absolutely sure, I dressed and packed up my kit inside the tent and then launched myself out into the blast. The loose surface snow snaked wildly out of the upwind horizon, and whirled past the tent, and the horizons all around were merged into the ice-scape by the snow particles whipped into the air. I shuffled around my tent for a good quarter of an hour, generating some body-heat while I agonised over whether to sledge today or stay tent-bound. But I realised that while I could travel, just, in such conditions, if anything went wrong I would be in very big trouble. There was no room for error whatsoever and I resigned myself to a day 'indoors'. I would have to stifle my impatience and wait out the storm once more.

It did at least give me time for some running repairs to the zip on my smock, which had broken the previous day leaving my right side more exposed to the wind than was comfortable. I couldn't fix the zip, so I had to sew the smock closed and wriggle in and out of it like a snake shedding its skin. The day off also gave me the chance to rest my back, which had been aching for the last couple of days – a reflection of the twisting and turning and the gruelling physical effort of manhandling the sledge over the pressure ridges while carrying a rucksack full of rations.

8

When I awoke on the morning of Day 8, I lay with my eyes closed, listening to the familiar sounds of the Arctic: the brittle rattle of the frozen tent fabric in the breeze, the hiss of loose snow as it surged past or was deposited around the base of the tent, and the occasional booms and pulsations of the ice-cap as it flexed and twisted under the pressure of the wind. It was still bitterly cold, but the sound of the wind was muted; it had obviously died down during the night. Even through my closed eyelids I could tell that a soft, diffuse light was permeating the tent. It would, I knew, be illuminating the thick layer of ice-rime covering the walls and the roof above my head and the intricate feathers and fans of ice crystals that had formed as my exhaled breath froze on contact with the hood of my sleeping-bag during the night. They would have been objects of wonder in any other circumstances, but they had long lost their appeal for me. From bitter experience I knew that my first movements would cause those delicate crystal structures to collapse and tumble down into the opening of my sleeping-bag. Even the most enthusiastic advocate of the benefits of a cold shower first thing in the morning would have second thoughts in an air temperature of around −40 °C − nearly three times colder than the average domestic deep-freeze.

I lay motionless, assessing my readiness for the day ahead. I didn't feel well rested, but that was scarcely surprising. I was putting in a huge physical effort every day and I hadn't been sleeping well for some nights now. Normally I'm blessed with the ability to sleep pretty much at will, regardless of any pressure I may be under, but at −40° I was so cold that I was waking up several times during the night, shivering from head to foot and with my teeth chattering like castanets. Even with my improvised 'smock' over it, my sleeping-bag was not rated for the temperatures I was enduring. It had been a deliberate decision on my part to keep the weight of my sleeping-bag system to a minimum, but I was paying the price for it in lost sleep. The bag was only rated to −25° − a good 20° warmer than the temperatures I was currently experiencing − and in any case the ratings were based on a well fed person who had not done any strenuous exercise, sleeping on a glacier for one night. It did not compare with having done seven days of gruelling physical work on a diet that was insufficient to replace the lost calories. In those circumstances, the bag probably had an effective temperature rating of nearer to −15 or 20 °C. I did what I could to supplement it, wearing not only my black thermal 'pyjamas', but my 'neckover' or 'headover' − a thick tube of fibre pile that covered my neck, blocking out the draughts at the top of my pyjamas, and pulled up over my chin. The custom-designed, thick fibre pile hat, that I kept pulled down to my eyebrows, left only my nose exposed to the cold through a tiny opening in the draw-stringed hood of the bag. I also took special care of my feet, since the more I could do to keep them warm, the more the rest of my body would stay warm as well, so I wore some specially made down bootees − and also filled my one-litre plastic drink bottle with hot water before I settled down for the night, using it as a hot water bottle for my feet.

I still woke cold to the core of my bones every morning but, even so, it was considerably warmer inside the sleeping-bag than the interior of the tent, let alone the ice-world that awaited me outside, and getting out of the bag into the bitter cold was one of the lowest points of every twenty-four-hour cycle. I delayed the inevitable a moment longer while I completed the mental tour of my body. As usual, my torso was reasonably warm, but my toes and feet and my face were numb with cold. In the temperatures I was enduring, my nose − the only part of me exposed when I was inside my sleeping-bag – was particularly vulnerable to frostnip and possible frostbite if my neckover worked its way down during the night, and I needed to get some warmth onto it straight away. That required movement, however, and that would inevitably bring the ice shower down on me.

Two things were driving me to get up. One was the need to strike camp, get in harness and begin hauling that sledge north. My whole life out on the Arctic Ocean was entirely down to me. There were no alarm clocks, nobody to kick me out of bed, and no boss waiting for me at work, wondering why I was late. I had only my own strength of character and sense of purpose to keep me motivated. I could break my self-imposed routines and no one but me would ever know, but it would be the start of a slippery slope that would end with failure to achieve my goal. Fortunately my desire to cover as much ground northwards as possible remained all-consuming but, even if that failed me, I had a second, even more pressing reason for getting up: the desperate need for a pee caused by the incompletely understood condition known as cold-induced diuresis that took place every night. As my body cooled during the course of the night, my brain automatically reacted to protect the temperature of the vital organs by withdrawing blood from the extremities of my body via the capillaries and veins; and one of the heart's chambers is consequently stretched. Another of the body's reactions to reduce its total volume of fluids is by extracting fluid from the tissue around and inside all its cells and from the blood supply, and to place this surplus into the bladder to be excreted. That was why, in the least conducive circumstances of my life, I often had to get up and have a pee during the night and also awoke every morning with my bladder at bursting point.

The moment could no longer be delayed; I was going to have to open the sleeping-bag. There were three different drawstrings to undo. One kept the hood tight around my mouth and nose, the second drew a ruff – a flap of extra material – around my neck above my shoulders to seal in the warm air generated by my body; the third was a crude drawstring of Kevlar cord that I'd improvised to replace the zip that had snagged and broken. I'd tried various ways of extricating myself from the bag, but whether I teased it open as gently as possible or exploded out of it in a blur of motion, the result was always the same – a torrent of super-frozen ice crystals cascading down my neck and into my sleeping-bag. By trial and error I'd found that sitting up in the sleeping-bag and leaning right forward over my knees before loosening the drawstrings was the best way to minimise the ice-fall, but that wasn't easy to achieve with my arms inside the bag and my lower back sore from sledge-hauling and carrying the thirty-five-pound rucksack.

I swung myself up, ignoring the stabs of pain from my back, and fumbled with the drawstrings, cursing as the inevitable ice found its way down my neck. I was working by touch, because my eyes were still firmly shut. I could not have opened them if I tried, since my eyelashes were welded together by my frozen breath. Such a thick encrustation of ice had built up that if I'd tried to open my eyes straight away, I'd have pulled out most of my lashes. As soon as I could work my hands out of the bag, I began to give my eyes a gentle rub, warming them and breaking up the ice. After a few moments I was able to ease my eyes open and I sat for a second, blinking in the light.

Even at the very start of the expedition, there was plenty of light between six and eight in the morning when I was getting up, and I only needed to use my torch in the evenings, initially to do everything, but later just to read and write my diary; and there would come a time before many more days had passed when it would be bright daylight throughout the twenty-four hours and the torch could be dispensed with altogether.

With my eyes now fully functional, I dragged myself into a kneeling position in the bag and grabbed the packaging from the previous night's freeze-dried supper. Once more, I'd saved weight by making equipment serve more than one function; each night's food packaging became the next morning's pee bottle. Having filled it, I drew back the floor sheet of the tent and poured the urine into the snow – if you poured it gently, the heat of the urine drilled a small hole down through the snow to the ice below.

The next job was to get the stove on and the day under way. I picked up the saucepan which I left upturned on the stove element to stop ice and snow falling into it from the roof of the tent, and causing problems in lighting it. I poured the still slightly warm water from my 'hot water bottle' flask into the saucepan, took my book matches from their perch against the outer edge of the fuel preservation unit, made for me by Peter Herbert, a brilliant engineer and local cub-scout master on Dartmoor, and lit the stove.

The stove was such a vital piece of equipment that I carried two whole stove units and a maintenance kit, including three extra fuel pumps – the most problematic and delicate part. It was just as well, for now, only a week into the expedition, the fuel pump of the first stove was leaking. I set it aside, got the first spare and discovered that the pump on that one did not allow the fuel to flow. Exactly the same thing happened with the third one and I was beginning to sweat. Every piece of equipment had been tested before departure and all were working perfectly. Now three fuel pumps were non-functional. The problem had occurred on previous expeditions when the temperature dropped to around −40 °C. The small 'O' ring sealing the fuel pipe to the pump would contract in the cold so much that when the fuel was pumped up to operating pressure it would seep past the seal and pool on the tent floor – a huge fire risk. I held my breath as I tried the fourth and last fuel pump; to my incalculable relief I saw the fuel at once begin to flow.

When I applied a light, the naphtha fuel – also known as

white gas or Coleman fuel – ignited with a slightly alarming *whooshing* sound; when first lit, the flames could be over two feet high. There was always a bit of tinkering to be done at first, pumping the air bottle to increase the fuel pressure, and opening and closing the fuel valve until the stove's heat had helped to fully vaporise the fuel; then it settled to a steady blue flame and a comforting roaring sound. I could have had a completely silent model, but it was a rather weedy looking stove, and lacked the 'Aga factor' of my preferred, more rugged one, and its homely roar that makes you feel a little less isolated and alone inside a tent.

That sound can spell danger, however, and as soon as the stove was lit, I increased the ventilation. My tunnel-type tent had air-vents near the top at either end and whenever I was using the stove, I had those open, covered with a fine mesh if it was windy or a more open weave mesh if it was still. I also had the zip at the downwind entrance to the tent open a few inches to create an airflow. Warm air rose to the roof of the tent and then escaped through the vents, while colder air was drawn in at ground level. I also made sure that I stayed awake while the stove was on because there was a significant risk of carbon monoxide poisoning; the risks have been well documented on other expeditions.

Carbon monoxide – CO – is both highly poisonous and heavier than air, so it builds up gradually, from the groundsheet upwards, and if you are lying down waiting for your water to heat up, you can't tell whether you're being dozy at the beginning or end of a long hard day, or whether it's the effects of carbon monoxide. In very crude terms, carbon monoxide poisons you by going through the lining of your lungs and grabbing all the oxygenated bits in your bloodstream, so less and less oxygen reaches your brain. It fixes very tightly to the oxygen and is very difficult to eliminate once you've got a build-up in your body. There are two easy tests for CO. If your stove is showing very little interest in burning fiercely, that's a big indication that there isn't enough oxygen at the lower levels inside the tent. The other test is to light a match and hold it at the top of the tent and then gradually move it down towards the floor. On previous expeditions I've seen the match start to gutter and even die out about two feet from the floor of the tent, an unmistakable sign that there's a layer of carbon monoxide . . . and of course if you're lying down, that's exactly the layer that you'll be breathing.

By the time you start to realise that there could be a problem, the CO may well have already deprived you of the ability to sit up, open the vents and get your head outside to get fresh air quickly – and it takes far longer to restore your internal oxygen balance than to lose it – so it is a particularly insidious and deadly hazard in a tent. Obviously you can't open up all the vents all the time and have huge volumes of air moving through – it would be unbelievably cold – but you have to ensure the minimum amount of ventilation to keep oxygen circulating. It's one of the very good reasons why tent manufacturers warn campers never to cook in a tent.

While the water was coming up to a decent temperature, I started packing more dense snow-blocks from my plastic rubble sack into it – the most fuel-efficient way of melting snow. I also fished out the tea bag, sugar lumps, and sachet of dried, full-fat milk to mix with my cup of tea and add to the porridge. Breakfast was always Readybrek, mainly because it's very quick to cook and gave a long, slow release of energy throughout the day. You just pour in hot water, stir and you're in business, but I'd also added crunchy coagulations of honey, oats, bran and the odd bit of dried fruit to it. Each day's ration was pre-measured into a breakfast pack, along with my tea bags and dried milk. I also took two effervescent vitamin C tablets and seven sugar lumps a day. One lump went into my first cup of tea in the morning, two into my second cup, three went into my tea thermos for the day's sledging and the final lump went into my first cup of tea in the evening.

My breakfast bowl was also my spare saucepan. If you lose or damage your saucepan you have no way of melting snow and creating water, so I always had a spare. The first of the hot water went into my tea so that I got some hot fluid into me; a true Englishman, my day was only properly under way when I had my first cup of tea in my hand – what Mavis and I used to refer to as 'our Tetley moment'. As I drank it, I reviewed my journal entry from the previous day and added a few notes; I often had a different perspective on it after a night's rest.

After I'd eaten breakfast, I prepared my two thermoses with everything I needed for that day: a litre of hot water in the stainless steel flask with sugar, milk powder and a fresh teabag, and another litre in the now insulated plastic flask, mixed with a sachet of energy powder and one of the vitamin C tablets. My breakfast, supper and all my tissues, matches and drinks for my thermos were all pre-packed in the day's ration bag, but my 'sledger's nosebag' – my pre-packed sledging rations for the day – were taken from a central store in the sledge and placed in the front of the sledge each morning. When I stopped for one of my scheduled breaks, I just fished out the 'nosebag', together with a flask, and delved into the bag – mostly a mixture of chocolate and nuts. Chocolate goes as hard as iron in very cold temperatures and you can easily break your teeth on it, so mine was in tiny drops, made by friends on Dartmoor who run Browne's Homemade Chocolates. The small size reduced the risk of breaking my teeth and also meant that I could melt them in my mouth and get more flavour from them; it's a shame to munch away on pieces of frozen chocolate that might as well be bits of wood. Mixed in with it were pine nuts, which have a very high calorific value, macadamia nuts and cashews – the honey roasted ones were particularly delicious – ten thin slices of fine grain salami and one shortbread finger. I'd dip into that at my ten-minute break between each seventy-five-minute sledging session.

For supper I always had a cereal bar as a starter and I'd eat that with a cup of tea using my remaining sugar lump. I had three main dishes in rotation: beef and potato stew, cod in a white cream sauce with potato, and chicken curry with rice. All were pre-cooked and freeze-dried, but after a long day's sledge-hauling they tasted like a gourmet dinner in a Michelin-starred restaurant. I also had a daily ration of a quarter of a pound of butter – a health nightmare in temperate England but a near-essential in the Arctic because it gives more calories per unit weight than almost anything else. I usually mixed part of it into my morning porridge and the rest into my evening meal. After supper I had a hot chocolate drink, adding any milk powder remaining from the day's ration.

The hot chocolate at night was a soporific, and the strong, sweet tea in the morning a much-needed reviver, waking me up and getting vital heat into me first thing. There was little warmth from the stove because it had such an efficient fuel preservation unit around it that almost all the energy was directed upwards into the saucepan, not outwards to warm the tent. I had to keep warm in my sleeping-bag, using any additional clothing I could muster. I only put as much of my body as necessary out of the sleeping-bag for as short a time as necessary to do any particular job, otherwise I retreated back into the bag.

I drank my hot drinks from a lidded, insulated mug – in an ordinary one, the drink would have gone cold far too quickly. It was black on the inside, a deliberate choice so that it didn't show all the bits that accumulated over the course of a few days. I cleaned it out every now and again with a tissue but for the most part it had quite a lot of grunge in it – all added nutrients as far as I was concerned, but in a white cup they would have looked pretty unappetising. I kept the lid closed whenever I wasn't drinking from the mug, so the likelihood of a spill – an ongoing hazard in a tent – was greatly reduced. Spills were a waste of the fuel used to melt the snow and heat the water; the spilt fluid also tended to soak into my sleeping-bag before I had time to react, and in any event the fluid was much too precious to waste. Given the energy I was expending during the day, I was already on a minimum fluid allowance for rehydration purposes, and even wasting a third of a litre would impact on my performance. If it ever happened, the best solution was to grab a chunk of snow from my rubble sack and let it soak up the spillage like a sponge.

As the expedition progressed and I got hungrier, I began feeling more weak and faint, particularly during the first sledging sessions of the day. As a result, I changed my breakfast routine a little, eating my porridge as early as possible to allow more time to digest it and release the energy it contained; I also upped the sugar content of my second cup of tea to three lumps and drank it just before I left the tent. That sugar 'hit' gave me a lift as I started the day's work, even if it was as much psychological as physical. For the first two days out on the ice I couldn't even eat all of my porridge and I wasn't interested in putting butter into it. I saved the butter and half the porridge to bulk up on later, or to keep as emergency food for the very end of the expedition. But by Day 3, I began eating more and more food and by Day 10 my body had realised that it was in for some serious work every day and was taking every chance to stock up on fuel; I was wolfing down every scrap of my daily allowance of food and was still hungry for more.

When my food and drink for the day was prepared, I packed my gear away. I always tried to do things as quickly and efficiently as possible because I either wanted to be in my sleeping-bag or out pulling a sledge over the ice and anything else, even doing the cooking, involved being cold. So I was raring to get out and start pulling that sledge, but when it's very cold your brain simply doesn't function as effectively – I noticed when I was doing my video recordings that I was switching words round and using the wrong terms to describe things –

and though I was desperate to get moving, I had to force myself to think ahead to the various sequences of actions that I was about to perform.

Ian later told me that when I spoke to him on the sat-phone, he was staggered by how slow and jumbled my speech was, particularly in the early stages of the expedition. As the temperatures rose later on, my speed of thought and speech increased. With my brain working so slowly and inefficiently, there was a strong inclination to simplify everything into single steps – I would find myself walking endlessly back and forwards carrying single items between the tent doorway and the sledge. I knew it was ludicrously time-inefficient to do this but in the mind-numbing cold I was struggling to convert awareness into remedial action. I therefore had to do much of my 'problem-solving' in the tent when I had warmed up a bit, and the solution to that particular problem was to pile everything onto the sleeping-bag and then drag it out alongside the sledge.

When I stepped out of the tent that morning the cold hit me like a fist. It was −45 °C, the coldest day so far and 10° lower than it should have been at that time of year, but fortunately the wind dwindled to a near flat calm and there was no wind-chill to trouble me. The early going was very difficult, with plates and blocks of ice stacked up in a series of walls that seemed to go on for ever. By halfway though the day I had covered little over half a mile, and I could feel my confidence ebbing away. I began to wonder if it was going to stay like this for a hundred miles or more. After the fourth break I even took out the sat-phone and tried to call Ian to talk things through with him, but I couldn't get a connection, so there was nothing to do but grit my teeth and grind my way through this morass of horrors, reminding myself all the time that what appears to be endlessly unbearable terrain is invariably very localised. So it proved to be, because within half an hour I found myself on the biggest, flattest ice-pans of the expedition so far, and by the end of my first eight-hour day I had completed 3.5 nautical miles – little

42. 'The Hamlet' – Resolute Bay, Nunavut, Canada

43. They don't come finer than this . . . Gary Guy, my rock in
Canada since 1997

44. The expedition's Canadian base some kilometres away from 'The Hamlet'

45. Activity in our base at Resolute was relentless over the final ten days – I am pictured here cutting down the chart to size

46. In training in -40°C with 30 kph winds giving a -70°C wind-chill effect

47. Limbering up for the main event (in Resolute)

48. Not what you want to see . . . bear tracks! But where's the bear now?

49. Practising night-time polar bear drills – with firearm

50. All the clothes I took, including spares

51. My sleeping system – 'mammoth smock' (a.k.a. outer sleeping-bag), sleeping pads (yellow), main sleeping-bag (green) and down bootees

52. The standard 1 kg ration pack including the 'sledger's nosebag' (second from right)

53. Ready for the off – the final attempt solo, without resupply to the North Geographic Pole, 2003

54. Tension builds as I fly in to the drop-off point – Ward Hunt Island

55. Ward Hunt Island, dominated by Walker Hill

56. The northern shoreline of Ward Hunt Island – the hut (circled), my refuge from the gale (the blue ice of the Ward Hunt Ice Shelf evident north of the island)

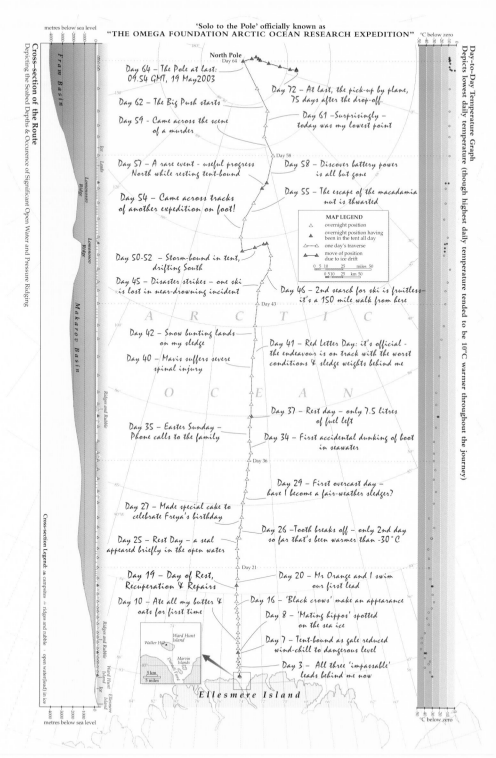

Cross-section of the Route
Depicting the Seabed Depths & Occurrence of Significant Open Water and Pressure Ridging

metres below sea level

Fram Basin

Lomonosov Ridge

Makarov Basin

Lomonosov Ridge

Ridges and Rubble

Ridges and Rubble

Cross-section Legend: ▲ campsites · ∧ ridges and rubble · ∿∿∿ open water(lead) in ice

metres below sea level

Day-to-Day Temperature Graph
Depicts lowest daily temperature (though highest daily temperature tended to be 10°C warmer throughout the journey)

°C below zero

°C below zero

North Pole
Day 64

Day 64 – The Pole at last:
09.54 GMT, 19 May 2003

Day 72 – At last, the pick-up by plane,
75 days after the drop-off.

Day 62 – The Big Push starts

Day 61 – Surprisingly –
today was my lowest point

Day 59 – Came across the scene
of a murder

Day 58

Day 57 – A rare event - useful progress
North while resting tent-bound

Day 58 – Discover battery power
is all but gone

Day 54 – Came across tracks
of another expedition on foot!

Day 55 – The escape of the macadamia
nut is thwarted

MAP LEGEND
△ overnight position
▲ overnight position having
   been in the tent all day
⋯ one day's traverse
〜 move of position
   due to ice drift

0 5 10   25   miles 50
0 5 10   25   km 50

Day 50-52 – Storm-bound in tent,
drifting South

Day 45 – Disaster strikes – one ski
is lost in near-drowning incident

Day 46 – 2nd search for ski is fruitless-
it's a 150 mile walk from here

Day 43

A R C T I C

Day 42 – Snow bunting lands
on my sledge

Day 41 – Red Letter Day: it's official -
the endeavour is on track with the worst
conditions & sledge weights behind me

Day 40 – Mavis suffers severe
spinal injury

O C E A N

Day 37 – Rest day – only 7.5 litres
of fuel left

Day 35 – Easter Sunday –
Phone calls to the family

Day 34 – First accidental dunking of boot
in seawater

Day 36

Day 29 – First overcast day –
have I become a fair-weather sledger?

Day 27 – Made special cake to
celebrate Freya's birthday

Day 26 –Tooth breaks off – only 2nd day
so far that's been warmer than -30°C

Day 25 – Rest Day - a seal
appeared briefly in the open water

Day 21

Day 19 – Day of Rest,
Recuperation & Repairs

Day 20 – Mrs Orange and I swim
our first lead

Day 10 – Ate all my butter &
oats for first time

Day 16 – 'Black crows' make an appearance

Day 8 – 'Mating hippos' spotted
on the sea ice

Day 7 – Tent-bound as gale reduced
wind-chill to dangerous level

Day 3 – All three 'impassable'
leads behind me now

Ward Hunt
Island
Walker Hills
Marvin
Islands

5 km
5 miles

Ellesmere Island

Ellesmere Island

57. A day-by-day progress chart, with an accompanying cross-section of the route
depicting the seabed depths and occurrences of surface open water and ridging
(incurring significant delays), and a day-by-day temperature graph (the latter two
graphics both correlated to the daily camp positions shown on the progress chart)

58. One of the three impassable 'leads', one mile wide of open water – trails of wind-driven spume line the dark water

59. 'Lunar' blue ice-scapes were one of my favourites

60. The foreground is the northernmost 'fast ice' (sea-ice locked in the permanent Ward Hunt Ice Shelf); beyond is the polar pack-ice thrown up, under compression, into the first of many pressure ridges I encountered

61. A 'still shot' (distorted by the deep cold) lifted from my video footage in -43°C at camp out on the polar pack-ice

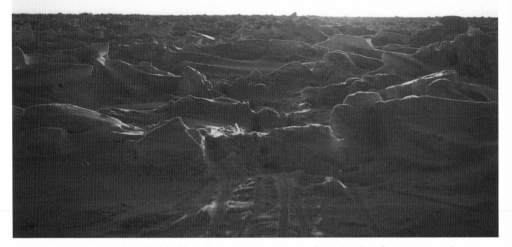

62. Minor rubble-fields like this were commonplace in the first twenty days

enough in terms of the overall distance to the Pole, but every hard-won mile was another step nearer to my goal.

On the morning of Day 9, I set off boosted by the prospect of crossing more second-year ice-pans – flatter and less weathered than multi-year ice, which is often carved into huge hummocks and depressions by the winter–summer thermal cycling of the surface and is also bent out of shape by the years of crushing by the ice around it. On the previous day I had experienced some dramatic mood swings, probably brought on by the hellish ice conditions and my wildly fluctuating sugar levels as I forced my way through them. Today I found myself thinking about my family, going about their daily business – the school runs, Wilf playing on the ropes-course in the garden and Freya sleeping while Mary worked in her attic office. I'd trekked only 22 miles so far – and still had almost 400 to go. I missed them all greatly but was as comforted by thinking about them as I was saddened that it was going to be a long time before I saw them again.

My hopes of a day on flat ice were soon dashed and I quickly found myself in a totally different ice-scape. I had now hit a series of exceptionally old pans. The old ridges had been completely infilled with snow and in some way weathered down, leaving huge mounds twenty or thirty feet high with vast banks of snow trailing off to the north-east. It was like a large, steep ocean swell frozen in motion, and the wave-forms overlapped so much that there was little else for it but to tackle it head on, dragging the sledge up at an angle to the wave to reduce the gradient and then plunging down the far side, only to repeat the whole performance within ten strides. As I took a last look around before settling down that night, I noted that I was still getting very 'lunar-coloured' night-scenes, though the twenty-four hour sun was not long away now.

Before setting off the next morning, Day 10, I emptied the sledge onto the ice and repacked it, taking advantage of the space that had already been created by eating ten kilos of food and using four litres of fuel. By doing so, I was lowering the sledge's centre of gravity and helping it to move over the ice as smoothly and efficiently as possible. Towards the end of the day I came into some second-year rubble-ice that had been partially filled in with snow and carved by the wind into the most striking anthropomorphic shapes. It was like walking through a garden centre full of animal sculptures – hippos and crocs being the most popular models, more often than not in a mating pose for some inexplicable reason.

When I stopped for the night, I again had problems with my fuel pumps. I hoped that rising temperatures would solve them, but there was no sign of those at the moment; they remained stubbornly the wrong side of −30 °C – and as low as −40° to −45° at night. Partly as a result of the problems that this was causing me, I was again struck by how little time I had to relax and think about anything other than operational matters. Every minute seemed to be spent either sledging and navigating, pitching or striking tent, multi-tasking while cooking, or sleeping. I still felt very strongly that I should be micro-managing every aspect of my daily sledge-hauling and tent-life, but it was made so much harder by the extreme cold; and yet every minor problem had the potential to escalate rapidly into some expedition- or even life-threatening situation.

However, there was one strong positive on which I could focus: I had reached the end of my first ten-day block. I visualised the sixty days of the expedition as a clock-face and I had now reached ten past the hour. It was a graphic representation in my head of what progress I had made and a useful distraction from the minimal mileage I had achieved. But I was now looking to pick up the pace a little. I wanted to be sure that I reached Day 20 having averaged at least three nautical miles per day, and, if necessary, I would do longer days to achieve this.

On Day 11, I was grateful for another day of progress over relatively flat pans, because my backache was growing steadily worse. Hauling the sledge was bad enough, but I also had the rucksack on my back to reduce the weight of the sledge and the combination of the two was making my back extremely sore. Just to give me some distraction from that, I was also developing 'sledger's elbow' – a repetitive strain injury like tennis elbow. Even so, I tried putting my rucksack on the sledge, and while it definitely made the sledge feel heavier, it instantly relieved my back, so I left it on the sledge over the flatter pans and put it on for the rough stuff. When I called Ian on the sat-phone that night, he read me a backlog of wonderfully funny emails that Mary had sent, about her action-packed social life in my absence and what the children had been getting up to. She was very good at describing amusing little scenes and scenarios that I could picture and carry with me through the next day and it was a great morale boost for me. Perhaps as a result, on Day 12, I found that my attitude towards and relationship with the ice-scape was changing. I was starting to relax now, realising that it was not going to be a bad year, at least as far as ridging and rubble were concerned, and knowing that I was now reaching areas with more first- and second-year ice – larger pans, fewer obstacles. I had weathered the storm and emerged reasonably unscathed, on schedule and with a manageable sledge.

I described the conditions in my diary as 'my Great Good Fortune'. The temperature had also risen a little from −40° to −35°, giving hope of warmer times to come. My only problem was my back pain, now bad enough to force me to start using some of my precious stock of painkillers, though I took them as much in the hope of getting more sleep at night as to lessen the pain. It seemed to have done the trick, because I set out that morning feeling better refreshed and rested than I had since I left Ward Hunt Island, and was rewarded with a record day of 5.5 miles. I was in such a positive frame of mind that I was singing songs out loud to myself as I crossed the flatter ice-pans. I was starting to enjoy my journey at last.

On Day 13 I again felt that I was making such good progress that the GPS reading of 4.4 miles came as something of a shock; it had felt like more. I even wondered if the ice-drift was beginning to kick in, but that would not start to affect my progress for a while yet. I made another call to Ian that evening and went to bed thinking how remarkably well he was doing his job. Nothing, however trivial, was too much trouble for him and, no matter what problem or question I presented to him over the phone, he always had a sensible solution. On the rare occasions when he couldn't provide one straight away, he made it his business to have found one by the next time we spoke. I felt that I had rock-solid support for my expedition through him, and that was a very comforting and reassuring thought on which to drift off to sleep. I was now ahead of schedule, but since the storm on Day 7, I had enjoyed a week of sunny, relatively windless days, and I knew that I had to take advantage while this lasted, for the Arctic weather could change in the space of a few minutes.

9

Day 14 began badly when I knocked over some hot water in the tent. My sleeping-bag was wet, I'd wasted the fuel to melt that water and I'd also wasted time, because I was on such a limited water ration that I didn't want to miss a single cup; it put too big a dent in my system. So I had to collect some more snow, re-light the stove and heat water again. Starting at a temperature of −40 °C, it took forty minutes to turn snow-blocks into drinkable water – time when I could have been out on the ice making progress northwards. And that just ramped up the psychological pressure that I was already feeling. I'd been travelling for a fortnight and I still hadn't even crossed the first degree of latitude since leaving Ward Hunt Island – I had been out there for two weeks and had done barely forty miles. With the rations I'd got, was the sledge really going to get light enough, fast enough, to enable me to make the necessary speed, or was I going to finish up out of rations and still well short of the Pole?

The day had dawned with a dark, brooding sky. It was a suitable omen for a day that, quite apart from the water-spill, was largely spent trying to find a way through or round a huge pressure ridge. This mountain of ice-boulders and rubble must have looked very impressive from the air, but from my perspective it was a hideous monstrosity that forced me into a three-hour detour due west, before I could find a way through it. In eight hours sledge-hauling, I only managed to make three nautical miles northwards. I also lost an hour when the skin of my left ski ripped clear of the screws holding it. I had to stop to repair it and within twenty minutes of setting off again, the skin on the other ski did the same thing. It was deeply frustrating because I was so focused on making the most of my sledging time that, if I even stopped to scratch an itch on my knee for a few seconds, I'd reprimand myself for unnecessarily breaking my rhythm and wasting valuable marching time.

Just to add a further layer to my frustrations, visibility was very poor. Although the sun kept trying to poke through the clouds, the low light levels and lack of shadow and contrast made navigation through the jumble of ice even more difficult. When the sun was shining, I could see a ridge up to about a kilometre away while crossing a pan, and occasionally I could see through or over as many as three or four pressure ridges ahead. Navigation was then relatively easy and I knew that I was taking the best available route. When the weather clagged in, whether through fog, snow flurries, ground-storms or dense cloud, the ice-scape became murky and nondescript and the worse the visibility, the worse my navigation – not in the sense of where true north lay, but in finding the line of least resistance. There was often no point in branching off to the right or left, because I had no idea whether that was going to be better or worse than the route I was taking.

I sometimes felt that I'd be better off blindfolded, because at least then my eyes wouldn't have been constantly tricking me into painful falls and collisions with unseen lumps of ice, or leading me out onto weak ice. In such horrible conditions, with minimal or no contrast, shadow, perspective or definition, the only consolation for the knowledge that there must have been at least a score of better routes was that I might also have blundered into some even worse ones. By going 500 yards to the east I might have saved myself three hours of thrashing through rubble but I might equally have dropped myself into the heart of an even more impenetrable ice-maze. It was very demoralising because moving the heavy sledge through rubble was strength-sapping, heartbreaking work, but I just had to keep moving it north the best way I could, accept whatever mileage I achieved as a bonus, and hope for better visibility and easier going the next day.

In part, I got my wish. It was the last day of March – another goal achieved – and for the first time I was now operating in twenty-four-hour daylight since the sun was now high enough in the sky to remain above the horizon right through the night. Day 15 dawned with brighter, clearing skies and a large, recently frozen lead gave me a flying start to the day with a good 800 metres of very flat ice. The going was rather less good for the next few hours – a continuous rubble-field that took me almost four hours to cross – but the ice-blocks were on nothing like the scale of those I'd encountered the previous day, and though navigating through them was time-consuming, it wasn't particularly arduous. In fact I was enjoying the challenges that it presented. After at last clearing the rubble-field, I then had a few hours of good ice-pans with minimal ridging and rubble. That was just as well because, probably as a result of the effort I'd had to put in the day before and the cumulative effects of a fortnight of gruelling effort on insufficient calories, I felt very weary all day. It was much too early in the expedition to be losing my edge and after I'd eaten my normal supper of a 300 gram pack of cod and potato, I allowed myself another half-pack and an extra mug of sweet tea to see if the extra fluid and calories would give me a boost.

Burning out before I reached my goal was one of the fears that haunted me throughout the expedition. I knew I was going to have to work very hard for the first twenty days to get through the big ice, with a heavy sledge in the coldest temperatures, but there was a danger that I would have had to push too hard, too early. I'd burned out on my second expedition, pushing so hard that I was very depleted, mentally and physically, and I'm sure that was a contributory factor in the decision-making process following the fall that ultimately forced me to abandon the attempt.

This time, I was trying to maintain a balance between the

urge to push, push, push, as hard and fast as possible, and the need to listen to what my body was telling me and try to be a bit more measured in my approach, confident that I would still succeed in the end. Months before I set out, I'd begun working with a sports psychologist, Juliette Lloyd, and she helped me to establish a few useful mental techniques and routines. The key thing was not to set myself cast-iron daily targets that inevitably would sometimes be missed. I needed to keep the bigger picture in mind, but also to be opportunistic when the chance presented itself. If I had only been making a relatively quick dash across the ice, then by all means go for broke and travel all day, all night and all the next day too – crack it and then relax afterwards. But on a sixty-day haul, I had to take a longer view. If the weather was fine and the ice conditions good, or if I was feeling particularly fresh and strong, I would certainly do an extra hour or three, but not the extra four or five that I had done in the past. It was a false economy because it overtired me and threw my sleep-patterns and my whole daily schedule out of shape. The key point was to relax, just do the hour and do the day, and eventually the Pole would come.

Burn-out was not the only deep-seated fear that I had to confront during the day. I also had an absolute terror of having to carry out self-dentistry. The risk was far from insignificant. I'm one of those people who has lots of metal fillings that I should probably never have been given in the first place, and they're starting to disintegrate. I'd been for a thorough check-up with my dentist before departure, but no check-up can prevent the sort of damage that can be inflicted during an Arctic expedition. I was constantly stressing my teeth and, more particularly, my fillings, which expand and contract at different rates to the teeth. One minute I was drawing in air at temperatures down to $-40°$ as I hauled my sledge along, and the next I'd be sipping a cup of tea at $+ 70°$ as I took my break. I was also biting on chocolate, nuts and other stuff from my sledging rations that were deep-frozen and as hard as rocks. Obviously

I was trying to protect my teeth but I only had to forget for an instant or catch one bit of food wrong and there would go a tooth. Inevitably it happened – during my first break on Day 15. I bit down on something in my sledging rations, heard a crack and felt a huge new cavity with my enquiring tongue – half a filling and part of a tooth had fallen out.

I'd never had any training in self-dentistry, and I was recoiling in my ski-boots at the thought of it. It would have been funny if it hadn't been so alarming. I'd have to use a dental mirror to be able to see into my mouth at all, but in those icy conditions the mirror would mist up in a fraction of a second anyway, leaving me working blind . . . and if an extraction did prove necessary, there were no door handles around that I could tie a string to.

I waited for the first waves of what dentists like to call 'exquisite pain' as the Arctic air hit an exposed nerve, but miraculously they didn't arrive; either the nerve was already dead, or enough filling and tooth remained in place to protect it. When I next spoke to Ian, he patched me through to my dentist, who advised me not to try to treat the tooth. It wasn't giving me pain so it was best not to try and repair it, particularly as I wasn't even sure that I could. If it did explode in pain, I'd just have to deal with it the best way I could. I had a little pot of clove oil for the local anaesthetic and five days' worth of pain-relief tablets, but my bottom-line thought was that there are people all over the world where there are no dentists, who get abscesses and all sorts of teeth problems, and they just grit their teeth and get on with it. If necessary, I'd have to do the same. But for the rest of the expedition, every time I ate anything during sledge breaks, breakfast or supper, I ate only on the right-hand side of my mouth. It became an instinct to try and minimise the likelihood of either pain or further damage. So it had been far from a perfect day, but it could have been an awful lot worse and, as I prepared to halt for the night, I had one solid achievement behind me: I was now a quarter of the way to the Pole – in days if not yet in miles. As I reached the end of Day 15, I'd done 25 per cent of the sixty days I expected to take; anything more than that I'd deal with when I got there. In a way, I was fooling myself. I'd only covered 46.5 nautical miles at this point and still had another 369.5 to go. But focusing on the days rather than the mileage wasn't a totally false perspective. In the early stages the sledge was at its heaviest and the ice conditions, temperature and weather were at their worst; every mile then was worth two or three further down the track. So I ignored the distances and focused on the linear track of the days. I'd done a quarter already. Five more and it would be a third, ten more after that and I was halfway. Once more, emphasising the days rather than the miles covered was an important strand of my psychological strategy.

There was one other reason for satisfaction. The winds were continuing to blow from the west, great news as far as I was concerned, because it meant that there would be minimal ice-movement from the north stacking up pressure ridges that I would then have to cross, and the weather had lifted again, allowing me to haul my sledge under blue skies, with great visibility. The high pressure and clear skies brought one other bonus; the temperature remained very low, −40 °C at night, and any leads opening at that temperature would refreeze enough within a few hours for me to walk across them in safety. The cold also meant that I was using more fuel, but that was more than outweighed by the speed I could maintain while I wasn't being held up by open water.

Towards evening, as often seemed to happen near the end of the day, I would find a natural stopping point – some rough ice, a thinly refrozen lead or a pressure ridge – but rather than use this as an excuse to pack it in for the day, I always tried to get to the far side of it before stopping. That way I knew that I'd set up a relatively easy start to the following day – always an incentive to get out of the tent and get moving the next morning. It was a way of looking after myself, almost as if I were two people: the evening person would do the extra mile to make sure he'd done his best to set up his partner for a flying start the next day. There was also the possibility that if I parked on the southern side of a newly refrozen waterway, covered by thinnish ice, by morning I could easily find that the lead had become active again overnight and had opened right up again. On this occasion, I crossed a lead of 400 metres of thin ice and pitched camp on the far side. I was woken by a rumbling and juddering during the night and discovered the next morning that ice-movements had driven the northern side of the thin ice right underneath the southern side. It was now half the width and twice the thickness, but it could just as easily have pulled apart and I'd then have woken to find 200 metres of open water on my doorstep.

Before I went to sleep that night, I read two chapters of my Herriot book, the first time that I'd looked at it. On all the previous nights it had simply been too cold to read, but though the outside temperature remained very low, it felt warm enough in the tent to do so now that direct sunlight was heating the tent throughout the night as the dark-coloured walls absorbed much of the sun's energy and re-radiated it into the tent.

Even though my sleeping-bag was full of ice, I managed to get a lie in on Day 16, 1 April 2003. I'd slept for twelve hours and felt well rested, and I was reasonably confident that there was little prospect of anyone playing April Fool's jokes on me. As I packed my sledge that morning, I spotted some nuts that I must have spilt in the snow the previous evening and they made a welcome tasty snack. I also noticed that for the first time, the sledge-load didn't form a hump. It now looked flat from end to end, visual confirmation that food and fuel were being consumed and the load to haul was getting lighter. Unfortunately it still wasn't warm enough to put my sleeping-bag on top of the sledge to dry it by sublimation. Although the sun's rays were hitting the top of the sledge, the sun still wasn't high enough in the sky to generate significant heat.

I had a gentle start to the day, but I soon hit a huge area of distorted and disfigured ice, even larger than the one the day before. I counted no less than twenty-five separate pressure ridges before I was clear of it. My log that night recorded my feelings about that in just four words: 'Baskers behaving painfully today.' These were very old ice-pans, very majestic and almost prehistoric-looking, perhaps decades old, and more than a little spooky at times. They had the form of giant sand dunes whipped and carved by winter storms. There were steep crests, rough crags, long bleak ridges and sinuous, snow-filled curves.

I tried to keep contouring while crossing each ridge, reluctant to lose height that was so hard won. In doing so, I was detouring big distances to each side, left and right, and barely going forward at all, but to go straight up and down the ridges was virtually impossible. It was easy to go down, but going up the ridges was such an aggressive and exhausting manoeuvre that even the longest detour around them seemed preferable. During the course of the expedition I encountered the ice in many different moods; it was like going from choppy waters to a flat calm and then a stormy sea on the ocean. And the only consolation I could take while battling through these ancient, rugged ice-ridges was that this difficult terrain might prove to be the gateway to an area of different and probably easier ice-pans.

Late in the afternoon I also experienced a phenomenon familiar from previous expeditions. After more than two weeks without seeing a single living thing, I began to glimpse 'black crows' on the horizon. They seemed to hover at the periphery of my vision and as soon as I looked directly at them, they disappeared. I knew that these were not really crows but merely specks of dirt – black gunge on the surface of my eye – but I could not stop myself from trying to track them as they drifted around the edge of my vision for the remainder of the day.

I had grounds for some muted celebrations when I took my GPS reading that night. I discovered that I had crossed the eighty-fourth parallel during the course of the day – 84° North – the first line of latitude I had reached since leaving Ward Hunt Island. It was still unseasonably cold outside, but there was enough power in the sun's rays to warm the tent walls and I was able to read another chapter of my book in relative comfort. I also opened the first of seven special cards I had brought with me that Mary and the children had made for each latitude reached. A vibrantly yellow, handmade silk daffodil dropped out of the envelope and I pinned it to my smock. Every time I looked at it, I thought of them all getting on with life on the moor – and it put a smile on my face as I got on with my life up here.

The morning of Day 17 was glorious, with skies of the deepest blue, almost shading into black, a genuine warmth in the sun and ice-conditions underfoot that allowed me to make steady progress. I covered the miles at a steady pace, troubled only by an occasional twinge from the knee that I had injured on my last solo attempt on the Pole. I always stopped within a stride and a half of any niggle of any sort anywhere in the body, just to relax, give it a shake out and then set off again thirty seconds later. I did not want to pull a muscle or tear a tendon through carelessness; only I was going to get myself to the Pole and I had to take care of me.

By the time I halted that night, after eight and a half hours sledge-hauling, I had covered 5.7 nautical miles, my best daily distance to date. I had 'budgeted' for an average of three miles a day for the first twenty days, and to have done almost double that in a single day was a significant morale boost. As I wrote in my log that night: 'Good ice, good weather. What a day!' I didn't want to get carried away with the idea – it was still very early days – but I was beginning to feel that reaching the Pole in less than sixty days was now a real possibility, and that would be a pretty good time. The quickest ever was forty-two days and that was by a team of three people, one of whom had to be airlifted out en route.

The bright sunshine that day hadn't been an unmixed blessing, because, with the sun getting higher and higher in the sky every day, it brought on the awful possibility of snow-blindness. Sunglasses are the obvious solution but in temperatures below $-35°$ they bring their own problems. Warm, damp air rising through your clothing, and especially from your breath, instantly converts to ice as it comes in contact with the cold surfaces of the lenses, and you are soon rendered partially or totally blind. So while the sun's daytime elevation was relatively low in the sky I had opted to do without sunglasses in the interests of better interpretation of, and navigation through, the sea-ice. But now I'd reached the difficult time when it was still too cold to keep the lenses clear, but the sun's rays were too high and strong to ignore. If you're snow-blind, you cannot open your eyes because they are supersensitive to any light. You get such extreme pain that you simply can't do anything, you can't even cook, you just have to lie in your tent and wait for it to pass. So snow-blindness was something to be very wary of. During that day I felt my eyes starting to feel unusually warm. I stopped at once and checked them; when I closed my eyes I saw a bright orange and red glow behind my lids – a real danger sign – and thought at once, 'Watch out!' I searched for my sunglasses that night but, though I knew they were somewhere in the sledge-load, I'd squirrelled them away so carefully that I couldn't find them. It was a bit of a worry – it's possible to manufacture sunglasses out of strips of material but I really didn't want to have to do that. Luckily, the next day was not as sunny and the following night they turned up, protectively wrapped in my spare thick socks at the bottom of my spare clothes bag. I wore them continuously from that moment onwards.

I spent some time on the satellite phone that evening and that was an unplanned development. My English base manager,

Ian, was in overall charge, and took my daily calls, but Gary and Diane Guy, who lived in Resolute Bay, kept an attentive eye on our operations in Canada – namely the air charter company. I'd scheduled phone calls to Ian every day for the first ten days, while we ironed out any bugs in the systems, but the plan was then to phase it down to every other day for the next ten days and then to around once a week. I was looking forward to that, because it really helped me to focus on my task. My brain function was too impaired by the extreme cold to be able to hold any extraneous thoughts. I didn't want my mind to be half in the Arctic and half back in Britain, worrying about domestic problems or the second Gulf War; I needed to be completely in the groove, concentrating solely on reaching the Pole.

However, Ginny Dougary's articles were starting to generate so much interest that the expedition website was being besieged by people wanting information on my progress. It had taken on a life of its own and people were logging on every single day from their homes and offices. None of us had been expecting to run daily progress reports on the website – it would be all I could do to reach the Pole without the substantial time commitment that daily updates would require – but with all this unexpected interest, it made the expedition appear poorly organised if we were not doing so. I therefore had to talk to Ian every day in addition to my scheduled long interviews down the phone with Ginny. It was great that there was such interest in what life was like on the Arctic Ocean and I was passionate about introducing as many people as possible to the existence and nature of the Arctic Ocean, but it did mean that the outside world was still a daily additional responsibility when I was already at full stretch and it entailed spending up to half an hour on the sat-phone every night, instead of just finishing my meal and going straight to sleep. That may not sound much, but, over the sixty days of the expedition, it came to thirty hours – the equivalent of three whole sledging days. And unlike a solo yachts-person who continues to sail onwards while at the chart-table or asleep, if a sledger is not straining in his harness, he's not going anywhere.

When I talked to Ian, I gave him a summary of the day's events and conditions: the number of pressure ridges, rubble-fields and leads encountered, (the overall terrain was graded from 1 to 5 – 1 being bad and 5 being great); the wind speed and direction; the atmospheric pressure and cloud cover; the navigational techniques I was using – solar or compass; and finally any equipment and health issues. From the data that was automatically transmitted to him by my Argos beacon, Ian then added the temperature readings; my position in the morning and evening; how many miles I had done so far and how many miles were left to the Pole; the ice drift if any; and the daily average necessary from this point onwards to reach the Pole. I wanted to generate quantifiable information that would be of use to me but would also give children in schools data that they could play with, to make maps and graphs, and generally get a feel for the expedition and its operating environment on the frozen ocean.

My conversations with Ginny were very different, more free-ranging and far more concerned with personal, human-interest angles. She seemed relatively uninterested in distances, ice-conditions or sledging strategies, but she came alive at the least mention of unusual thoughts, psychological developments or actual incidents, and she loved the anthropomorphic treatment of my equipment, so much so that Mavis the sweeping brush became a personality in her own right. She obviously knew her readership much better than I did, but it was a minor, though growing frustration for me, that she seemed so uninterested in the physical process of getting to the Pole, but so fascinated by what seemed in my head to be irrelevant trivia. It was irrational of me to be so concerned about it, but I felt very vulnerable and found it impossible to see our interviews in any wider published context, so it was an issue that would not go away. These long chats with Ginny and Ian were also using battery power much faster than I had planned. Before the expedition, we had estimated the required number of hours and minutes for talking by sat-phone to Ian and to other people, but it wasn't a precise calculation because battery-use was affected by the ambient temperature – and it had been unusually low right through the expedition so far; the budgeted battery-use was being bent right out of shape and that might have a significant impact by the end of the expedition.

I had one other chore to perform before I could sleep that night: de-icing my boots. I made myself do this not less than once every other day because the encrustations of ice that built up inside them in Arctic conditions, both from sweat icing to the frozen surfaces and external moisture from the snow that would leach its way in through the seams, are at best uncomfortable and at worse positively dangerous. If left to accumulate, there could be as much as a quarter of a pound of ice in each boot, a significant additional load when seen in the light of the number of times that I would raise and lower my feet in the course of a day's trekking across the ice-cap. But ice building up inside my boots was also an invitation to frostbite. Your feet – the body parts furthest from your heart – are always vulnerable to cold and, if the ice inside your boots is occupying space designed for insulating air, your feet will inevitably be affected; you could easily lose your toes to frostbite.

Removing the ice from my boots was therefore essential but it was a time-consuming and surprisingly gruelling task. First, I pulled out the double fleece liner. There was ice along the seams and the lower section and also around the toe line and the heel. At $-30°$ or so it didn't come off easily; I had to work it out by rucking up the material and rubbing it together to loosen the ice and then scraping it off with furious brushing by Mavis. Below the fleece liner was a thick foam insole. That had to come out as well. I chipped off the worst of the ice-encrustations with the handle of Mavis, then banged and rolled up the insole to loosen the rest of them, and chipped and picked those off as well. After that was another insole, a green, plastic, fine mesh that also had to be de-iced, and then I had to pick the remaining ice from around the inside of the boot. When I'd done all that, I had to put it back together and start the same process on the other boot.

It was a real physical effort that left me with aching hands and arms and bleeding fingers. The deep-frozen ice was as sharp as razors and I had to do all the work with bare hands; if I got my gloves wet with melting ice, they'd lose their insulation value and I might end up with frostbitten fingers on the next day's trek. By the time I had finished, there was blood everywhere, and my thumbs and forefingers were skinned. I made myself do it before I ate my food because I really hated to do a horrid job like that after I'd eaten my supper; it spoiled the one relaxing time I had in the whole day.

I woke the next morning, Day 18, feeling very tired. I was still sleeping badly – far from normal for me – and I could only think that the fault lay with my sleeping-bag. I'd saved weight by bringing a lower-rated one, and I would have been fine at the normal temperatures for this time of year, but it had been much, much colder than that and I was simply too cold to sleep properly. I even tried taking off the 'elephant smock' – even though it was supposed to keep the inner bag relatively ice-free – because it had so much ice in it that it was probably now draining my body-heat rather than augmenting it. But, even without it, I still didn't feel any warmer.

Despite my weariness, I managed another 5.4 miles that day, over an ice-scape of very old pans. Whenever the going allowed, I let my mind drift off to one of a number of pet projects. I ran through a typical day for Mary, Wilf and Freya in the finest detail and tried to guess what each was doing at exactly this time of day back in the UK. I could almost see Wilf moving the coloured drawing pin higher and higher up the giant chart we had pinned up together on the kitchen wall as he tracked my position each afternoon after school.

I compiled guest lists for dinner parties and special occasions, and landscaped and planted up swathes of our garden in a variety of styles and colour schemes. I was also mentally designing a pocket classic yacht that had so many additional features and gadgets that it would assuredly have sunk without trace within minutes of starting its maiden voyage, but I loved tinkering with and fine-tuning the plans. It all helped to distract me from the endless drudgery of putting one foot in front of the other, as the sledge dragged behind me like a sea-anchor.

For the first time, the sun was now high and hot enough to burn some of the ice out of my sleeping-bag. I spread it on top of the sledge during the day and it was noticeably lighter and less lumpy when I took it into the tent that night. It was a big psychological boost and I looked forward to some better nights' sleep from then on. I felt I was right in the groove on my navigation, helped by clear skies that allowed me to navigate by the sun, and I was making good progress, but I'd felt very washed out in the middle sessions – weak, wobbly and listless – and I decided to take a rest the next day, regardless of the weather. It was an unusual decision for me. Normally I just seized the moment: wild weather, take a rest today. It was perhaps symptomatic of my tiredness that when, late in the day, I hit a huge refrozen lead about 800 to 1,000 metres wide with ice only two to four centimetres deep – too thick to swim through but too thin to walk on – I did not even try to find a way round it so that I could finish the day on the northern side of it. I simply set up my tent a few metres from the edge of the lead and decided to let nature do my work for me by freezing it to durable ice over the rest of this day and the next.

Despite the reduced ice in my sleeping-bag, I didn't sleep well that night, reinforcing my decision to take a day off. Day 19 was therefore a day of rest, recuperation and repairs, though thanks to a northward ice-drift – the first I had encountered –

I did end the day 0.12 nautical miles nearer to the Pole than at the start. The weather was still set fair, but I didn't beat myself up about wasting a day that could have taken me a few miles nearer to the Pole. I looked on it just as taking some cash out of the bank. I'd been paying in plenty over the previous few days, racking up big mileages for this stage of the expedition, and I was comfortably ahead of schedule. The sledge was feeling significantly lighter and running more smoothly and quickly over the ice-surface, and the weather was definitely warmer. Things were looking up, and it would do no harm to give my body a break, and catch up on some of the routine maintenance and kit repairs that would stand me in good stead further down the line.

As it was a rest day, I put some of the chocolate drops and pine nuts from my day's sledging rations into my morning porridge as a treat and had an extra cup of tea before I began work. Then I suspended my outer sleeping-bag from a ski stuck upright in the snow to burn off more of the ice; and every four hours or so I'd pop out with Mavis to brush off the ice fronds drawn to the surface of the pile. I spent the rest of the day doing running repairs and also gave myself a full body wash in the tent, scrubbing my naked body with blocks of snow and spare tissues I'd been saving. It was heart-stoppingly cold and the hard-frozen snow was as rough as sandpaper on my skin, but I felt great afterwards, and it was a real morale boost. I turned my thermals inside out before I put them back on and they felt as clean as new against my skin. Later that day I gave Robert Elias a call to report on progress so far. Just before we hung up, he told me 'If you have any problems or if you need help of any sort, just ask and it will be there for you.' It was a typically thoughtful and generous gesture and nice to have in reserve, but I had no intention of allowing myself to get into a situation where I would be tempted to take him up on it by asking for a resupply or an emergency flight out.

Whether because of the rest, the loss of ice in my sleeping-bag, or the rising air temperatures, I slept better that night, and set off refreshed early the following morning, Day 20. It was another fine and sunny day and I made reasonable progress – another 4.5 nautical miles – but there was the first sign that the summer thaw was beginning: a lead stretching across my track, the first open water I had seen since setting off. The lead ran broadly east–west as far as I could see in either direction. I tracked it westwards for around twenty minutes and then said to myself, 'Come on. It's the first water you've actually seen, the air temperature feels warm, it's not windy or nasty, this'll be good practice. Get the immersion suit out.'

I stood on the brink and studied the lead carefully. There was about twelve metres of open water and the division between it and the ice-banks on each side was clearly defined – there was only a short apron of thin ice that might or might not bear my weight. I wasn't unduly nervous. I was more intrigued by what it would feel like and how I'd feel doing it. After all, this would be the first time I had used the immersion suit on my own, with no one to dive in and rescue me if things went wrong.

I ate a little extra chocolate, both for energy and as a reward to myself for agreeing to do this, then hauled the sledge onto its 'lilo' – the inflatable raft that would keep it higher and better stabilised in the water as I towed it behind me. I could even straddle the sledge and hand-paddle it along like a surfboard or use my shovel as an oar, but it was very cumbersome and, in practice at Resolute Bay, I'd found it easier to tow it behind me while I swam. When I'd secured the sledge to my satisfaction, I put on the immersion suit over my sledging gear. All I had to take off were my skis, though I also removed one mitt so that I could work the zips and do some fiddly adjustments with the hood. All my other clothes and gear, even my sledging harness, stayed on. I worked the suit up to my waist, then wriggled it up to my chest and shoulders.

At the last minute I took off my sledging hat – my head was seriously cold without it, but if I kept it on while I was swimming it had a habit of working itself down over my eyes so that I couldn't see where I was going; I stuffed it down inside the suit and then used the long drawstring to help me pull the hood over my head. When I'd finished, I crouched down into a tight ball to squeeze the excess air out of the suit, so that when I stood up again it was vacuum-formed against my body. The suit had to be roomy to fit over my clothes but, given my fear of inverting when wearing it, I didn't want to go into the water with air trapped all over the place. I then put the sledging-trace round my waist. I had loops every metre of the trace, so I hooked two together around my waist – a tight fit – and clipped them with a climber's metal clip to make a crude belt-harness for the sledge that I could drag behind me as I swam across. I was almost ready to go. I took a few deep breaths to relax myself and, as I did so, I took a long, hard look around. If a polar bear came along while I was in the water, I would be exhibiting classic food-source behaviour – swimming around just like a seal – and I would be unable to reach, never mind fire the rifle stashed on the sledge. I scanned the foreground, middle distance and horizon in every direction, every sense attuned, looking for the least movement or unusual shape or colour. As far as I could tell, there was nothing out there but ice and snow.

It still took a few moments to steel myself to get into the water. The contrast between the snow and ice and the menacing, black, black water was almost panic-inducing but after a brief exchange of views with Swerves, Curves, Baskers and the rest of the team I was ready. I sat down on the ice and worked my way out towards the lead on my bottom, keeping the sledge right up behind me so that it would only need a gentle tug to get it into the water; I didn't want to be yanking on the trace to move it and have it come flying into the water and crashing into me. I inched further and further, until I could feel the ice bending beneath me. I paused at the brink, feeling very self-conscious, had one last look around, then took a deep breath, pushed my feet down through the thin ice and dropped down into the water.

Even though I knew that my immersion suit would protect me from the cold, I'd been holding my breath in the tension of the first few moments. I let it out with a gasp of relief. I could feel the pressure of the water compressing everything, as if I were being shrink-wrapped. Despite that, and all the air I'd been squeezing out of the suit, there was still a lot of trapped air and I felt unnaturally buoyant, riding unnervingly high in the water like a swimmer in the Dead Sea. I turned around to face the sledge and put both feet up against the ice to brace myself as I pulled it in after me. It was a bit scary, because I was almost pulling the sledge in on top of me, but I couldn't just swim off towing it behind me because, until it was in the water, there was too much inertia and friction to overcome. As I pulled, the sledge slid to the edge of the ice. It caught on a projection and teetered for a moment, then slid into the water with a soft splash. A few icy drops hit my face and the bow-wave set me rocking in the water as if in the wash of a passing boat. I turned over in the water and began breaststroking my way towards the other side of the lead. The sledge skimmed along behind me, putting no drag on me at all. Just the same, I was glad that the lead was no wider, because the exertion of swimming wearing this giant bin-liner around me would soon make me pour with sweat.

In what seemed like no time at all, I was breaking through the small apron of thin ice on the far side. Even then I was still harbouring paranoid thoughts about inverting in my immersion suit. Although not strong enough to walk on, the marginal ice at the edge of open leads was often too strong to be easily broken with my arms. Instead, I had to pull myself up onto the ice and load it with my body weight until it broke. When it did, often quite suddenly, I would drop back into the water, and each time there was a tiny, niggling fear that the air trapped inside the immersion suit would suddenly shift, tipping me head-first under the water like a dabbling duck. If that happened, the trapped air would make it impossible for me to right myself and I would drown.

I pushed those unhelpful thoughts away and broke my way through to some slightly thicker ice, then, kicking with my legs and hauling on the ice as much as the slippery integral mitts of the suit allowed, I launched myself upwards onto the surface of the ice. Streaming water, and still lying flat to spread the load, I worked my way across the thin ice and onto the more solid platform beyond, then stood up and hauled on the trace to bring the sledge out of the water after me. It took another twenty minutes or so to take the suit off, rub it in the snow to soak up the moisture and shake it dry. I then rolled it up from the feet and secured it in a neat bundle, tying it with the drawstring of the hood. It might have taken three hours to walk around the lead; it had taken no more than an hour to swim across it. As I made ready to move on, I noticed that the stealthy movement of the ice-pan had already caused the width of the lead to shrink. Had I just sat on the ice and twiddled my thumbs for two or three hours, I could probably have walked straight across. Nonetheless, I was extremely pleased to have used the suit; it was good practice for the times when I'd have to do so again, perhaps several times a day in leads far wider than the one I'd just crossed. But I was never entirely comfortable about using what I christened 'Mr Orange' – the colour of the suit. Putting him on always seemed to be admitting some sort of defeat that I could not find a quicker way around, and deliberately immersing myself in the forbiddingly black waters and with no one around for hundreds of miles always seemed to be an unnatural act. But we all have our own mental barriers to break down, go around or push through and this one was probably my greatest. Every time I finished a swim, I'd say to myself, 'What on earth was difficult about that? This is the answer. I'll not waste a single minute looking for a way around it, the next time I hit a lead.' But every single time I saw a thin black strip emerging on the horizon, my heart would sink at the prospect of another encounter with Mr Orange and, if there seemed even the slightest possibility of getting off the hook, I'd waste up to twenty minutes trying to find a way round.

As I sledged over the ice, I felt significantly warmer than the previous days. In fact the ambient air temperature was actually two to five degrees colder than on the previous five days, but my all-black suit was paying dividends as it soaked up the heat of the warming rays of the sun. As proof of that, as I moved on to the north, I was progressively loosening and then removing items of clothing. The first thing was to fold back the ear flaps on my hat to expose my neck, then I unzipped my smock, took off my gloves and put them in my day-bag – a pocket sewn on to the top of the sledge for quick access to things I often needed in the course of the day. I kept my mitts on a while longer and then took them off and put my gloves back on. Sledging without any head-covering was too cold, but I took off my hat, and just wore my neckover over my ears and a bit of my forehead, but with the top open like a chimney. I must have looked a real state like that, but there was no one around to see and it kept my head at the right temperature. I couldn't set off at the start of the day and know what I was going to be wearing all day; it required constant tinkering, trial and error, to maintain the right body temperature. Too cold and I was shivering and not able to work efficiently, but being too warm was even worse, because that meant sweat-soaked clothing dangerously accelerating the cooling of my body when I slowed down or stopped.

I rarely clock-watched during the sledging sessions – only twice in the entire expedition can I remember thinking that the time was dragging and wishing that it was time for the next break. My standard day was six seventy-five-minute sessions with a break of eight to ten minutes between each session. If there were jobs to do or problems to sort out – checking the screws on my ski-bindings, changing the film in my camera, or tightening my boot straps – I tried to save them until the next break, otherwise I was continually stopping and starting, and the endless interruptions ate away at the time when I should have been heading north. And if I had jobs to do, I hurried my food and drink in that break so as to minimise the time lost before I was moving again.

In mid-afternoon on Day 20 I came across another recently active lead, where an ice-pan had pulled apart and then refrozen. The surface was thin ice, just about walkable, but there were signs of activity to the west where the two halves of the pan were crunching together, with plates of still dripping ice freshly lifted above the waterline. In the course of a single day I had now come across a stretch of open water that I'd had to swim and a currently closed but obviously still active lead – confirmation not only that the spring thaw was now under way, but also that I was entering an area of more active sea-ice. The phases of the moon were also a significant factor; there had been a full moon and a spring tide, greatly increasing the stresses on the ice-cap. The resulting frequent minor ice-movements had created a series of waterways over two metres wide that were even more time-consuming to deal with than one or two monster leads, involving many short, time-wasting detours in the hope of finding a dry route across, as the far banks were too high and steep to climb.

The increased warmth – if an air temperature of $-30°$ can ever be said to be warm – helped me to sleep well that night and I woke to another beautiful morning, Day 21, Sunday 6 April, feeling refreshed, rested and raring to go. Ice conditions were good too, and as a result I put in an extra couple of seventy-five-minute sessions at the end of the day and achieved my best mileage yet – 7.5 nautical miles. Although I was meant to be increasing my daily average to five nautical miles a day between Days 21 and 30, 7.5 miles was really hammering along. But it was just as well that I'd put those extra miles in the bank because the noises and ice-movements that accompanied me all day indicated that, in this part of the Arctic Ocean at least, the spring break-up of the ice had now begun in earnest. There were continual rumblings and rending noises and, every now and then, a crack like a pistol shot as the ice, stressed beyond endurance, fissured and split apart. There was such a big jolt as the ice moved during one tea-break that I slopped some precious tea over the side of my mug.

These were potentially alarming developments – Day 21, barely north of 84° and already the sea-ice in this sector was breaking up. Perhaps this was going to be an unseasonably warm year, with endless expanses of rotten ice and open water. But I had to keep telling myself that this wasn't the beginning of the end for the expedition. My experience over many years was that these conditions were nearly always localised. I'd led a dozen Last Degree expeditions to the Pole much later in the year and often found very little open water at all. I tried to keep calm and just told myself to work my way through it. In time, despite the fact that it was getting warmer, I would get back onto better ice.

The only other blot on the day was that, towards evening, I'd entered a zone of very active ice-movements. I kept going for a while, wiggling around to east and west in the hope of striking a patch of cleaner ice, but I only seemed to be succeeding in getting myself into worse and worse areas. Had it been earlier in the day, I would have pressed on in the hope of finding a better place to halt, but after ten hours' hard walking and with no sign of any imminent change in the ice-surface, I decided the risks of continuing were greater than those of staying put. If I carried on, I might find myself irrevocably committed to a really complicated area without any safe site to put up my tent. Even the area where I now stood was bad enough, a large expanse of bad ice with a number of cracks and fissures in the surface.

I picked the best area I could find, a flattish slab with a

number of straight-line cracks running across it. One or two might have been a metre or more in width, most were no more than a few centimetres, but all were moving and 'breathing', pulling apart and coming together again with an impact that sent ice fragments tumbling into the cracks. I still had the strong sense that I was not in a good place to camp and, as a result, I packed everything away after supper so that I was ready for a quick smash and grab to get everything into the sledge and pull away as fast as possible if things turned ugly during the night and the ice-pan began to break up completely. I slept fully clothed, with my boots at the ready, not wrapped up in a plastic bag as I would normally do to keep them dry, and as I settled down to an uneasy rest, I wrote in my log 'Let's see what the night brings.'

It certainly brought very little sleep because I was kept awake by the deafening noise of the pressure ridges erupting around me all night. It was like trying to sleep near a forge or a metal-works. There were screeching, rending and grinding noises, underpinned by a rhythmic *boom, boom, boom,* as if a giant hammer was pounding some massive lump of iron. When it came to an abrupt stop, the ensuing silence was in some ways even more menacing and disturbing; then it would begin again in a different, faster tempo. The banshee screams and metallic hammerings and crashings grew so loud and seemed so close that twice during the night I dragged myself out of my sleeping-bag to check that I wasn't about to find myself in an impossibly smashed-up area, unable to retreat or go forwards or sideways to get onto better ice. But, as if the ice had achieved its aim by forcing me out of bed, it began to settle down soon afterwards and all was quiet again by morning. I took the chance to make up for some of the lost sleep and had a lie-in before making a late start to the day.

Once outside the tent, I could see dramatic changes brought on by the night's events. The ice-pan was now riddled with hairline cracks, extending around and even beneath the tent, and a new pressure ridge had appeared about forty metres away, rising four metres above the surface of the ice-pan. It was an unwelcome obstacle to clear at the start of the day, Day 22, but I reflected that my situation could have been an awful lot worse. Had the ice been pulling apart rather than grinding together, I could have been plunged into the Arctic Ocean, this time without my immersion suit.

I set off at 2.50 in the afternoon and covered 5.8 nautical miles in eight hours' sledge-hauling. I was pleased to have covered so much ground because there were several other pressure ridges to clear, the worst a huge quadruple ridge. They were no more than a few yards apart and each was composed of large, jumbled blocks that made navigation through them difficult, while the physical effort of dragging the sledge over them left me trembling on the verge of hypoglycaemia. My consolation was that the going did not really get much worse than this and I had managed to clear all these ridges without needing to shift the load in relays at any point; the weight of the sledge was now sufficiently reduced to be manageable in even the most difficult terrain. I could even start to think about getting rid of my rucksack and transferring its contents to the sledge; unencumbered, I could really really start to motor. I was also convinced that carrying the rucksack was damaging my back – I was suffering a lot of pain in the lower back and between the shoulder blades – and I could not afford to let that get any worse. I enjoyed sledging into the night but it got quite cold after nine o'clock as the sun dipped low towards the horizon, and I stopped at eleven o'clock. I put up my tent and ate my supper at top speed to ensure I could get to sleep at a reasonable time and not have another delayed departure the next morning.

Fortunately, there was no repeat of the previous night's scrapyard symphony and I slept well. Day 23 dawned bright and clear again, the twenty-third consecutive day of visible sun, but, despite that, I still had around five-pounds weight of ice in my sleeping-bag, as there still hadn't been enough energy in the sun to burn it all off. I had my first serious piece of kit failure that morning when my sledging-harness broke. A circular steel clip – brand new when I set off – had completely worn through and it snapped as I was sledging along. I didn't want to have to stop for ages to fix it, but equally I couldn't allow it to be a continuing problem for the rest of the expedition. I'd had that sort of problem with my ski-bindings on the last expedition and it had been irksome in the extreme. I needed to improvise something that would be a quick but lasting repair. The first thing that came into my mind was a miniature climber's metal clip – not a particularly strong piece of kit – but I just clipped it through the harness and found that it fitted and worked perfectly. I was expecting it to buckle and break the first time I put some real loading on it, but it didn't happen and in the end I stopped worrying about it. It was worn down to bare metal but still working perfectly well at the end of the expedition. I was very chuffed about it: problem solved in less than a minute.

Day 23 also marked the point at which I planned to start doing extra sledge-hauling sessions every day as a matter of course. I'd held myself back at the start, making sure I kept some fuel in the tank, but now was the time to press on. The weather was good, the ice conditions acceptable and the sledge getting lighter; this was the time to pick up the pace. At the start of the day, doing the standard eight hours twenty minutes often seemed as if it would be more than enough, but I invariably found that I'd get a second wind by the time I reached the end of the main set of six sessions and would actually want to do more. I covered 7.7 nautical miles in ten hours' sledging and felt that I could have done even more. I was not even in a hurry to get to sleep and read some more of the Herriot book; sadly, this was now nearly finished – I'd have to start re-reading it, or rely on my imagination for evening entertainment from now on.

Day 24 started well and I was making fast progress under clear, sunny skies until I met more evidence that the summer break-up was well under way – another lead of thin ice and open water. It was progressively thinner towards the middle, following the usual pattern of a lead that had repeatedly frozen, pulled apart and frozen again, and just looking at the dark colour of the ice, the surface texture and the density and formation of the ice flowers – the crystal structures formed where salt had been squeezed out of the sea-water as it froze – I could tell that the ice was too thin to bear my weight. I'd have to swim, smashing the ice ahead of me as I went.

For the second time in five days I put on the immersion suit, lowered myself into the water and set off, pulling the sledge along behind me, but this time the lead was a good seventy-five metres across and I severely underestimated how long it would take me to break through all that ice. Battering it with my arms was very tiring work. I couldn't just go smash, smash, smash, at anything like the speed of normal swimming because the ice wasn't brittle like freshwater ice, it had more of the resilience and plasticity of thick perspex. Each time I loaded it with my weight, it would bend down and down and down into the water before it finally gave and a plate of a foot or more wide broke off. I really had to force the ice down through the water and the muscles under my arms, ones I would never normally use, were soon protesting and cramping up. I was getting shaky and having to take repeated thirty-second rests, hanging in the water before thrashing my way onwards again.

I also had major struggles with the sledge. Even kicking my legs and thrashing with my arms, I couldn't generate enough forward momentum to pull the sledge along at the same time as I was breaking through the ice; that was simply too much to ask of my body. Instead I had to move forward a few feet through the ice and then pause, get my breath and strength back, and then drag the sledge after me. In theory it should have pulled along the narrow channel I was making easily enough, but all the plates of loose ice that I'd broken were floating to the surface and piling up in front of it, blocking the channel. So every few feet I had to turn on my back, brace my feet against the underside of the unbroken ice on either side of the narrow channel, and then heave and haul at the sledge to pull it through or over the floating ice-plates.

I wasn't panicking because, though I hoped I was going to be able to get to the other side, I knew I could always swim back along the channel I'd broken through the ice behind me, but I was getting exhausted. The rest periods grew longer and more frequent and it took me about an hour just to get through those seventy-five metres of ice. I was so knackered at the end of it that I barely had enough strength left to haul myself out of the water. I made myself strip off the immersion suit at once and repack the sledge ready to move on, but I then gave myself a double break to allow a bit more recovery time, and an extra portion of sledging rations to rebuild my strength.

Although the muscles under my arms continued to ache, I was pleased to find that I was soon feeling strong and eager for more work. I pulled well all day on the sledge and was ready for extra sessions at the end of it, but then I encountered another lead. This one was enormous, between 800 and 1,000 metres from bank to bank. Wraiths of gunmetal-blue frost-smoke were hanging in the air above the surface, as molecules of relatively warm water vapour fogged as they rose from the lead and met the super-cooled air at −30 °C. I climbed up onto a block of ice and looked east and west, searching for a way round or a point where the lead narrowed, but it was like a giant motorway running across the ice. The trail of frost-smoke stretched away to the horizon, a menacing line etched against the ice.

Open water was not such a huge issue; it would have been hard work but I could have paddled across it on my sledge, but the ice covering the lead was a real killer: too thin to cross on foot or skis but also too thick for me to break with my arms. I had struggled to swim 75 metres through similar ice that morning; I certainly wasn't going to be able to get through 800 metres. None of my devices would work. The immersion suit was irrelevant; I didn't have enough strength to break the ice with my arms, and I couldn't put the sledge on its 'lilo' and then paddle across on it like a raft, because once I was up on the sledge I couldn't get enough purchase to smash the ice. It had to be done with my body weight. Hammering at it with a ski-pole or even a shovel simply wouldn't break through; it was just too strong.

I'd been going for eight hours and had covered a respectable 6.8 miles and, though I could certainly have kept going for another couple of sessions I didn't think there was much to be gained. I could have spent several hours tracking left or right with a heavy sledge and still had no guarantee of getting round the lead. It was better to stop for the night and see how things looked in the light of a new day. I was very frustrated though, because I really had thought that with the equipment I'd brought there would be no obstacle I couldn't cross. I now knew that I was wrong.

Before I went to sleep that night, I did a thorough 'inventory' of my physical state and it was obvious that the expedition was already taking its toll on me. When I tested my resting heart rate I found that it had dropped from its normal rate of about forty-five to thirty-five, and I suspected that it would fall even lower by the end. I was getting a bit bony on the hips – I'd lost a lot of weight, perhaps a stone and a half so far – and I'd also lost the sensation in my fingertips and toes. It wasn't frostbite but nerve tissue damage, and I knew from previous experience that I would not recover from it until about six months after my return to warmer climes. In the meantime, I had to be even more aware of the danger of frostbite at my extremities because my nerve endings could no longer send the danger signals to my brain. Better news was that my back had miraculously improved. A few days earlier it had felt as if I'd had an axe buried between my shoulder blades and it even hurt when I breathed deeply, but now I'd moved the weight from my rucksack to the sledge, my back had improved out of all recognition. So, despite having a body physiologically well suited to polar work, with small hands and feet reducing the risk of frostbite, a high body volume to skin surface ratio minimising heat loss, a slow heart rate increasing the use of body fat during exercise and a genetic predisposition to endurance activity, I was still not getting away unscathed in doing what had to be done to make it to the Pole.

IO

I broke camp on Day 25, Thursday 10 April, pulled the sledge east for about two hours along the edge of the lead and achieved precisely nothing beyond sighting a seal that popped its head out of the water just by me. It was the first living creature I had seen since the Arctic hares at Ward Hunt Island but it wasn't a particularly welcome sight. As ever, seals meant more water about, and polar bears. The lead was even wider than the day before because the ice had pulled apart in the middle, leaving a stretch of black, open water, and the ice flanking it was still not strong enough to support my weight. I could have gone on for another six to eight hours and still not found a way round it, so the only sensible course of action was to bow to the inevitable, take the day as a rest day, and hope for a change of fortune in the morning. At a temperature of −30 °C, provided the lead did not pull yet further apart during the night, the ice would have thickened enough by the following day to allow me to ski across in safety. But if the lead widened again, I would be in trouble.

Even though I felt that I'd made the logical and correct decision, I could not stem the frustration inside me. This was my third rest day in twenty-five days. One was for very cold winds, and one because I needed a break, but now I faced another day of enforced rest which felt more like idleness for not trying to find a way round the open water. I was averaging roughly one day off a week and it had not been my plan to take anywhere near that number – around Days 15, 30 and 45 was what I had anticipated. I had only a finite supply of rations. If I fell behind schedule I risked being caught in a classic double-bind: needing to make more and more miles on less and less food. I could not afford many more unscheduled hold-ups.

I was woken by the rumbles, screeches, groans and shocks of ice-movement during the night and I felt a great deal of trepidation as I prepared to leave the tent the next morning, afraid that I would see a fresh cloud of frost-smoke hanging over an even wider expanse of open water. But this time the fates had dealt kindly with me. Far from opening further, one side of the thin new ice covering the lead had simply slid straight under the other during the night. It was a well-known process that even had its own name – 'rafting' – but I had never seen such an epic example of it – 800 metres of open water and thin ice had now been converted into 400 metres of ice, ten centimetres thick, more than enough to bear my weight. When I set off I was able to walk straight across it. The worst-case ice scenario had been converted into the best with no intervention on my part at all.

Day 26, Friday 11 April, was the eve of my daughter Freya's first birthday and I set out determined to give her a personal best that day, so that when she woke up the following morning back at Wydemeet, Mary could show her the mileage achieved, my birthday present to her. I pushed myself really hard that day – so hard that I actually found myself dropping off to sleep while leaning into my ski-poles to have a quick breather towards the end of the day, but I just couldn't achieve the personal best I'd so wanted to do. I was upset and would have kept going, but I was beginning to get very wobbly, lacking glycogen and going hypoglycaemic. I wasn't going to break into my rations for the next day to try and give me that extra mileage because that was a very bad habit to get into, so I just had to stop for the night, knowing that I had given Freya the best present that I could. Once in the tent, I found I had done 7.5 nautical miles, within 325 metres of my previous best daily distance, and the reason I wasn't able to do even better was probably because

I'd encountered my first negative ice-drift – the ice was now moving southwards as I tried to go north. I was walking up the down escalator and in reality had probably travelled around nine miles in the course of the day.

However, I also had reason to be very pleased because during the later stages of the day I encountered my first 'first-year ice'. It would have been open water the previous summer, freezing during the autumn and then being driven by the prevailing winds and currents over the ocean to its position here. Such new ice was invariably pretty flat and it was a very encouraging sign that I was now leaving the pressure ridges and rubble-fields behind and moving into an area of flatter, smoother ice, where I could really begin to pick up my speed and make serious inroads into the mountain of miles that still separated me from my goal. When I checked my log that night I also discovered that the distance I had travelled that day was enough to take me to a significant milestone; I had now covered 100 nautical miles – 100 down, 'only' 316 to go . . .

One other sign of change was rather less welcome. On Day 27, I noticed that although the outside temperature was still −33 °C, the sunshine had now warmed up the tent to the point where all the frost that had formed on the inner surfaces during the night melted with the heat of the stove, and water was running down the sides of the tent and dripping onto the sleeping-bag and me.

It was 12 April, Freya's birthday, and I faced south-west to Britain and shouted 'Happy birthday, Freya!' before setting out for the day. I imagined her with her friends at her birthday tea party, all sitting round the table near the map on the wall where Wilf was marking my progress every day. Often, as I plodded northwards, I wandered around the house and the garden in my imagination, picking daffodils with Wilf or watching Mary groom her horse, Philbo, or Freya smilingly smearing jam into her white-blonde tresses. Those thoughts of Freya and Wilf gave me such a powerful jolt of homesickness that I had to thrust the thought away at once and busy myself getting ready for the day's travel.

Ice and weather conditions were again good and I covered another seven nautical miles in nine hours' sledge-hauling, but once more I was feeling pretty wobbly and faint by the end of the day. I camped on a tiny area of snow on a huge refrozen lead, a giant ice lake four miles across. Normally I would have carried on to the far side before halting for the night, but I was so exhausted that I stopped and camped right in the middle of the frozen lake on a small islet of thicker ice, not much bigger than the tent's footprint, that must have been caught when the lead refroze and now stood almost a foot proud of the surface of the thinner, newer ice. It was the only place within a mile that I could have pitched the tent and there was only just enough snow on it to be able to anchor the tent and fill my sack with snow for drinking water. Weary or not, had it not been there, I'd have had to go on for another hour to the far side to get back on to the snow-covered ice.

I hadn't eaten my chocolate drops and the shortbread finger that usually went in my sledger's nosebag for the day – probably the reason I was feeling so feeble by evening. Instead I'd saved them for a special dessert. When I'd put up the tent and fired up the stove I brought some water to the boil, and then put my thermos mug in the saucepan as a *bain marie* to melt the chocolate drops. While it was heating, I fashioned a little dish from a piece of aluminium foil, put my shortbread finger inside it and poured the melted chocolate over the top. I put it on the floor of the tent to let it set – at −30°, it only took two or three minutes – and, just as it was firming up, I pushed a wooden match into the middle of it with the pink head uppermost. By now I was salivating and really looking forward to my special cake, but I made myself wait until I'd eaten my supper and had my Fruesli bar. Then I struck a match, lit the improvised candle on top of the cake and blew it out again, and, in three of the most delicious and memorable mouthfuls I've ever had on the Arctic Ocean, I ate this extremely rich home-made birthday cake. As I did so, I thought very fondly of little Freya. Even though she wouldn't know or understand what her Dad was up to at that moment, I knew that one day she would hear this story of how I celebrated her first birthday, and I hoped that it would make her feel good.

After the birthday celebration I had to carry out some repairs on my mitts. The constant friction from the handles of the ski-poles had already worn out the palms of both mitts, but they had deliberately been designed to be reversible, so I merely had to sew up the holes and then switch the mitts over so that the back of the left mitt was now the palm of the right one and vice versa. Of course, if they wore out again, repairs would be rather trickier, but by then the temperature should have risen enough to allow me to wear my thinner spare pair.

The next day, Day 28, exactly four weeks since I'd set off from Ward Hunt Island, I had three further reasons to celebrate: I encountered the best ice conditions of the expedition to date, crossed the eighty-fifth parallel during the course of the day and, by the end of it, had travelled 9.2 nautical miles in ten hours – over two nautical miles further than I'd managed on any previous day. To celebrate reaching 85°N, I opened another of my treasured cards from Mary, exhorting her husband to 'keep at it' and not worry about her and the children. The 'Big Four' factors – ice, weather, health and equipment – had all been good that day, which was an extremely rare event. Good weather conditions entailed good visibility, and that in turn meant good navigation over the ice. Surface conditions were excellent – flat, fresh ice-pans with plenty of gateways and low-level ridging between them, made for far faster progress than the rubble-fields, pressure ridges and leads of open water or newly frozen thin ice that I'd been encountering on previous days. Now that I was no longer carrying a huge rucksack, my back was much improved and, with no other health worries, aches, pains or injuries, there was nothing physical to hold me back. My kit was also working well; there was no need to keep stopping for running repairs, and that made a big difference. If you've got problems with your bindings, or your boots are starting to break up, or the ski-skins keep falling off, or the sledge is getting a hole in it and can't be pulled over open water, that can really affect the routeing and speed of progress.

I was also deep into the expedition psyche now, and most of my actions – even navigation – were becoming semi-instinctive. As the ice-pans got bigger and the navigation became less technical and challenging, I could let my mind wander and that really helped to make the time fly by much faster than in the early stages when I had to maintain complete concentration on the job of just taking the next step. As I've told all of my Polar Travel Company clients at one time or another, polar expeditions are mostly about: 'Just putting one foot in front of the other, interspersed with a few cups of tea.' But the flipside of that is that, as a rough average, around once a fortnight something major is going to happen. It may start as a trivial incident but it can easily escalate within minutes into a very serious problem. That's just one of the incidental dangers of operating in an extreme polar environment. So you have to be on your guard and be aware that you're never going to get a completely incident-free run to the Pole.

As well as a fearsomely dark tanned face, I now had a passable beard and moustache as well, which needed trimming back for the first time as part of the evening's routine mainten-ance. And I was grateful that the days of trying to melt the large bobbles of ice out of my moustache with my tongue had now passed with the arrival of the warmer weather. At forty below, I often briefly froze my tongue to my beard in the same way that fingers can become frozen to items in a domestic deep-freeze.

It was a constant unwelcome reminder of a gruesome

episode that occurred at Gary and Diane's house in Resolute. An Arctic fox scavenging in the night must have smelt some cooking grease on the side of the forty-gallon drum that served as their dustbin. When it tried to lick the grease its tongue must have frozen instantly to the super-cooled metal of the drum. Trapped, in pain, and panicking for its life it had eventually ripped it away only to leave its entire tongue, including the root, sticking to the side of the drum and a trail of blood going off into the snow.

As if to remind me that good days in the Arctic would always be the exception rather than the rule, the following morning, Day 29, broke with high winds and drifting snow. It made me realise just how lucky I had been with the weather up to now. It had been wonderful waking up every morning with the sun ever more discernible through the thin wall of the tent, and on such days I couldn't wait to get out there and start pulling the sledge. Today there was no sign of the sun, just a dull, matt-grey light, and the wind was making the tent flap and snap. I had to wonder if I was turning into a bit of a fair-weather sledger, because my whole heart sank at the prospect of a day of wind and snow in my face and it took much more mental energy to make myself get out of the tent, put on the harness and start pulling the sledge, and I was dragging my heels a bit.

Before I set off I made a quick call on the satellite phone to Simon Murray's home near Bath, to thank him for the finest and most encouraging letter I could ever have hoped to receive from a friend, which I'd been saving since he handed it to me just before he flew out of Resolute. In it he reminded me of the French Foreign Legion's motto: 'Marche ou crève' – 'March or die' – and it had made me remember that however hard life may be out here sometimes, it was as nothing to what others had to endure. Simon's confidence in my ability to succeed also served to remind me that it was a privilege for me to be here on the ice, and not a punishment to be endured. I could choose at every hour of every day whether I smiled or grimaced – and I would stand a much better chance of arriving at the far end if I chose the former. Put like that, the choice was surprisingly easy.

Simon wasn't there, but I spoke to his wife, Jennifer. It seemed surreal; there she was in their conservatory, drinking a glass of red wine with a friend on a beautiful, sunny English spring evening, and here I was trying to gird my loins to get out into the teeth of a blizzard at 30° below zero. The call was a distraction and, though I enjoyed the contact with the outside world, I was equally happy without it. That's not to say I didn't miss my family and friends but, even in my darkest hours, I never felt lonely for a single minute during any of my solo expeditions. I never considered it a trial to be going to the Pole alone and I relished the solitude as much as, in other circumstances, I enjoyed company; I suspect that solo yachts-people are the same. Certainly there are additional demands and challenges in going solo, but they are the very things that can also bring about the greatest benefits. In some ways the journey is purer, more absolute and more extreme, and that can bring out the best performances and the most valuable insights and experiences.

Rather than filling me with negative 'I wish I was there' kind of thoughts, the conversation with Jennifer inspired me to get out of the tent and get on, and I was quite proud of myself for having forced myself to do it rather than looking for excuses to take another rest day. The wind was whipping up the fallen snow into drifts and fresh snow was still falling, but the faint outline of the sun was visible through the layers of cloud, offering the promise of a return to better weather later on. I gritted my teeth and forced myself to head north, navigating by compass in near white-out conditions, but after a couple of hours the skies began to clear, my pace picked up and my spirits lifted. I did my normal six-session day and put another seven nautical miles on the clock. This gave me confidence that the weather didn't really matter. I had done a day without the sun and it didn't make any difference. Life goes on.

Day 30 dawned bright and clear, but I found it hard going and struggled for rhythm all day because, although the weather was good, the ice conditions were poor – new snow on rough, multi-year ice with a few leads and pressure ridges. The nature of the ice-surface meant that I was constantly having to focus on the technicalities of finding an optimum route rather than setting my mind free to wander. As a result, the time dragged a little, but I did my full sessions and covered another eight nautical miles.

Day 31 was a hard, hard day. I was looking for a regular working day of ten to twelve hours by this point, but I was struggling to achieve it. The newly fallen snow was still hampering my progress, the ice conditions were miserable that day and during the last of the two extra sessions I was doing, I became very hypoglycaemic, trembling and sweating.

Day 31 was the birthday of a friend of ours, Ann Daniels, and also the day she was due to have a baby. She had been helping me with my preparations during the early stages of her pregnancy and had really stuck at it, determined to do all she could to take over some of the ever expanding workload from me. She was due to go into labour today and the thought of all the experiences awaiting her put my own exertions right into perspective. I was intensely grateful for the support she had given me so I had decided that I was going to dedicate my day's mileage to her.

With that thought in mind, I had set off like a train and the early part of the day had gone fine. I was on ice-pans that had been open water the previous summer, there was virtually no ridging at all and there was a flat ice-surface on which I could pick up my speed substantially . . . or at least I could have if the ice had not also been riven with cracks and fissures. I couldn't see them until I was almost upon them but, suddenly, looking ahead about 100 metres, I saw an area that looked a little suspicious, a discoloured line running across the ice. When I got nearer I realised that the line was caused by the inky blackness of open water reflecting on to a ragged bank of ice, giving it a very different colour from normal – mud-brown or rust. And when I reached it, I found that there was a two-metre lead of open water. Looking ahead again, I saw the line of another lead and another beyond that, and I realised that the apparently perfect ice-surface was broken by these narrow leads every 100 metres or so.

Suddenly it had turned into a less than perfect day. I was zig-zagging around because it didn't seem worth putting on the immersion suit to cross a two-metre-wide strip of water when it looked as if the lead petered out after a couple of hundred metres. But when I skied to the vanishing point I found that the lead had merely taken a dogleg and was running on beyond it in a slightly different direction. I skied on to the next vanishing point and found that I'd been suckered again. I kept on doing this for more than twenty minutes, growing more and more annoyed. If I'd put the immersion suit on I could probably have jumped the lead. But then 100 metres further on there was another and I'd have the same dilemma again.

I eventually found a way over, and rounded or crossed a few more, sometimes going west of them, sometimes east, trying to keep to a broadly northward course, and then I found that I'd crossed onto a floating island of ice. As I walked over it, it swung like a gate in the wind and though I plodded north, north-north-west, north-west, west and then south-west, I couldn't find a safe way off it. Even backtracking to try a different route looked closed to me, because the ice-island had swung far enough to prevent me from going back the way I had come.

I'd now spent a further thirty or forty minutes getting nowhere fast and I was starting to get really cross with myself; I was losing time and the day was wasting. I had to try to stride or jump across a two-metre-wide crack, and though that wasn't a great distance, the ice on either side of it looked rotten – my ski-poles left wet holes if I pushed them into it. The alternative was to put on my immersion suit and swim it. If I backtracked to look for another route, I might put myself in an even worse position, because I could tell from a smudge of frost-smoke in the air that there was a larger lead over to the west.

I decided I had to have some food while I planned my next move, but for some reason – maybe anger – I wolfed the entire day's rations in one go. I started getting into it as a comfort factor, a reward for taking the tougher option – I'll do the dodgy ice but I'll just have my chocolate first – but then I just kept on munching my way through it. Having had nothing in the first break, I'd now eaten the whole lot in the third one. Now I was really furious with myself. There was no way I was going to start raiding any future day's ration bag so, apart from the odd cup of tea, I was going to have to march for the rest of the day on what I'd just eaten.

When I finally steeled myself to cross the dodgy ice, I discovered that, even though my ski-poles were indeed puncturing it at every step, I could actually get across it and bridge the two-metre gap over the open water on my skis without any great problems at all. That did nothing to improve my temper; I'd been messing about for hours trying to find a way round and then eating all my food and all the time I could have gone straight across it. How stupid was I exactly? Then, towards the end of the day, I was feeling really wobbly and washed-out but I was just making myself go on as a sort of punishment. So all in all, it was a pretty mediocre day. Considering I'd crossed seven leads and two ridges in the course of the day, seven nautical miles probably wasn't a bad rate of progress but it had taken me over ten hours and left me exhausted. From now on I had to plan my days, and particularly the allocation of rations, with much more care.

Of course, my wobbliness towards the end of the day might just have been psychological, brought on by anger and frustration with myself, but it seemed pretty physical to me, so I thought: 'Right, if I don't eat anything in the first break, when

I've still got breakfast and a few cups of tea with sugar kicking in, and then have a relatively small amount for the second break, I'll have saved some snacks for the latter part of the day.' That would give me a couple of extra hours sledge-hauling and hours equal miles. If I only did one extra mile every day for the next thirty days that would be worth a half degree of latitude – the equivalent of two long days' sledge-hauling at the end of the expedition.

On Day 32, the signs of the break-up of the ice were even more pronounced. It was a gruelling day. I had to put on the immersion suit again and swim a fifty-metre lead – one of eight I encountered in the course of the day, though I managed to circumvent the rest – but, even on relatively good ice, the normal process of sledge-hauling north was a backbreaking task. The snow was about fifteen centimetres deep and as viscous as treacle, and dragging my sledge through it was a constant, strength-sapping burden. I couldn't get into any sort of rhythm and the physical effort and the noise of ice activity made it impossible even to hold a train of thought for more than a few seconds. There was a constant backdrop of crashing, splashing, groaning and grinding from the ice, punctuated by booms like distant cannon fire as the tortured ice tore apart.

The wind was usually the big mover of ice but there hadn't been any wind to speak of for a few days. The influence of the ocean current, the Transpolar Drift Stream, on the ice was negligible most of the time here – it only really kicked in as a significant force in a big sheer zone around 86°30'N, well to the north of my current position – so I had to assume that the tides were driving the ice-movement, or gales occurring far away on the ocean. Whatever the cause, the effect was massive.

As I skied along, I heard a huge disturbance somewhere ahead of me, a rumbling and crashing, like great ice-blocks rolling downhill or smashing into the water. I paused at once, straining to locate the precise direction of the noise. If it was behind me, it didn't matter, I had no intention of heading south, but if it was in front of me, was it directly ahead, or to the north-west or the north-east? Another crash as I looked towards the north-west gave me a fix on it. I spotted a pressure ridge in that direction and ran my eye along it eastwards; did it peter out before it came to my line heading north? If not, then I was probably OK to continue on this heading.

One of the tricks in this situation was to aim for the point where the ridges petered out downwards into the horizon because when two plates were moving in relation to each other, there was often a metre or two of ice at the axis of the movement that was neither being thrown up into a ridge nor pushed apart to reveal water, and thus simple to walk across. I managed to cover just six nautical miles in the course of the day and the effort so exhausted me that, despite the previous day's resolution to complete extra sessions at the end of every normal working day from now on, I was forced to stop and pitch camp at the end of my standard six sessions. Maybe tomorrow would be better.

In fact, it was worse, another tough, tough day. It was a special day for me, Good Friday, the anniversary of my father's death, and I so wanted to put in a big effort for him, but once more the ice conditions were terrible and it was a debilitating struggle even to achieve the modest total of five nautical miles in over eight hours sledge-hauling. I was now privately conceding to myself that sixty-five or sixty-six days might be a more realistic target than the fifty-eight to sixty I had been hoping for, but even on that revised schedule, Day 33 saw me beyond the halfway mark, in time, if not yet in mileage. I made a concerted effort to regroup and refocus, but trying to keep positive was extremely difficult in the face of the atrocious ice conditions of these last two days. There were cracks and small leads everywhere and my only hope was that it was localised activity and not continuous all the way to the Pole.

Meanwhile, no matter how nervous I was feeling and however inconvenient the ice, I just had to keep grinding out my sledge-hauling sessions one by one, and accept whatever mileage I could achieve even though the day's total was woefully poor at this stage of the expedition. Along with my worries about my rate of progress, I also had anxieties about fuel. Since the start of the expedition, the temperature had been well below normal for the time of year – never warmer than −30 °. As a result, I was really getting through fuel at an alarming rate. There was no way I could be more efficient in fuel use; I was already consuming the absolute minimum amount of fluids, just four litres a day, including the liquid required to reconstitute my porridge and evening meal. If I drank less I would save fuel but become seriously dehydrated over time. Only significantly warmer weather could help me to prolong my fuel supply.

That night, reviewing my previous few diary entries, I was struck by the ubiquity of words like 'concern', 'nervous' and 'anxiety' sprinkled across the pages. This was partly because success on this attempt was so important to me and anything conceivably threatening it was identified and worked through till it had been resolved, but partly because my diary was also a place to bury such concerns at the end of each day. Just the act of committing them to paper seemed to lessen them in my mind, and for the vast majority of my waking hours I was infinitely more relaxed, focused and positive day by day than a reading of my diary would suggest. I was on schedule, as I had been almost from Day 1, and if I was occasionally keen to scour the horizons for potential problems it was often for no other reason than my hunger to seek out and destroy any obstacles that could threaten my progress.

Day 34 was again hard work, but I'd conquered my depression of the previous couple of days and managed to stay in good spirits. It was Easter Saturday, when my whole family were due to gather at my ever supportive mother-in-law, Esther Nicholson's house in Dorset, and, knowing that my family and all my in-laws, nephews and nieces were all monitoring my progress every day, I wanted to give them an Easter present of a really big mileage. Breaking my normal habit, I kept the GPS in my pocket to keep the LCD display and the batteries warm and checked my mileage at the end of my normal six sledge-hauling sessions. This didn't seem a particularly good idea when I discovered that, despite pushing hard all day, I had only covered 5.6 miles. That was absolutely unacceptable – what kind of a present was that? – so I made myself carry on and, helped by some better ice and my decision to start dipping into my extra sledging rations (originally planned for Days 66–9), to maintain my blood sugar levels. I then did a further three miles in just two hours.

I felt much happier as I made camp that night. The conditions had been horrendous again, which made for pretty slow progress, but at least I felt that, after a couple of bad days, I'd got the measure of it. It had been another really hard day, but I was more relaxed knowing that I was still doing the miles and would get through it. Those last three miles were a great boost, a signal that when conditions improved – as they were bound to do – I would really be able to fly over the ice.

My new-found equanimity had even survived the shock of getting one of my feet wet – the first time it had happened on this expedition. In the late afternoon I'd come to yet another small lead about ten metres across. I walked along it a little way and reached a little headland of ice, jutting out from the other side. There was about a metre and a half of open water and another sixty centimetres of relatively thin ice on both sides of it. I stood there thinking what to do. I was pretty tired and didn't really fancy struggling with Mr Orange or the 'lilo' for the sledge and I suddenly decided that I could solve the problem without either of those, simply by using my sledge as a bridge. I took my skis off and then pushed out the sledge until it was resting across the thin ice on each side. I was leaning forward onto the back of the sledge, trying to test it before committing my full weight to it, when I felt my right foot slowly start to sink through the ice. I just managed to pull myself back and get back on to firmer ice, moving very gently to avoid doing further damage, but by then my foot was soaking wet.

My policy was never to allow that to happen because it was indicative of having taken some avoidable risk, and it also greatly increased the risk of frostbite. I gave myself a well-deserved dressing down. 'You idiot. What are you doing getting your foot wet? You've got all this kit you've been lugging around for precisely this kind of situation. Why don't you use it?' So I inflated the lilo, dragged the sledge onto it, and was just about to push it out when I suddenly felt my ice-pan start to judder and move. The lead began to close and in under three minutes I could step straight across it. It was as if someone up there was saying 'Right, you've got your boot wet. Smart move. But you've got the right things now, so I'm going to give it to you anyway.' Having switched to a dry boot-liner, I carried on walking, but I had to dry the sodden one on a ski-pole outside the tent during the night and then spent precious time scraping out the accumulations of ice in the linings and insoles.

I didn't let it spoil the day, Day 35, Easter Sunday. I thought of my family and remembered the previous Easter morning when we'd all been together, going to church at St Raphael's in Huccaby on Dartmoor and having an Easter egg hunt in the garden. This year was very different, but I pledged to myself that I'd put in a big day today, both for Mary, Wilf and Freya, and for all the rest of my supporters – my back-up team, family, friends and all those who were tracking the expedition on the website and leaving messages of support.

In lieu of an Easter egg, I gave myself a portion of extra porridge as a treat and some extra nosebag rations for the long day ahead and then set off. The weather was fine and sunny and the ice conditions much improved; the new snow that had given me such trouble was now hardened and compacted and I made fast time. I had done 7.4 nautical miles by the end of the normal sledging day – good in itself – but I then put in another four hours, completing a twelve-hour day and adding another 2.6 miles, taking me to 10 for the day, a new personal best.

I rewarded myself with a superb Easter supper. I gave myself an extra serving of cod and potato with my main meal and put some of the extra milk powder I'd saved from the early days of the expedition into my hot chocolate, along with an effervescent vitamin C pill. It sounds disgusting, but tasted delicious – a rich, creamy, orangey chocolate drink. I put off opening my Easter presents until after supper. Knowing my addiction to chocolate, Mary had put in a Cadbury's Creme Egg (frozen solid but soon warmed through enough to eat). Wilf had given me an iridescent green clothes peg from which to suspend my drying socks in the tent, and Freya's present was a 'must-have' micro four-wheel buggy, measuring all of an inch by an inch and a half square, with two moving mechanical brushes to sweep up any crumbs from the tent floor. There were also some miniature Easter cards and airmail letters from close friends.

It was remarkable how these little gifts, coming on top of a good sledging day, a few extra miles and a little extra food could lighten my mood. I was now confident that, even though I knew anything could yet happen to throw my calculations off track, sixty-five days to the Pole would be a worst-case scenario. So I told myself that it would be perfectly OK to eat the rations for Days 66 to 69 which I'd begun yesterday. I didn't eat the whole day's allowance in one lump, but it would allow me to give myself 30 per cent extra porridge in the morning, 30 per cent extra sledging snacks during the day and 30 per cent extra supper at night. That would not only do wonders for my morale, it would also propel me faster and further over the ice. On that basis, sixty-five days was beginning to sound like a self-fulfilling prophecy.

Day 36 was Easter Monday, the excuse for another breakfast treat, this time finishing off some of the porridge I'd saved from the first days of the expedition, together with my newly sanctioned extra allowance. The porridge was a mixture of oats, dried milk and honeyed, crunchy bits and, for the last few days, I'd been snacking on the next day's crunchy bits while reading in my sleeping-bag at night, but now it was getting a bit out of hand. I was not only stealing from the following day, but in my desperation for extra food, I was even eating spoonfuls of dry porridge oats and dried milk before I went to sleep.

I made a good start to the day, moving fast over relatively open ice-pans and finding many fewer cracks and leads than the previous few days, but by the afternoon I was encountering light rubble-fields, which slowed me down considerably. In the circumstances, seven miles in ten hours was a reasonable rate of progress. When I checked my GPS that evening, I also discovered that I had crossed the eighty-sixth parallel during the day. Even with all the bad ice conditions, getting from 85°N to 86°N had only taken eight days, an average of 7.5 miles a day, but I hoped to go even faster as I approached the Pole.

Another treasured card from the family marked the latitude and served to remind me how much Mary continued to support my endeavour. Even when so far away and so long apart, she was still determined to give me all the support she could, unswerving in her belief that I could and would make it to the end. Her faith in me was more than just words on a card. She had enabled us to survive financially and, in my absence, was willing to run the household for long periods to make sure I could realise my ambition.

I spoke to my base manager, Ian, later on. He was in the garden of his home in Chagford on Dartmoor, bathed in spring sunshine – another warming reminder of home. Ian informed me that, by his calculations, the weight of the sledge was now under 100 kilos (around 220 pounds). Even though he was thousands of miles away and hadn't laid eyes on the sledge since my departure, I had no reason to doubt his maths. Everything I had with me had been weighed and logged before

I set off, and every time I emptied a fuel bottle or discarded something, I told Ian and he deducted its weight from the total. However, one part of that weight-loss was giving me increasing concern. With about thirty days to go, I only had 7.5 litres of fuel left. I kept my fingers crossed that rising temperatures would reduce my fuel consumption, but just in case, I began serious fuel rationing that night, aiming to use no more than 0.2 litres per day from then on.

The following day, Day 37, I took as a rest day. In one way it was a quixotic decision, to rest so soon after I had been chafing at the delays to my progress and with shortage of fuel such a growing concern, but my exertions over the previous few days had left me very tired, I had a backlog of repairs and maintenance and I had grown further and further out of synch with the calendar day. I was going to bed and getting up later and later every day, partly because of the extra sessions I was doing, but partly because of the time I was having to spend on the satellite phone each night, making sure that the website was updated with the latest information and statistics and that Ginny had the copy she needed . . . and, as I had already discovered, that was not a quick process. I enjoyed doing it but it was really bending my schedule out of shape, and as a result, I was now walking from roughly one in the afternoon till eleven at night, and although there was now twenty-four-hour, continuous daylight, after eight in the evening the angle of the sunlight directly into my face, and the consequent dark shadowing of the ice-features ahead, made route selection surprisingly hard and much more challenging. It was slowing me down a lot and, after a rest day, I planned to get up at four the next morning and walk with good light all day.

The latest I had set off was about 3.50 in the afternoon and ten hours' sledge-hauling had taken me to 1.50 in the morning before I even began my evening work and sat-phone calls. It was four in the morning before I finally got to sleep. If I got up at eight to get myself back on track, I'd only have had four hours' sleep, which would have been crazy. So the only thing to do was to take a day off. The sun was shining the next morning, so I had thrown away a good weather day, but I didn't dwell on that. If I put the day to good use and was well rested by the following morning, I'd make up the lost time in short order.

I first hung out a lot of my gear to dry, spreading my sleeping-bag and my 'elephant smock' over the sledge to let the sun burn off some more ice, hanging my wet boot from the previous day on a ski-pole, and draping my gloves and socks over the skis anchoring each end of the tent. Everything I had was black or very dark blue so that it absorbed the maximum amount of energy from the sun and things dried or de-iced surprisingly quickly. Even lumps of ice the size of my fist had disappeared by the end of a full day in the sun.

I next had the tricky task of changing my contact lenses. I was wearing lenses that could be left in for a month but these had now been in for about forty days and were getting a bit dirty and smudgy with excessive use, so it was time to change them. It was a bit of a hoohah because, after over five weeks without a proper wash, I was filthy and my tent was not the most sterile of environments. I was also catching the occasional whiff of fetid body odour, which was eye-watering in itself. I was paranoid about getting conjunctivitis, so I cleaned my hands thoroughly with some sterilising wipes before I even touched the packets, let alone the lenses. The saline solution in which the lenses were stored was of course frozen solid, so before I could insert the lenses, I had to slide the packets up inside my thermal sleeves and let them thaw with my body-heat. While they were doing so, I faced a protracted struggle to extract the old lenses, which seemed to have become part of the eyeball. In comparison to that, slipping the new lenses into my eyes was child's play.

My only problem with my eyes was a slight irritation in the left corner of the left eye, almost certainly caused by the sun striking the tiny gap between my sunglasses and the corner of the eye. When I set off each morning, the sun was behind and to the right of me, but by around five o'clock in the afternoon it had swung around enough to hit the chink at the side of my sunglasses and cause some irritation to the eye. It was bearable at the moment, but snow-blindness was a potential expedition-wrecker and if it became any worse I'd have to modify the sunglasses to block out even that tiny area.

I'd taken a leaf out of the book of the numerous women I had worked with on polar expeditions and begun applying some antiseptic cream to my face to start the repair process for the damage that was accumulating in the form of windburn and frostnip on my cheeks and the sides of my nose. It was impossible to avoid minor tissue damage of this kind in temperatures as low as −45 °C, but that was no reason not to keep trying to minimise it and reduce the risk of infection using the limited amount of cream I carried – like my toothpaste – defrosted, up my sleeves morning and night. Having sorted out my personal problems, I next set to work to repair the lilo straps. I'd over-tightened them the first time I used the lilo and one of them had ripped off during the crossing so I sewed it back on with a huge needle that I had and some thick thread. The watertight seal around the support bar at the front of the sledge had pulled apart under the stresses and strains of crossing the ice, and I had to fix it with jubilee clips so that I would have a dry sledge even if it nose-dived into the water. The base of my thermos had also come off, so I superglued it and mended the torn covers of my diary and my data log.

Having completed all my running repairs, I went through my clothes and equipment and had a ruthless sort-out. If anything was worn out or no longer needed because conditions had changed, it had to go. I bagged up four useless fuel pumps, a spare wire stand for the stove, some spare black rubber hosing and the tent bag, which I no longer needed. My duct tape and spinnaker tape were both on circular card stands which seemed to be unnecessarily weighty, so I threw those out, together with two spare toe-strap leathers and two extra cables for my ski-bindings. That left me with no spares at all, but, having assessed the damage to the existing cables, I felt that as they were under much less strain from the lighter sledge they would last out the remainder of the expedition. Some of my clothing was also surplus to requirements now that the temperatures were rising. I didn't need a spare hood or a second hat any more, and I also threw out two spare pairs of gloves. It didn't make a vast difference to the weight of the sledge – no more than a couple of kilos – but it was a psychological benefit to know that I was only carrying stuff that was actually going to help me get to the Pole.

The full programme of works had taken five hours, but it was time well spent, because it was great to have things back in full working order again and, with everything absolutely squared away, it was as if I was starting on a new expedition. I was up early as planned the next morning, Day 38, and set off full of optimism, bathed in bright sunlight under clear blue skies. Eight hours later I was reflecting on the worst day of the entire expedition so far. Within half an hour of setting off, I had left the light rubble-fields behind and entered a region that had seen considerable ice activity. The ice was making all sorts of noises: groaning, grinding, juddering, squeaking, and it sounded to me as if my sledge, 'Baskers', had taken to copying the noises. I got so irritated by this that I stopped, turned round and snapped, 'For God's sake, Baskers, stop making those noises,' when I suddenly realised that a pressure ridge was forming and the ice was splitting under my feet.

I crossed that one without trouble, but I was soon hauling and manhandling the sledge up the first of a succession of pressure ridges that were steeper and of larger, more unmanageable blocks than any I had seen since the early days of the expedition. I was to cross eighteen such pressure ridges in the course of that gruelling day. Around noon I witnessed a rare and extraordinary sight. In front of me, running in from the west and tapering out ahead, was a vast ridge of particularly huge blocks of sea-ice. The largest block in this pile was about as large as blocks get, almost twice the size of a London double-decker bus, its facing side a vivid blue and showing its layered growth over the years. Despite its prodigious weight – hundreds of tons – it had been jacked up high above the waterline by the pressures in the ice-cap. There was a steep-sided, canal-sized lead in front of the ridge, but it appeared to come to an abrupt end a little to the east of the end of it, and I was hoping to walk around it, crossing along the axis of the relative movements of the two ice-floes. I was about thirty metres from the crossing-point when I heard, fractionally before I saw, this gigantic block of ice begin to move. Gathering speed at a frightening rate, it hurtled down into the water. The next moment I saw a huge wave rearing up. Accelerating and growing as it surged between the narrowing walls of the canal, it blasted into the air like a breaking storm-wave smashing against a harbour wall. It had exploded across my path and the wash reached to within less than a metre of my skis before it subsided, gurgling back into the canal and soaking into the snow around it like a spent wave sinking into a sandy beach. For over a minute, the air was full of spray that turned instantly into ice crystals, creating a miniature frozen rainbow, but I had little appetite for the beauty of the scene. I was reflecting that if I had been thirty seconds earlier that day I might well have been swept to my death.

My one consolation for the horrendous ridging I had encountered was that this was also the warmest day I had yet seen – a positively balmy −26 °C. I was so warm that, for the first time, I wasn't wearing a hat of any sort, not even my 'chimney' hat, and I was only wearing gloves, not mitts, on my hands. That was not to last, however. I sensed a change was coming before any visible sign of it. The sun was still shining brightly, but the air began to feel damper and the temperature started to drop. A few minutes later, I saw that a low fog-bank was starting to build up across part of the horizon. A couple of minutes more and half the sky had been obscured, and within ten or fifteen minutes of the first faint signs, I was enveloped in thick fog. I could still just discern the outline of the sun through it, but the temperature had gone down five or ten degrees as the damp air rolled in. The hat and mitts went back on, and I began to plod through a grey, formless and totally silent world. The terrain had also changed again to an eerie ice-scape, a flat plain broken by small plates of ice, perhaps a metre high, rising at all angles from the surface. They looked for all the world like tombstones in some lost and long-forgotten graveyard. I could pick my way through them easily enough but it was a creepy and very atmospheric place. The fog-bank took around ninety minutes to pass over me and, after a brief interlude of sunshine, there was another and then another. I could have few complaints; I had been travelling in near-continuous sunshine for almost forty days, and it had to stop some time, but as I plodded on to the north, I thought to myself, 'Today's the day. It's all over, I can't expect the sunshine to continue, I'm now into the tough times. I'll really have to grind it out from now on and, with poor visibility, navigation is not going to be much fun at all.'

It wasn't just the cold, the damp and the poor visibility; the fog was also a warning of dangerous conditions ahead. Fog tells you that there are large areas of open water around. That open water generates its own weather; frost-smoke and fog come off the relatively warm water as it meets the frigid air, and are then driven along on the breeze. The fog-banks were moving in from the north-east, so I had to assume that there were large areas of open water in that direction. It wasn't necessarily a catastrophe, they might be tens of miles away – several days' travel – and they might pinch out to the east of my track north, but it was another sign of the times: the spring thaw was now accelerating.

At the end of the normal sledging day of six sessions, I checked the GPS. The day had been a complete disaster. At a time when I was looking to break double figures each day, I had covered just 3.6 nautical miles in eight hours. It couldn't be allowed to stand there, I had to go on and do some more miles – even if only a couple – before I stopped for the night. Fortunately the last of the fog-banks had now passed over and it turned out that I had also cleared the last of the pressure ridges. I found myself on large, smooth ice-pans and travelled so fast across them that by the time I called a halt two hours later, I had more than doubled my day's mileage, covering four miles in that short space of time.

When I read the figure on the GPS, my depression at once gave way to elation. Without knackering myself completely, I had been travelling at two nautical miles an hour. If I could just string a few good ice-pans together over the course of a day, I could really pile up some serious miles. But even as I thought that, I knew that you almost never got a whole day of good ice. I was resigned to that, but it was good to know that, even after such a horrendous start to the day, I could still achieve a reasonable mileage by the end of it.

To my great relief, when I woke the next morning, Day 39, the sun was once again shining through the tent wall. It made starting the day so much easier; when it was foggy, windy or cloudy, I really had to push myself to get out there, but the sun was still there today and I was really grateful for it. I thought quite a bit about the sun, and the difference it made to my mood, and I even found myself talking to it every now and again, exhorting it to burn its way through any obscuring cloud and thanking it when it finally won through.

I encountered another seven big pressure ridges during the course of the day, and a couple more fog-banks rolled over but, despite those hazards, I made good progress, covering 9.3 miles in ten hours' sledge-hauling, close to my personal best. The fog had cleared and the sun was shining strongly during the evening, so I managed to dry lots of my gear and burn yet more ice out of my sleeping-bag, which also boosted my morale. I spoke by sat-phone to my Canadian base management team, Gary and Diane, that night. Ian was overall base manager, but I also liked to touch base with Gary every now and again. He was a great character with a terrific sense of humour, but some of his advice and anecdotes, delivered absolutely deadpan, had a habit of unsettling me. He thought that I was such a hard case that I could take any amount of banter, and I don't think he realised how fragile my mental state could be when I was out on the ice. I was telling him about using the immersion suit when he suddenly said, 'You've got to watch out for those Greenland sharks, you know, they're absolute bastards. Once they see you, they just go for you. You don't get any warning, you don't even see the fins above the water.'

I said, 'I don't want to hear this.'

'Oh yes you do. It's all for your own good. Forewarned is forearmed!'

He was roaring with laughter as he told me this, and I was laughing too . . . in a rather nervous way. Of course it was rot, but like all good scare stories, it contained enough elements of truth to make it both memorable and all too believable. The Greenland shark, *Somniosus microcephalus*, also known as the sleeper shark, does live in polar waters. One of the largest of all sharks, it can be four or five and, occasionally, even as much as six or seven metres long, and though it does have a dorsal fin, it is small. It is omnivorous and its reputation for sluggishness is belied by the salmon and other fast-swimming fish that it catches. It also eats seals, carrion including whale-flesh, and one specimen has even been found with a whole reindeer in its stomach. It suffers from a parasite called a copepod that infests its eyes and makes them glow an eerie whitish-yellow in the dark Arctic waters. The Inuit use its razor-sharp teeth and eat its flesh, which is poisonous unless repeatedly boiled. With the seed planted in my mind courtesy of Gary's little joke, every time I went in the water from then on, I was imagining those bloody sharks in the depths below me.

I slept relatively well that night, without too many dreams of sharks severing my body parts, and awoke to another fine morning. It was Friday, 25 April, Day 40 of the expedition, two-thirds of the way in time, though less than half that in actual mileage. Even so I'd passed another milestone during the day – the 200-mile mark. I had now covered 203 miles, but still had another 213 to go. I was counting in blocks of five and ten days, rather than ticking them off each day like a prisoner in his cell, but reducing the expedition to manageable segments certainly seemed to help, giving me a sense of real progress as I reached each milestone. The end of each five-day period was never too distant and each ten-day chunk felt like a major achievement – only six of those and I'd be there. It was just one of an endless series of mathematical games I'd play, always looking for the most positive gloss to put on any given situation.

Almost every day there was a reason for having another milestone, if not in days or weeks, then in miles or degrees of latitude or even days of the month. And if those failed, there were always special occasions of family and friends, national holidays or anniversaries of expeditions on the Arctic Ocean that I'd noted in advance in my diary. That way, I always had a reason to be positive and looking forward to the day ahead. I also found that it helped to discuss things with my anthropo-morphic 'team' – Mavis, Swerves, Curves and Baskers. I'd been doing so for a couple of weeks by this stage and at every break I would have a chat with them. During the first day or two I'd felt a bit self-conscious about holding a conversation with a couple of ski-poles, a sledge and a de-icing brush, but since there was no one within a hundred miles to overhear me, it very quickly became a non-issue. My daily briefings to the team covered everything from route plans, warnings about potential problems or hazards and appeals not to lose vital bits of kit through carelessness and inattention, to generalised appeals for ever greater efforts – 'We're just going to have to take it up a gear today, everyone. Come on, we've got to raise our game' – that sort of thing. I found that just verbalising things made an enormous difference to my mood. If I needed to be more positive, just saying it out loud really did seem to do the trick, whereas trying to change my mood simply by the power of thought was markedly less effective.

It wasn't hard to find positives at the end of this particular day. I'd travelled eleven miles in ten hours – my best day so far. It was amazing how fast things could change; two days ago had been my worst one. Today the surface conditions were very good and the weather near-perfect. The Big Four – ice, weather, health and kit – were all good now, and it was all systems go as everything came together: the sledge was lighter, the coefficient of friction was reducing on the sledge runners as the ice temperature rose and I was getting more and more of the newer, flatter Siberian ice coming across. One big fog-bank did come rolling up out of the west, but luckily I just missed the edge of it. The temperatures were rising steadily day by day and were now in the low minus twenties – warm enough to have long since burned off the ice in my sleeping-bag. Of course, every night it built up again as my breath froze on the hood lining while I slept and moisture from my body radiated out into the body of the bag, but as long as I could drape it over the sledge during the day, the sun would remove the accumulated ice.

The only slightly troubling factors were that my right hamstring was almost going into spasm – I spent some time rubbing and massaging it and trying to get it to calm down – and, rather more worrying, my powers of concentration seemed to be waning with every passing day. Sometimes the ice conditions were so rough that I couldn't think about anything beyond the next footfall, but on good days with good surface conditions, I could let my mind wander. When I did so, I found that I was struggling to maintain a thought pattern for more than about ten seconds. It was a sign of just how physically and mentally tired I was becoming; I didn't recognise it at the time, but that's undoubtedly what it was.

This otherwise perfect day was also marred by a bitter personal tragedy in the shape of the sad demise of the lovely Mavis, the de-icing brush who had been through so much with me. While cleaning ice and snow out of my sleeping-bag that morning, she had suffered a terrible spinal injury – her metal body broke. She had been looking very tired and dishevelled for several days – her hair was falling out in clumps and that once proud, bottle-blonde Afro was a threadbare shadow of her former glorious self, but she was a special bit of kit to me. She had worn herself to a frazzle and beyond, and was still making herself available for duty, broken in body, but not in spirit. I continued to use her, holding her torso, and I kept all her body parts so that, in a sense, she would still be seeing it through to the end with me.

A good night's sleep helped me overcome the worst of my grief and Day 41 was another storming day with exceptionally good ice and weather, and another personal best of 11.2 nautical miles. I wrote in my diary that it was a Red Letter Day because I now realised for the first time that, after fifteen years, it really was going to happen – I was going to reach the Pole solo and without resupply . . . always providing that I could just keep it together for another twenty days or so. I had seen off the worst of the cold weather and the worst of the ice conditions. I had plenty of food and, with the timely warmer temperatures, it looked as if the fuel was going to be enough after all too – and, although I was mentally weary, I was carrying no injuries and felt as physically fit as when I'd set out.

When I spoke to Ginny on the sat-phone that night she picked up on my mood and did her best to get me to say that I was as good as there, but it was one thing to think it and quite another to commit it to print and I wasn't going to set myself up for that kind of fall if something went wrong later on. Hard though she pressed me, I refused point-blank to play that game. 'I know exactly what the paper would like to report, Ginny,' I said, 'and I'm not going to bloody well say it. It's not what I think. I feel cautiously optimistic, but I would absolutely not say it was in the bag.' I was certainly not going to start counting my chickens yet, not even in the chicken curry that I ate that night.

There was also one cautionary sign; I'd seen fox tracks for the first time, running across the snow for a few metres and then disappearing as they reached a patch of hard-frozen snow. It was another indicator of the changing season and another reason to maintain vigilance at all times. I had already seen a seal in the huge lead that had held me up. Now I'd seen the tracks of the second member of the polar trinity – the Arctic fox. All that was now missing was the third.

The next day, Day 42, saw yet another personal best: 12.5 miles in twelve hours. The day's mileage would have been even more impressive but for the loss of a quarter of an hour to mend a broken trace (the rope that attached my harness to the sledge) and another forty-five minutes when I had to retrace my steps to retrieve the basket that had become detached from one of my ski-poles – Swerves. I had been going for almost an hour when I realised that the basket was missing. I couldn't believe that I hadn't noticed it straightaway because, as a rule, I was instantly aware of anything even the least bit unusual or awry. I can only think that the tiredness I was feeling had dulled my senses. It wasn't a disaster but it did mean that every now and again the ski-pole could just plunge straight through the snow, throwing me off-balance and risking a fall that could be critical on bad ice. So I unhitched the sledge, slung the rifle on my back and started to ski back the way I had come. It was easy enough to follow the tracks I had made, and without the sledge I made fast time, but, inevitably, I had to ski virtually the whole way back before discovering the basket within ten yards of where I had set off from that morning. I fixed it back

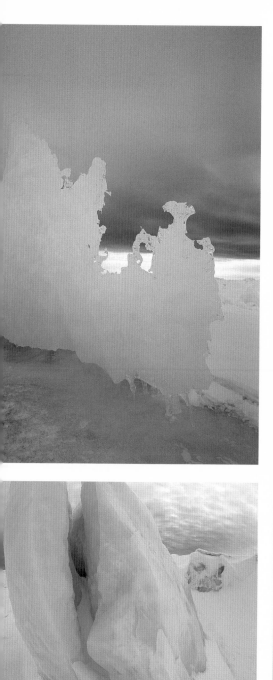

63/64/65/66. 'Freya moments' would capture beautiful ice-scapes like these

67. Preparing camp on the sea-ice below -40°C (image from the video distorted by the cold)

68. Introducing my faithful companion, 'Mavis'!

69. Relative chaos resulted when converting my tiny tent into a workshop to modify my binding – everything had its place 99 per cent of the time. Promise!

70. An area of recent activity, evidenced by the angularity of the uplifted ice with no wind-driven snow yet filling in the cracks or accumulating on the lee sides. The layering of the thicker ice reveals phases of freezing

71. Not what you like to discover ahead coming up over a ridge!

72. In the final third of the journey, clean multiple fractures of younger, larger, flatter ice-floes were routine, but a crossing point on foot was rarely far away

73. Self-portrait, Day 20

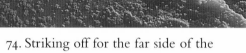

74. Striking off for the far side of the lead, 'icebreaking' through the 'dark *nilas*'

75. 'Mr Orange' – my immersion suit in all its glory

76. Envisaging this scene changed my whole approach to thin ice

77. Self-portrait, Day 60

78/79/80/81. Breaking up an ever wider area of ice in search of the lost ski involved all manner of manoeuvres

82. My original ski tracks heading north on the 'light *nilas*' of the refrozen lead before the incident . . . and the booted tracks heading back after a narrow escape (minus one ski)

83. The penultimate reading – logged at 09.54 GMT on 19 May. Within seconds I had drifted onto the Pole at 90° North. My embroidered family crest is visible on the sledge

84. The ninth, and final, day waiting in the tent for the pick-up plane

85. First came thoughts of Dad – my vow fulfilled
86. Then the feeling of 'utter, utter relief'
87. And suddenly the unexpected realisation '. . . at last, I was free'

88. This is the scene of 'my North Pole' – taken the day I was finally picked up by aircraft – a large, seemingly flat pan with pressure ridging all around its perimeter

89. All four pilots busy de-icing the wings of their Twin Otters at Eureka

90. Arriving safely back in Britain – and re-united at last with Mary, Freya and Wilf

91. 'The last place on earth' – the Arctic Ocean

on to Swerves with some spare wire and hurried back to my sledge to resume the northward journey.

As if to compensate for such minor irritations, I had a magic moment as I took my regular nosebag break at the end of that sledge-hauling session. I was sitting on the back-end of my sledge, keeping my back to the breeze as I warmed my face in the sun, when I sensed as much as saw the faintest disturbance, a fluttering in the air. I looked around slowly and could not believe my eyes. A snow bunting, a bird no bigger than a sparrow, but with more white plumage, had landed on my camera on top of the sledge. It must have got lost on migration and strayed hundreds of miles off course, before spotting this unusual surface feature – perhaps an inhabited island. Now it was taking in the scene, showing no fear whatsoever, its bright eyes fixed on me. It was a beautiful, almost spiritual moment: a brief encounter between two lonely, stressed-out travellers in the middle of this vast empty ocean of ice. It stayed there for only a minute or so, and then took off. It circled overhead as if getting its bearings and then flew southwards, disappearing almost at once into the glare of the sun. I felt a sense of loss but wished it well on its own long journey, as I stood up and prepared to resume mine.

The sun was now relatively high in the sky both by day and night, giving a stark light that wiped out the pastel tones of the ice-scape, replacing them with a harsh, unyielding white glare that forced me to wear sunglasses all the time and made photography a nightmare. If I took my sunglasses off even for a few moments, I simply couldn't look at the snow – its brilliance was too dazzling.

Towards the end of the day, I came to a huge frozen lead, so vast that I could not see the other side. It had obviously been open water a few days before – perhaps the source of one of the fog-banks that had rolled over me – but now the surface was smooth, bare ice. It made for very fast travel, but it was less than ideal as a campsite, because no snow had accumulated on it, and there was nowhere to anchor the tent if the wind got up, nor any snow to melt for drinking water. I was resigned to carrying on until I reached the far side, at least another hour's travel away, when I came to a small area of disturbance in the middle of the lead where there were a few small plates of ice and a tiny patch of snow, barely enough to anchor my tent. As I wrote in my log that night, 'If I sneezed it would fall down!' By the time I had scooped up enough snow for water, there was none left to weigh down the outer valances. Luckily there was no wind and very stable weather conditions, so I was not that worried about waking up to find my tent on its way back to Ward Hunt Island.

By contrast with the near-euphoria of the previous day, Day 43 was a day to be endured. I had stopped walking at one in the morning and didn't close my eyes until 3 a.m. Then I couldn't get to sleep, tossing and turning for another couple of hours, and, as a result, I slept until three in the afternoon – absolutely hopeless time keeping. I then had a bad phone call with Ian, who told me that some press information had been sent out without first having gone through the agreed protocols with our various media partners. As a result, I thought that they were about to be scooped by their rivals and I was beside myself with anger, and working myself up into an ever more towering rage as I came off the frozen lead into a huge rubble-field on the far side, where I encountered some of the worst pressure-ridging of the whole journey. It felt like a succession of Great Walls of China, some with only metres between them.

As had happened before when I was in a filthy mood, I then gorged myself on my sledging rations and had eaten the entire day's nosebag and two-thirds of a spare bag of chocolates by the end of the second break. This compounded my problems and made me even more furious. However, I then got back in control of my temper and myself, struggled through the rest of the bad ice and had a flying finish to the day, on a series of big flat pans of ice, making up much of the time I had lost. Despite the obstacles, I had still covered ten miles in ten hours, and had crossed the eighty-seventh parallel just before I stopped for the night. There were now only 180 miles to go. I checked my main meal stocks that evening, and discovered that, at current rates of consumption, I still had thirty-two days' supply of fuel and twenty-three days of food – 2.5 servings of cod in sour cream and potato, 6.5 of beef stew and potato and 14 of chicken curry and rice (my favourite, that I tended to save till last, when I would appreciate a little extra boost).

I had recently been planning for a worst-case scenario of reaching the Pole on Day 65, but aiming for Day 57, and so had just the right amount for that; but there was the possibility of increasing my food intake and getting there faster by further extending the duration of my sledging days with the extra food. Should I do that, or keep the food in reserve, just in case conditions deteriorated, and accept that I would be moving a little slower and taking a little longer to reach my goal? I was accelerating as planned and, always subject to the constraints of weather and ice conditions, I now estimated my fastest time to the Pole as fourteen days. Still breaking the journey into smaller, bite-size portions, I was hoping to cover the sixty-mile sections between the remaining degrees of latitude in progress- ively shorter times. I had taken six days to reach 87°N, I estimated it would take another five to 88°N, five again to 89°N and a final four-day dash to the Pole. Part of me wanted to go for broke, capitalising on the good ice and good weather by moving forward as fast as possible, but I had spent enough time in the Arctic to know that ice and weather could change with bewildering rapidity, and that a conservative strategy was always the safest, if not the quickest way to achieve my goals. In the end I arrived at a typically British compromise, 'borrowing' a proportion, but not all of the potentially spare rations, to fuel a charge to the Pole while the weather and ice remained in my favour.

During a call to Ian back at base that morning, he had

suddenly told me that Wilf wanted a word with me. Wilf had been great for the first few weeks that I was away, but he'd begun doing mornings at primary school, and I felt it was really bad not to have been there for him at the start of his school life. I'd wanted to tell him how proud I was of him, so I'd left a voice-mail message for him a couple of days before. That may have been a mistake – perhaps it rekindled all the thoughts and memories he had been suppressing – and now he wanted to talk to his Dad. Given the opportunity like that, I didn't think too hard about it, I just said 'Yes, I'd love to.' If that was what my boy needed then I was going to speak to him straightaway. It would have been a lot better to have waited a few minutes and thought about all the things that I wanted to say, so that I could control the conversation rather than being reactive to Wilf, but I didn't and the conversation did not go very well. I had been away for a long time now. Of course I had been away for a long time before, but he had been very small then. Now he was going to primary school and Freya was no longer a baby but a little girl in her own right. Mary was working really hard coping with the house and the children and their school life, looking after the horse and still running a business to try and make some money for us. It was an impossible workload. Wilf found himself often looking for his Mum, just for someone to chat to or mess about with, but when time was available Freya also needed attention. The result was that he was not able to have all the parental attention he deserved. That was distressing for everybody and I felt very bad about it. He had really tried to be so self-controlled, sensible and mature about everything but he was only a little boy.

I told him, 'I'm missing you so much, Wilf, but I'm trying not to be too sad, because I know that there's only another three or four weeks, then I'll be coming home to give you the biggest hug in the world. That isn't too long to wait, is it?'

I heard his brave little voice saying, 'No, Daddy,' but I knew that he was thinking it was an eternity.

278

The call ended with both of us sad and upset. I couldn't give Wilf the news that he wanted: that his Dad was on his way home there and then, and I found it very unsettling, because it got me thinking about all sorts of things that I couldn't do anything about; I was also a bit cross with myself for having taken the easy quick fix of talking to Wilf, without thinking it through first.

Perhaps spurred by the need to get back to my family as fast as humanly possible, I posted another personal best on Day 44, 14.6 miles in ten and a half hours, the equivalent of almost a quarter of a degree of latitude in a single day. I achieved that despite having to repair the basket on Swerves again, use a compass for navigation for part of the day when the sun was hidden by cloud, and cope with another upsurge in ice activity. That was really motoring and it felt like the Pole was rushing to meet me. Tomorrow was looking as if it was going to be a monster fifteen-miler.

When I came out of my tent in the morning, I saw that the tides had torn the ice-sheet behind me apart, leaving a broad lead, with steep, sheer banks of ice on either side. At the temperatures now ruling, −19 °C and still rising, the lead would refreeze only very slowly, if at all. I'd been posting personal bests on four of the previous five days, building up from 10.9 nautical miles on Day 40 to 14.4 on Day 44 and today, Day 45, I was ready to crack the fifteen nautical mile barrier. These were big mileages that would normally be achieved only in the final push to the Pole. To be doing it three-quarters of the way through the expedition was really exceptional. I was feeling on top of my game and sure that I would reach the Pole in under sixty days – a good time even for a resupplied expedition.

On almost every previous day the sun had been visible – sometimes behind a veil of mist, fog or high cloud, but for the most part shining from clear blue skies, allowing excellent visibility and accurate solar navigation, and it was now sufficiently high in the sky that there was no dusk as the day progressed. The sun just rolled around the sky, staying above the horizon all day and all night, though temperatures still dropped about 10 °C during the 'night'. Day 45 was the first completely cloudy day since I'd left Ward Hunt Island, and the dense overcast made it quite dark. Perhaps that affected my mood; I quickened my pace still more, as if fearing that some dark force might be overhauling me. I'd already been looking ahead to reaching the last degree of latitude, and comforting myself with the thought that I had done that last degree so many times with clients that the conditions I would encounter should hold few surprises for me, but the other thoughts occupying my mind that morning were much less constructive.

I was becoming increasingly preoccupied and concerned by the nature of the media coverage that the expedition was being given. It was absurd; I obviously wasn't getting the papers delivered to my tent every morning, and so I had no real idea of what was being written. But perhaps that was the problem, because I'd got it into my head that no one was really able to understand what I was thinking, feeling or doing, and that through my own tiredness and inattention I was making the situation worse rather than better. Was I, through my own ill-chosen words, bringing down the monument I was trying so hard to erect in my father's memory? I felt like a ladybird scuttling across a huge white tablecloth, being peered at through a magnifying glass by someone who was trying to count the spots on my back, while all I was concerned about was if I could make it to the other side of the table before events overtook me. The one benefit of this mounting paranoia was that it served as a potent motivating factor, and I was using it to push harder and harder. If I could do fifteen nautical miles every day from now on, I would reach the Pole in just two weeks. I even wrote in my journal: 'Just fourteen days to go.' But just getting to the Pole wasn't enough. I desperately wanted to succeed, but how and how fast I got there were just as important, as if I had to demonstrate, both to my father and the world at large, that I hadn't just got lucky with the ice and weather conditions; I really had mastered my craft.

Late that afternoon I was skiing along under the overcast skies, making really good progress, when I came across a series of refrozen leads, each about 100 metres across and stretching out of sight to the east and the west. All had probably opened on the same day, and refrozen to the same degree in the relatively warm temperature of about −15° to −20 °C. The overcast skies meant that the coloration of the ice was slightly different from previous days, conveying a meaning that I had to be careful to interpret correctly. On a bright day, an expanse of freshly set ice might look pale-brown, suggesting it could be crossed in safety. In lower light levels, the same ice might look dark-brown, suggesting danger. Indeed, as the surface lost its sparkle with the disappearance of the sun, it took on a much more sombre and brooding air. I had to readjust my senses to accommodate the changed situation but, tired and preoccupied by my obsession with the way the expedition was being reported, I was heading for a fall.

I always divided thin ice into three categories: marginal-good, marginal and marginal-bad, and I had decided at the start of the expedition that, for safety reasons, I wasn't going to be crossing any marginal or marginal-bad ice. On previous expeditions, I'd undo the leather toe-straps on my skis before crossing marginal ice, so that if I fell through the ice I could kick off my skis and swim to safety. To start undoing my toe-straps on this expedition would therefore be a clear indication that I was ignoring my previous resolution.

Up to now, every single time I had been about to cross thin ice, I had only to think of a three-second mental video clip of Wilf in his shorts on a sunny spring evening, picking wild daffodils from the garden to give to his mother, and I would instantly stop, shocked by the awfulness of never reliving that scene. That simple mental technique had prompted me to re-route scores of times when otherwise I might have taken an unnecessary, and potentially fatal, risk.

I crossed the first lead without any problems; I didn't even have to undo my toe-straps. I was dimly aware that I really would not want to face these tracts if they hadn't frozen over completely and I was moving into an area and a time of year where this was going to happen more and more often. These might well be the last few days when temperatures were cold enough to freeze open leads sufficiently for me to cross them. I thought no more about it than that. I crossed a succession of four of these leads in the space of a few hours, and I was into my sixth seventy-five-minute session of sledge-hauling of the day, when I came across yet another lead. I was feeling strong, going well, and was planning to do another one or two extra sessions, pushing me well past the fifteen nautical mile mark for the day.

This lead was wider – about 125 metres – but otherwise it looked no different from the previous four. Before I even set foot on it, I studied it carefully, assessing the general surface texture and colour, and looking for any shimmering of light that might indicate a very thin strip of open water – perhaps as little as a foot wide – in the middle of the lead. Over years of travel across Arctic sea-ice, I'd built up a vast data bank of ice textures, colours and contexts, and I was able to look at this particular refrozen lead and almost intuitively compare it both with those I'd crossed earlier that day and those I'd encountered on previous expeditions. The obvious questions uppermost in my mind were: Is this identical to the leads earlier today? And if it's fractionally more marginal, is it still crossable?

These leads were giant slashes across the Arctic Ocean, like fault lines in a rock formation. They sometimes run for 50 to 100 miles, but I suspect I could have walked around this particular one in no more than three to four hours; that's normally the case this far north, however big they look at the time. Having looked at the lead as a whole, as I moved out onto the refrozen ice I also studied the area directly in front of my skis with great care, scanning the 'ice-flowers' – salt crystals – and the other minute surface features that offer a big clue to the age of the ice, and therefore its thickness and strength. This lead still looked exactly the same as the previous four I'd crossed, but as I approached the middle, I could see there had been some sort of disturbance there.

Judging by its increased opacity and the density of ice-flowers on the surface, the ice on the far side actually looked to be fractionally stronger, but the few metres around the fault-line seemed to be thinner. There were noticeably fewer ice-flowers there and it was darker in colour, always a major clue. Even wearing skis, which spread the load of your body weight, young dark *nilas* isn't safe to cross, but medium to thick light *nilas* is usually passable. I gave it the classic ski-pole test: three hard, well aimed blows into exactly the same spot in the ice. If I could puncture the ice through to the water below on blows one or two, it was too young to bear my weight. If it went through on the third, it was my call, but by any count it was marginal ice. I judged there were perhaps two metres of dodgy, marginal and marginal-bad ice, but it then seemed to be stronger on the other side.

The problem was the fault-line that ran through the middle of this weaker area. It had a slightly crinkled edge, three or four centimetres proud of the ice-surface, suggesting that there had been a little bit of movement and friction between the two sides of the lead as the surrounding ice-pans rocked to and fro. If you have a continuous surface of marginal ice, you can usually get across it but if there is a crack down the middle of it – even if it's only a few centimetres of water or very thin ice separating the two ice-pans – the surface tension is broken. If you then stand near the edge, it can just cave in, dropping you into the water like a trap door. If you bridge the crack by putting your skis on marginal-good ice on each side, you may get across, because your weight is spread along the length of the skis and the weight of the sledge is similarly spread across its runners. But the wider the crack, the more dangerous it becomes because, even on marginal-good ice, there's going to be a degree of flexing as you move from one edge of the ice-pan to the other, and if, as on this occasion, there was marginal-good ice on one side of a crack, and marginal ice on the other, then the odds were moving out of my favour.

Whether through tiredness, inattention or impatience, on this one occasion, for the first time in the whole expedition, the little clip of Wilf picking daffodils didn't pop into my mind. I should have just walked away, saying 'Well, I'm not doing that, I'm off to find a better route. There's always a better way, so stop being idle and keep concentrating.' But I didn't do it and I still can't explain why. Even worse, I actually undid my toe-straps, the reflex action that shows that a part of my mind had accepted that I was probably going to go into the water.

What was I thinking about? I suppose the answer is that I was far more mentally tired by this stage of the expedition than I realised, and I was pushing hard to do another personal best and hit the fifteen nautical mile mark. I was also fired up – illogical though it may have been – by my perception of the way that I was being presented in the press. For all those reasons, for that crucial two minutes out of all the hundreds of hours I had been travelling over the ice, I allowed my obsession with making progress north to overshadow my basic guiding principles.

As I prepared to cross the danger area, I noticed that there was a little platform of thicker ice less than a metre from the edge of the crack. It was about a metre by two metres across, and had obviously been floating around in the open water and had then got locked in to the ice when it refroze. Rather than the four-centimetre thickness of the rest of the lead, this piece looked to be double that. I wanted to be unencumbered and not worried about the sledge snagging behind me at a critical moment, so I parked it on the ice-platform and put my traces on the maximum extension so that I could cross the marginal ice without having to pull the sledge at all. I had to be clear of the bad ice before I hauled the sledge after me, because the action of pulling the sledge would greatly increase the loading on the ice at my feet. I tested the ice by putting a bit of my weight on it, releasing it and applying it again, then, completely absorbed in the fine detail of this crossing, I moved my right ski tip up and over the crack, keeping my left one back so that most of my weight was on it. So far so good. I pushed my right ski a little further forward, until it was straddling the crack and moving onto the better ice beyond it. Things still seemed to be OK, even though the ice was bending slightly. I could feel it going downwards, flexing where the surface tension was broken at the two edges. Even now, alarm bells should have been ringing deafeningly loud and it still wasn't too late to pull back, but I was so deep 'in the moment' that someone could have been shouting to go back from the other side and I probably would have been unaware of it.

My right ski was fully on the marginal ice, and I now slid my left ski forward. I was committed, but I knew at once that I'd made a big mistake – possibly the last one that I would ever make. My first instinct was: 'Right, ski on. Don't wait around. Go, go, go!' If I could keep moving, continually shifting the load on to new ice, I might be all right, but within a split-second of having crossed onto the marginal ice, I knew I was in deep trouble. It wasn't the trapdoor effect that I'd certainly have had if I'd been walking rather than skiing across, but I could feel my rear ski sinking inexorably downwards. Everything went into slow motion. I tried to ski forward for another couple of strides and then realised that I wasn't going to make it. At once I veered hard left, trying to get the ski back onto the more solid ice. But as I skied in a very hard tight circle, I was already sinking faster and faster. The ice didn't disintegrate at first; it just bent down, down and down; then finally it broke. My ski tips were still proud of the ice but behind me it had broken up. I sank up to my knees, up to my waist and then the ice gave way underneath me completely and I was plunged up to my neck in the icy water.

The first thing I felt was shock, not at the cold – my multiple layers of clothing gave me enough temporary insulation to prevent that – but that I could have let myself get into this situation. The next thought, following hard on its heels, was to leave the inquests for later and give my total and absolute focus to getting out of the water, back on to firm ice. I didn't really panic, I'm not someone who's prone to it anyway, which is just as well because panicking when completely alone and up to your neck in the freezing waters of the Arctic Ocean is not a constructive exercise. Shouting for help was hardly going to be of any use either, so I just channelled everything – my whole physical and mental being – into survival.

Over the next ten or fifteen seconds, the water seeped through my clothing to my skin, but even then it didn't feel heart-stoppingly cold, partly perhaps because I was so focused on other things – saving my life for one – that the sensation of cold just didn't register as a priority. Submerged to my armpits, I went into front crawl motion, thrashing my arms down ahead of me to break through the thinner ice, while I kicked with my legs as hard as I could – no easy feat wearing skis – trying to create some propulsion. It's almost impossible to find enough purchase on the ice to haul yourself out when you're hanging vertically in the water, so you've got to get your body horizontal on the surface, and then generate some forward momentum to help reduce the load on the surface of the ice as you drag yourself out.

I made a few attempts to get out, but each time the ice crumbled beneath me. It was like a flashback to the time I'd fallen in on my first expedition to the Pole, when the ice kept breaking as I'd tried to drag myself out. The same thing was happening again. How many mistakes was I going to be allowed to make? That question was running in parallel with other, less philosophical thoughts, and I remember thinking that it was down to me and me alone to give the answer. What I did in the next two minutes would decide my fate. I hauled myself up and the ice broke, plunging me back into the water. I hauled myself up and it broke once more. Then a curiously detached, but helpful thought burst into my head, a lesson I had drawn from previous near-drownings: keep aware of your surroundings, look for options, don't focus on just one route, it may not be the one that can get you out. Slowing down and taking stock even for half a second was the last thing I felt like doing, but I just managed to whip my head around each way to see if I could take in any useful information. And for the first time

I saw my sledge and remembered that I had positioned it on that little platform of thicker ice.

I changed direction, swimming towards the platform, smashing the thinner ice before me like an icebreaker. But my water-logged boots and salopettes, and the layers of saturated clothing, made the effort of kicking my legs so incredibly draining that almost at once I felt so exhausted that I was forced to slow down. The overriding feeling was still not the cold, but the heaviness of my legs. I felt that my muscles just could not continue at that pace.

It was a frightening feeling, but I took a breather, a little rest just hanging off the edge of the ice for a few seconds to gather my thoughts, and then had another go. I didn't allow myself to accept even as a possibility that I wouldn't be able to get onto the ice, that what I was doing wasn't going to work. I was determined to get out – how I did it didn't matter – but I was going to get out. As I drove myself forward again, everything seemed to go into slow motion. I was hyper-aware of every tiny detail and sensation, scanning the ice in front of me for crenellations, lumps or bumps on the ice that might give my clumsy, frozen hands enough purchase to haul myself out. I worked my way left, towards the platform, its upper surface pocked with lumps and small hollows in the ice, and powered myself up onto it, kicking with all the remaining strength in my legs while my hands groped at the ice, searching for grip. One hand caught at a projection, then the other and the next moment I was inching my way up onto the ice next to my sledge and out of the water.

For a moment I lay prone across the ice with my feet still dangling in the water. I felt a huge wave of relief, tinged with the continued shock that I'd got myself into this dire situation. Then I noticed that I was only wearing one ski. The left one had fallen off as I struggled in the water. At one level, there was no cause for concern – that was the whole plan, that's why I loosened the toe straps in the first place, so that I'd be able to kick it off as I thrashed around in the water – but if I couldn't find it, I had a major problem on my hands.

I knelt on the ice and scanned the jumble of broken ice and mushy, part-frozen sea-water around me. The ski was nowhere to be seen but I assumed that it would be floating just under the surface somewhere. I knew that I was going to have to search for it at once, and that I was going to have to go back into the water to do it. If I couldn't see the ski, there was no way I was going to be able to use a bit of kit from my sledge to locate it and pull it out. So within no more than a minute of getting myself out of the water, I was rummaging around in the sledge for my immersion suit. I got straight into it, still wearing my saturated clothes, because I knew that it was vital to begin the search at once. I was on a fault-line in the ice and movement would often take place there. If I put up the tent, had some food and water and a night's rest, by the time I came back out in the morning it was quite possible that movements of the ice would have carried the ski half a mile away from me, never to be found again. I was soaking wet but, at this point, only my hands felt really cold and I was confident that I had a little more time before frostbite began to set in. I lowered myself back into the water in my immersion suit and began a search. It was no easy task. I was searching as much by touch as by sight among pieces of broken ice suspended in a morass of semi-frozen mush the colour and opacity of wallpaper paste. I tried to work in a systematic way, moving backwards and forwards in the area of broken ice, a few metres square, but I could find no trace of the ski. I was now growing increasingly concerned. I could have carried on searching but I knew in my heart that it wasn't there. By now, after twenty minutes in the water, my hands and fingers were getting really cold, and, despite my exertions, I wasn't generating enough body-heat to stave off the risk of frostbite. I hadn't found the ski but I had made a thorough search of the obvious area and now I had to start looking after myself. If I developed frostbite, my worries about the fate of the ski and the expedition would be trivial in comparison.

I dragged myself out of the water and, still wearing the immersion suit, I tied the single rope trace around my waist and hauled the sledge back in the direction I had come from less than an hour before. I kept about a metre away from my ski tracks because the ice had already been loaded with my weight on the way in and I had no desire to risk another plunge into the water by applying my weight to the same piece of only marginal-good ice, particularly as I was now only on one ski and applying much greater weight per square inch than when I had been on two. I moved quickly so that I wasn't standing on the same piece of ice for any length of time, and shuffled rather than walked, like a decrepit old man.

I didn't allow myself to wallow in my predicament and kept my thoughts firmly on each step I now had to take, as if this was just another routine stop for the night at the end of a sledging day. I remembered an area of firm, level snow where I'd come down from the ice-pan onto the frozen lead, and, as I approached it, I rehearsed in my mind the sequence of actions I had to take. I pulled the sledge up over the bank onto the thick ice, an old pan probably around four metres thick, then unhitched the sledge, took off the immersion suit because I couldn't work wearing it, and exchanged my wet mitts for dry ones. Then I began erecting the tent as fast as I could, without even bothering to fill the snow valances. I didn't do it in record time – you can never work as fast as you really want when you're shivering and your fingers are numb with cold – but I kept focused on the immediate task in hand, deliberately pushing aside worries about my situation and whether my fingers were going to get frostbitten.

As soon as the tent was up, I unrolled my sleeping-bag onto the snow next to the sledge and loaded it with the routine night-time kit – stove, fuel, food – plus the additional things I needed in this situation: dry clothes. I didn't carry many spares but I had some thermal trousers that I'd been using as pyjamas and my much cut-down mammoth smock. I added them to the pile of things on my sleeping-bag and then dragged it into the tent. I folded the sleeping-bag over so that it was sandwiched inside the waterproof sleeping-mat. I could then kneel on that without any moisture seeping into the bag. I sorted out my kit, put snow in the saucepan to melt for drinks and food and even took my clothes off before lighting the stove. I was always very fuel-conscious and, although I was cold, I didn't think I was in a critical condition and I wanted the discipline of going through all the usual evening procedures. The more normal the routine, the more confidence-building that was for me, and I was trying to instil the belief in myself that falling into the water and losing the ski were not going to have a disastrous impact on my progress to the Pole.

I fumbled with my matches, my numbed fingers struggling to hold them firm enough to strike a light, and eventually I managed to light the stove. Then I changed into my dry clothes and got into my sleeping-bag, made myself a cup of tea and some hot food. I had time to gather my thoughts while I was having my brew and I then called my base manager, Ian Wesley, on the satellite phone and gave him the full story, not least because he would often come back with some useful comments or ideas that might not have occurred to me. 'Ian, my friend,' I said, 'I'm really sorry to wake you up in the middle of your night, but there's been a development' – the phrase I always used when relaying problems. 'Everything's fine now, but I wanted to put you in the picture.'

When I'd finished explaining what had happened, his first reaction was that it was very important that I made a second search for the ski, if only so that I would know, as I foot-slogged my way north for the rest of the expedition, that I had done my level best to find it and that there had been no possibility of recovering it. He pointed out how awful it would be to have the nagging thought in my mind that I was having to walk the whole way to the Pole simply because I'd not bothered to make the extra effort to find the ski. He didn't have to argue hard to convince me; I could see at once that he was right.

Before I settled down to sleep, I wrung as much water as I could out of my sodden salopettes, smock, socks and boot-liners, and put them into a spare plastic sack. They would freeze overnight and I wasn't looking forward to getting back into some of them in the morning, but it would have to be done. I had the spare dry socks and boot-liners that I'd used earlier in the expedition, but they were pretty worn – there were giant holes in the heels of the socks and, having already been worn for thirty-odd days before I switched to the other pair, they were extremely crusty as well, but they'd have to do; I had no others.

As I closed my eyes, I thought through the impact that the loss of the ski might have on my progress, if I couldn't find it. That morning, Day 45, I had been convinced that I would be able to do twelve to fifteen nautical miles a day and reach the Pole in fifty-nine days. Now all bets were off, and I had no clear idea of how long it was going to take. It was unsettling and unnerving to wonder what impact it was going to have on my speed. I had been pacing myself, increasing the effort with the finishing post in sight, and now the line was being moved back again out of sight. In certain conditions I might even be able to walk faster without skis, but the odds were against that for most of the journey ahead. It was far more likely that I would be slowed down, perhaps by a little, perhaps by a lot. My best guesstimate was that walking rather than skiing would probably add as much as 20 to 30 per cent to the time it would take.

In the back of my mind, there was now the dark possibility that I might even need a resupply, even though, in my eyes at least, the expedition would be tainted and corrupted by it. I was certainly going to do my best to carry on without skis, but there was a possibility that they might be essential to reach the

Pole at all. The sky was now overcast, the temperatures were rising and if snow started to fall, I would experience more and more difficulty in making northward progress.

Even without a new snowfall, I was very unlikely to get a firm, hard-packed surface all the way to the Pole. The snow and ice had started to decay as the temperature rose, and though it still looked as hard as cement, its structure was weakening. With no skis to spread the load of my weight, I was at ever greater risk of breaking through the crust as I walked. I might just break through an inch or I might sink up to my knees at every step, greatly increasing the effort levels and decreasing the speed I could achieve. I was hoping that I was going to be no more than 20 or 30 per cent slower – an extra five days – but the only way to find out was to do it.

I was very determined, if at all possible, not to allow the loss of the ski to impact on the expedition. I was going to be the master of the situation rather than its victim. By continuing to post big mileages in the succeeding days, I wanted to reassure everyone – my family, my base team, my sponsor, my suppliers and the thousands of visitors to the website, as well as myself – that I wasn't just going to stumble my way to the Pole. Instead, the message would go out loud and clear: 'The expedition is still in hand and will continue to the planned schedule.'

Despite all my troubling thoughts, I slept pretty well and woke on Day 46, Thursday 1 May, full of resolve to get the expedition back on track. I ate breakfast and then gave myself a bit of extra chocolate as I often did before I used the immersion suit, partly to sugar the pill of having to do so, but it also served a practical purpose in putting a bit of sugar into me for all the hard work I'd have to do swimming around in the suit for anything up to an hour. The suit was frozen on the inside because I'd got into it in my wet clothing yesterday, and I turned it inside-out and hung it up to dry in the sunlight. Even though it was −20° or so, the thin covering of ice dispersed quite quickly and I was able to brush out the remaining ice that had collected in the seams. But still I dawdled over beginning the search, partly because I was dreading the likely result and partly because I was never happy using the immersion suit, perhaps because its bulk and awkwardness, not to mention its potential for turning turtle in the water, gave me a feeling of not being in complete control.

Finally I'd run out of reasons to delay. There was no point in putting on my wet smock and salopettes – it would just have made me very cold and miserable, since I was not going to be generating much heat doing this search. I climbed into the immersion suit wearing my pyjamas – my thermal trousers and my mammoth smock – my newly darned dry socks, and my dry gloves and mitts. I positioned my sledge at the edge of the lead as a sort of emergency life-raft, and tried to set up the video to film myself, the first time I'd done so for a while. I spent a long time explaining my predicament for the benefit of posterity, but I later discovered that I'd forgotten to turn on the sound, so only trained lip-readers would find watching it an enlightening experience. Having set up the camera for the action sequences, I then lowered myself into the water. I didn't have to break up much ice; it was only semi-frozen because the overcast conditions during the night had kept the tempera-ture to no lower than about −15 °C. I completed a search of the open water without finding the ski and then decided to break up the thinner ice on the edge to increase the diameter of the search area. I succeeded in moving the edge back by about two metres in all directions but there was still no sign of the ski. Next I hung from the edge of the ice-sheet with my hands and slid most of my body under the ice, until I was right up to my armpits with the waterline just below my mouth. I stretched my feet out against the underside of the ice, reaching as far as I could – about a metre and a half from the edge, and then raked my feet back towards me, trying to drag anything lodged under the ice towards me, but though I worked my way right around the edge of the open area, I still didn't find the ski. I worked my way back, smashing up another two-metre-wide strip of ice and then repeated the search with my feet under the remaining ice, but still found nothing. The writing on the wall could no longer be ignored; I wasn't going to find the ski.

I decided to keep my other ski, even though it broke the absolute rule I'd set: if something was no longer going to help me get to the Pole it had to be jettisoned. I'd been ruthless about that up to now, but I couldn't bring myself to part with my ski. We'd been through a lot together and I felt it was a memento that I'd want to have. It was deadweight – around two kilos – but the sledge was getting lighter and I did find a use for it as a stake for the upwind guy-rope on my tent, maybe the heaviest tent-peg in history.

I trudged back to the tent wondering how things were going to pan out from now on, but constantly telling myself that it was all going to be OK for the remainder of the journey, just a bit harder than I'd expected. Back at home I often used to say to myself, 'A day without a challenge is a day incomplete.' Well, today's challenge was to override the negative impact of foot travel and keep to my current schedule. If that meant harder days or longer days or both, so be it. I steeled myself to get into my frozen, sodden salopettes and smock, put my dry clothes away and broke camp as fast as possible, keen to get moving north again both to generate some heat to dry my clothes and to put the scene of my near-disaster behind me. However, first I had to cross that wretched lead. I sledged east for around twenty minutes but there was no evidence of the ice improving, and I decided to cross the lead there and then. I put my immersion suit on again and very cautiously shuffled out across the ice, testing its strength by my weight. Now I wasn't wearing skis, the load I was exerting per square foot of the ice had greatly increased. But even at the crack in the middle it didn't give beneath my weight. Either all it had taken was another night's sub-zero temperatures to freeze the ice a little more, or I had picked an area where the ice was already fractionally thicker and more opaque. I spent a few more minutes trying to find exactly the best route across and then I made it to the far side without any serious alarms. I hauled the sledge across after me, then took off my immersion suit and headed on to the north. I was at last beyond that wretched lead and on my way again, resolved that, from now on, I would be taking no unquantifiable risks. One soaking in the Arctic Ocean was enough.

12

I set off at about five o'clock in the afternoon. It was well after my normal starting time but since there was now bright daylight twenty-four hours a day, it was of no other consequence. I kept a close watch on my progress throughout that day, taking a reading from the GPS at each break. I did 1.3 nautical miles in the first session, 1.9 in the second and 1.7 in the third. It was an even better average speed than I had been doing on skis over the previous few days, and it was a great relief. Just as I was starting to relax and enjoy myself, I came to a rent in the ice-surface, exposing swirling, dangerous waters below and instantly I was back on full alert. It looked narrow enough for me to jump over comfortably, but the banks of ice on either side were sheer and steep. If I fell in, I wouldn't be able to get out again, because I wouldn't be able to reach up high enough from the water level to pull myself out. It was too wide and too deep to use my sledge as a bridge, so the choice was either to jump it or spend precious time trying to find a way around it – and I suspected I'd face a long detour before I found a narrowing or closure. I deliberated for a few moments, thinking about all the other cracks I'd be encountering with ever greater frequency, and decided that the time had come to change up a gear and go for it, but this time I would check every facet before committing myself.

I first measured the gap. It was exactly the length of my ski-pole so I laid it on the ice nearby and did a test jump over it. I cleared it with a good half metre to spare, but it was one thing to be doing that on solid ice and quite another leaping from one ice-floe to another with a strip of icy, ink-black water awaiting me if I slipped. I checked that the ice was not going to crack and break as I jumped and spent some time preparing my take-off point, packing the snow down by stamping it with my feet. I also tried to build in some capability for self-rescue. I adjusted my sledge-trace to its maximum length and pushed the sledge right up to the edge of the ice so that if I did fall in, I could pull it in after me and clamber onto it as a sort of life-raft. Then I walked back to the end of my run-up, psyched myself up, took a big, deep breath, sprinted down the runway, took off and cleared it with ease. I hauled the sledge across after me and was on my way north again within five minutes of first sighting the lead. There were several more in the course of the day – there were fresh cracks and water all over the place, like crazy paving – but I cleared each one in the same manner and by the end of that first day on foot, a short one because of the late start after the fruitless search for the ski, I had covered 5.4 miles. With 264 miles behind me and only 152 miles to go, if I carried on at that rate I would actually finish in 60 days.

Some hope. The next day, Day 47, was extremely taxing. The ice was rumbling all day – the usual sign of the spring break-up – and though I set off in sunshine, within an hour or two it clouded over and then began to snow. It carried on all day, producing a near-total white-out and, without my skis, I was struggling to make headway in the soft, newly fallen snow; there was much stumbling into snowdrifts and falling into small fissures. Even worse, I was now well into the region of negative drift – the escalator was moving steadily southwards as I attempted to go north. I finished the day walking through extremely broken ice and had to keep on walking longer than I wanted to before I could find a suitable place to pitch my tent for the night. Not exactly a perfect day – no sun, poor visibility, loose snow and negative drift were far from an ideal combination – but, in the circumstances, eight miles in ten hours was not bad going.

I slept badly that night, for no more than four or five hours, leaving me feeling weary the next day. When I awoke on Day 48, it was still snowing and once more, it carried on doing so all day. Visibility was barely fifty metres and forty-eight hours of continuous snowfall, albeit fairly light, left a mantle of snow averaging about ten centimetres thick, but three times that in hollows, holes and fissures. I needed some wind to really blow the snow about, break up the crystals and pack them down tight to form a dense, hard-packed surface. In the absence of that, it was horrible going underfoot; Sod's Law, just when skis would have been really useful, I couldn't use them. The snow shrouded every surface feature: thin ice, cracks, gaps between the rubble and even sheltered water – snow will settle on open water because it's below zero, so you can be walking along thinking you're on snow and find yourself far out on open water. It made heading north a hesitant, staccato process as I was probing in front of me with a ski-stick as I walked. The sledge had to be dragged through snow as cloying and glutinous as my breakfast porridge, and the snow stuck to my boots and then melted, soaking them through and adding greatly to their weight. Every footstep I took, I sank into the snow to a different depth, sometimes only an inch or two, but sometimes floundering deep in drifts of snow as fine and soft as talc.

In lightly rubbled areas, I'd often stumble, try to break my fall as best I could, and then immediately restore my forward momentum by crawling across the awkward surface and then flicking a ski-pole into firm ice to lever myself up and onward. The thing was not to collapse, stop, think about the fall, and restart, but push away any thoughts of the hopelessness and frustration of the situation and relentlessly head north. Once or twice I did just lie in the snow, spread-eagled after a fall, but it was with a smile on my face, relaxing, because I knew it didn't have me beaten. I needed that feeling because often the top layer had melted and then frozen again, leaving a brittle crust over a hugely variable layer of soft snow, and this surface was the hardest to bear because it was so unpredictable: one moment a gentle drop of a few centimetres, the next footfall perhaps twenty, then no drop at all, then thirty centimetres, and so it went on until the inevitable sudden, jarring descent into a deep, snow-filled fissure. As I wrote in my log that night, "Travelling by foot, as opposed to ski, offers few pleasures." But once more, nine miles in eight hours was better than I had feared, especially given another day of negative drift. I was still knocking out good distances in the course of a day, but it was far more tiring without skis and to keep doing so was purely a question of mind over matter.

On Day 49 the sun was shining first thing, but during my morning call to Ian he warned me of a developing depression, with gale-force winds and ground-storms forecast. He'd looked at the weather maps and seen densely compressed isobars slowly tracking in my direction. Sure enough, it soon clouded over and the winds began building from the north-east, veering east-north-east – the beginning of the wild weather that Ian had promised. Under the influence of the winds, there was heavy drifting of the loose snow, but I managed nine nautical miles in the course of the day – reasonable progress, but below the 10.7 I needed to average if I was to reach the Pole inside sixty days. I also soaked my foot in a patch of mushy ice, a scary moment for me because I had no dry pair of boots to change into. I had saturated my other pair in the wet snow of a couple of days before and there had been no sun since then to dry them out. The one positive factor was that by the end of the day I had moved out of the area of heavy localised snowfall and was finding the conditions underfoot much improved, but the winds were still building and I fell asleep that night to the sound of the tent fabric drumming as the gale shook it.

As soon as I opened my eyes the next morning, I knew that I would not be going anywhere that day. The wind was shrieking around the tent, blowing at forty knots with stronger gusts. If

I had any remaining doubts, they were literally blown away when I went outside to check the sledge. An unexpected gust was so strong that I was blown off my feet and had to crawl back to the sanctuary of the tent on my hands and knees with drifting snow, like sand in a desert storm, forcing its way into every crack and crevice, filling the cuffs of my unsecured mitts and penetrating the inside of my smock and the back of my hood. The exposed flesh on my face was stung viciously by the wind-whipped snow particles and, such was the intensity of the ground-storm, it was impossible to keep my eyes open properly and even breathing was uncomfortable.

Instead of heading north, I was forced to lie in the tent all day listening to the storm, while all sorts of thoughts and worries preyed on me. I had just fifteen days of full rations left and was still 125 nautical miles from the Pole. I had to average over seven miles a day to reach the Pole before my food ran out. I could reduce my daily rations and create another three or four days' supplies but if I was going to do that, I had to start now. I was also praying that the storm was not ripping the ice-cap apart, pushing up enormous pressure ridges or creating leads that might not refreeze until the summer was over. I could feel my stomach knotting with the tension. This was my third attempt on the Pole, my target was within my grasp, but was something going to go wrong at the last minute and rob me of success? To complete my black mood, the storm coming out of the east-north-east was pushing me west-south-west; by the day's end I was two nautical miles further from the Pole than I had been twenty-four hours earlier.

Day 51 was even worse. Once more the storm kept me pinned in my tent and the drift cost me another four nautical miles of hard-won progress. The enforced rest was undoubtedly doing me some good but whether it was outweighing the accumulating stress as I saw my remaining rations dwindle still further and the Pole drift ever further out of reach was another question. I had mended everything that there was to mend, written all there was to write, checked all there was to check, and still I had time on my hands, with nothing to do but twiddle my thumbs, brood on things and wait to see what tomorrow would bring. While out sledge-hauling I was continually having to deal with issues, but, stuck in the tent, all I could do was worry about them instead.

All kinds of factors were now conspiring to make what remained of the journey to the Pole really hazardous. Overcast conditions, blizzards and strong winds kicking up the existing snow all made visibility poor, increasing the risk of straying onto bad ice. I was no longer on skis, which had helped to spread the load on marginal ice. The powerful winds were driving the ice before them with potentially disastrous consequences and the spring thaw, now well advanced, was making the entire ice-cap weaker. The thickness of the ice is only one of a number of factors dictating its strength. The cumulative effect of the sun's rays on the surface also produces an effect known as 'candling' whereby the structural strength of the ice is significantly reduced, so that even apparently thick ice can become unsound for travellers. And the worst fear of all was of drifting snow covering expanses of thin ice. There was no way of knowing that until you were committed and then it might be too late. I was faced with the prospect of having to go round a lot more dubious areas of ice, rather than taking straight lines across them as I had been able to do so far, and endlessly putting on Mr Orange in case of a fall through the ice. In the worst case, I would have to walk north wearing the suit, a dismal and dehydrating prospect, like being encased in a bin liner.

Day 52 was another total write-off, the third in a row. The storm continued, if slightly abated from its peak, and ice-drift saw me another 2.3 miles further from the Pole. It would now take a day's hard walking just to get back to where I had been on the eve of the storm. Late in the day, the winds moderated a little more, giving hope that I would be able to resume my interrupted journey the next morning. In the absence of anything better to do, I cleaned out the sledge completely and repacked it so that the heaviest items were in the centre of the sledge and as near the bottom as possible, making it more stable and easier to haul.

I didn't sleep well that night. My worries about the ice conditions when I finally got moving north again were now being reflected in a vivid, recurring nightmare. In the year leading up to my departure for the Pole, I had been having a nightmare about drowning in the Arctic Ocean. Even in my waking hours I had a growing sense that this was going to be how I would die. Now, for the first time on the expedition, the nightmare had returned and my sleep was constantly disrupted by images of myself trapped under the ice or floundering helpless as black, icy water closed over my head. I drifted back into an uneasy, fitful sleep.

I was still tired when I woke – Day 53, Thursday 8 May – but I lay still for a moment listening and then I started to smile. After three days of booming and snapping as the winds tore at it, the tent fabric hung limp and still – the best greeting I could have had from the new day. I hurried through breakfast, eager to be under way once more, and though the overcast skies and snow flurries made it a less than perfect day, I was not going to let that spoil my mood – Freedom! – I was back on the road again. After three days lying motionless in a sleeping-bag, my legs were understandably wobbly to start with, but within a couple of hours I began to hit my stride. With a white-out and light snow falling all day, I had to use the compass for navigation. To my huge relief, the ice did not seem to have been broken up too badly by the storms and conditions underfoot were pretty good all day. The only hold-ups were caused by two massive leads, each extending in a semicircular arc. Unfortunately, I hit both of them almost at the apex of the arc and was then forced to backtrack to get around them, a more attractive, if not quicker, proposition than donning Mr O. As a result, each of them cost me an hour or so in lost time, so the 9.9 nautical miles I covered in twelve hours walking was not too bad a day. Even better, I crossed the eighty-eighth parallel just before camping for the night; just two degrees of latitude to go.

On Day 54 the sun at last began to show itself between the clouds and not even a couple of fog-banks rolling in from the west, suggesting substantial leads of open water in that direction, could dampen my spirits for long. I covered another eleven miles in just short of twelve hours and was delighted with my progress, because, in the course of the day, I'd had to swim two substantial leads, so wide that I could barely make out the bank on the far side. I was getting a bit less apprehensive about swimming in the immersion suit by now, though I was well aware that it was the single most dangerous thing that I did. With the far ice-bank at such a distance from me, there was no question of carrying out a preliminary survey before I set off. I just had to get in the water and go for it, knowing that if I wasn't able to get out on the other side, I'd have to swim all the way back again. There was also the usual range of other dangers to worry about: getting inverted in my suit and not being able to right myself, and being vulnerable to whatever was lurking in the depths of the black waters beneath me – damn Gary and his tales of Greenland sharks!

I also had to cross an area of saturated, rotten ice about half a mile wide, with an upper surface that was flush with the level of the sea-water. It looked heavy and leaden and was so weathered that it had probably formed off the Russian coast several seasons previously and been caught in the ocean's Beaufort Gyral system to the south-west before being spun out here. It was cracked and fissured in all directions and it had soaked up water like blotting paper, sinking lower and lower as it did so until the surface of the ice was at sea level. There was no option but to wear my immersion suit when crossing it as all the dips and depressions were full of sea-water and I could not tell if there was a solid bottom to them or a hole straight through the ice, and the edges were nowhere near as strong as normal ice. If I jumped from, or even just stood on an edge, it could easily have broken off and taken me down into the water with it.

I crossed a narrow peninsula of more solid ice onto this rotten pan and had gone no more than a hundred metres when I saw a myriad glints of water to either side of me. I pressed on ahead and reached the edge to find a broad stretch of open water beyond. I then went right, working my way slowly around the edge of the ice-pan, completely focused on how I would get across. Then suddenly I came across some sledge-tracks and a line of boot-prints in the soft, mushy surface of the ice. I stopped dead, shocked. No one could have been here; I knew that I was the only person in the whole of the western Arctic Ocean this year. Perhaps I was looking at tracks that had somehow survived from last year, but it was wildly implausible that they should have done so, let alone that I should then have stumbled across them. I began looking round for other evidence when the blindingly obvious solution hit me. As a Winnie-the-Pooh fan, I should have recognised the situation at once, for the same thing had happened to that Bear of Very Little Brain during a walk around a spinney near the Hundred Acre Wood. Now it had happened to me as well: I had crossed my own tracks, working my way in a complete circle around the ice-pan.

After a rueful pause for reflection, I retraced my steps to the peninsula of ice that had led me onto this time-wasting ice-pan in the first place, crossed back onto the solid ice and found another way north. There were many more cracks and minor leads and patches of thin ice on my route north and I had to use all sorts of bridging techniques to get across. I couldn't jump many of them and sometimes I slid the sledge forward, walked along the top and stepped off on the other side; sometimes I braced the ski and two ski-poles to the back of the sledge to effectively extend the length of the sledge to make a precarious bridge; sometimes I used Mr Orange; and sometimes I even belly-crawled across thin ice, spreading the weight of my body over as big an area as possible. To help me recover from these exertions I'd now taken to stretching out on my sledge during some of my ten-minute breaks: five minutes to eat and drink and a five-minute catnap. Anyone would think that I was doing a hard day's work . . .

The time I was now having to spend near open water was adding to my anxieties and I made a discovery that evening that greatly increased my paranoia. When I checked my rifle that night I discovered that the barrel and breech mechanism had rusted so badly that it was questionable whether it would fire at all, and even if it did, there was no way that the cartridge would eject – it had rusted to the ejection clamp. The thought of facing an angry bear with at best one shot, and at worst no shots in my locker at all, was scarcely designed to give me untroubled nights.

When I was inside my tent, I normally kept the rifle in its red nylon sack with the butt just inside the tent and the drawstring of the tent entrance drawn tight around it. The trigger, all the other working parts and the barrel were thus outside the tent, protected from windblown snow by the sack and safe from condensation from cooking and my breath inside. Even with this precaution, as the air temperatures rose, condensation from the moist marine air had begun to form on the gun and, once that had happened, it rusted in a remarkably short time. Within two or three days the barrel was no longer gleaming gunmetal, but a dull, rust-coloured mess. I'd been congratulating myself on remembering to bring absolutely everything that I needed for the expedition but it now turned out that I had made one small, but potentially life-threatening omission – a tiny tube of low-temperature gun-oil. I used butter as a substitute – an example of having to be prepared to improvise to deal with a potentially serious problem.

I used my knife and one of my old socks to scrape and rub off as much of the rust as I could from the exterior of the rifle. Then I strung my spare tent poles together to form a cleaning rod and used it to work old rags and then some tissue paper down inside the barrel. Having cleaned it as well as I could, I melted some butter and rubbed it all over the inside and outside of the rifle to try to protect it, but in that marine environment it was always going to be a constant battle to keep it rust-free. I had to keep the gun loaded at all times, but though I began checking the rifle and the bullets twice a day, I began to find that they wouldn't eject properly because they had even rusted into the barrel during the course of the previous twelve hours. Even worse, the gun had also been battered when the sledge overturned on a pressure ridge, and as a result, the stock was damaged across the middle, where it 'broke' open for reloading, causing the barrel to wobble ominously and preventing it from locking securely into place when I snapped the gun shut. So not only did I now have the risk of a round rusting or seizing immovably in the breech, I also had a wobbly barrel that would make accurate shooting difficult, coupled with a locking mechanism so precarious that it might fly open as I fired it. It was so bad that I had to have one hand around the trigger and the other clamped over the top of the barrel just to try and keep it closed. This greatly increased my nervousness because if I did have to fire this gun it would probably do me more damage than the target.

With a few more miles under my belt I began to plan for my arrival at the Pole. I had now reset my goals. The three storm days meant that to reach the Pole in sixty days was no longer possible without pushing to the limit and while I would have given it my best shot if I had been making the decision in isolation, I was also getting input from Ian at base. For safety reasons Ian was urging me not to push too hard just to break a fairly arbitrary time-barrier. As a result, I was planning to ease back a fraction and arrive at the Pole at lunchtime on Sunday

18 May, Day 63, just nine days from now. Despite that level of detailed planning, there was still no complacency on my part. There were still 109 miles to go and I knew that ice and weather might have a few more surprises in store for me.

Day 55 was a very good day – every day in every way, things were getting better. The omens weren't that good when I set off; very light snow was falling, with mid-level cloud overhead, but looking towards the west, where the weather was coming from, I could see what looked like a dense black overcast, promising serious snowfall and probable blizzard conditions. Luckily, it turned out to be a trick of the light, for, as the banks of cloud rolled overhead, they seemed to lighten and the snowfall got no worse. When I'd been tent-bound in the middle of the blizzard, I'd imagined it snowing for hundreds of miles in every direction, blanketing the entire ice-cap but, just like the other phenomena I'd encountered – areas of pressure ridges, rubble-fields, bad ice and open water – the heavy snow proved to be very localised. I'd crossed the region of heavy snowfall and was now moving beyond it. Even better, I passed another significant milestone in the course of the day: the Pole was now less than 100 nautical miles away and, best of all, the snow that had fallen over the previous days had settled and compacted, and instead of sinking into it, I was walking on top of it.

That made the going underfoot the best so far and I was making very good time, scarcely noticing the loss of my skis. I managed eleven nautical miles in fifteen minutes under ten hours; on previous days it had taken twelve hours to cover the same distance. The ice was quite active but quite a lot of the leads were running north–south – my direction of travel, making them easier to avoid. When I did have to cross them, I found that I was having a lucky day; I'd aim for a particular point and more by luck and instinct than judgement, I'd find that I'd got it spot on. To the right and left of me, the lead would widen to open water, but straight ahead it would be narrow enough for me either to stride or jump across, or bridge it with my sledge. My only anxious moment was when I climbed a pressure ridge about two metres high and felt it start to move and sink. I got off again with remarkable speed!

I also had a novel experience after one of my breaks, when I started to feel a pain in my left ankle. I assumed that my sock had slipped down inside my boot and my policy was always that if something was wrong with my feet, to stop and sort it out at once; why incur a blister by waiting until the next scheduled break? I sat on my sledge and took off my boot and socks, but I could find nothing out of the ordinary, so I shrugged my shoulders, put them back on and set off again. The discomfort was still there. I stopped again, and this time I took out the insoles as well, both the thick foam lining and the plastic mesh. Nothing there. I felt around the inside of the boot. Still nothing. This was getting ridiculous. Finally I pulled the bootee apart – it was composed of an inner and outer layer – and out fell a macadamia nut that had been nestling in the innermost layer. It must have fallen down the collar of my smock as I was eating my sledging rations, and by some curious process of osmosis, it had then migrated south under my salopettes through several layers of clothing before burying itself in the interlining between my bootees. Obviously I ate the nut because I'd carried it that far, and I wasn't going to let it get away. The great escape of the macadamia nut was over . . .

I could once more hear the wind howling around the tent and lashing it with particles of drifting snow when I woke on Day 56. It was already blowing at almost twenty knots, and over the course of the day it picked up to over thirty knots. These were big winds, but the air temperature was only −14 °C and, even with the wind-chill, it still felt quite mild, so I decided not to sit out the gale but to press on northwards. I walked all day in a partial white-out due to both the overcast skies and the ground-storm kicking up loose snow from the surface and reducing visibility to 100 metres or so, but the conditions underfoot were still generally good and the winds were steadily backing southerly. That not only gave me some wind assistance as I walked, but also meant that the ice was being pushed in the same direction. For once the escalator was moving my way and at an accelerating speed – I'd even gained 5.6 nautical miles during the night while I was asleep.

I had to cross a series of leads during the course of the day. Most were mere cracks, no more than about two metres wide by 1.5 metres deep, and I bridged them with my sledge and crawled across it to the other side. But in the late afternoon I came to another, much wider lead, perhaps 150 metres across. I didn't want to waste time by walking round it and it appeared to be completely refrozen from side to side – certainly the ice at the near edge felt solid enough – but I couldn't see the state of the ice because the surface was obscured by snow, and, as a precaution, I put on my immersion suit before starting to cross it.

The first half of the lead was reasonably solid ice, but near the middle, where it had recently opened and refrozen, it began to thin and I could feel it flexing and bending beneath me. Once it broke, the surface tension would disappear and it would keep on breaking all the way to the bank fifty metres away. There was no point in backtracking; having come this far I might as well keep going. I went into a fast shuffle – you can't sprint when you're pulling a sledge behind you – and this helped to spread the loading on the ice. I wasn't banging my feet down but sliding them gently and quickly forwards over the ice – the less time spent standing on any one area of ice the better.

It soon became apparent that even this was not going to be enough. I sensed as much as heard the ice begin to give way beneath me. I had fifty metres to go. I didn't want to have to swim the rest of the lead, doing my usual icebreaker routine with my arms, because it was so exhausting, so I kept on shuffling forward faster and faster, trying to keep ahead of the breaking ice even as I was starting to sink through it. At the same time the sledge-trace kept slipping off my waist and down my legs and I was trying to haul it back up, while still pulling on the sledge and shuffling forwards as fast as I could go. By now I'd sunk to my waist but, half-crawling and half-swimming, I broke through the ice for a few metres and then managed to crawl back out by spreading my body horizontally over the unbroken ice in front of me. I cat-crawled forward very gingerly for a few metres, then got to my hands and knees, using my ski-poles to spread the load of my hands on the ice, and covered the last twenty metres that way, moving flat-out, the ice still breaking behind me and the sledge actually in the water. My hood kept falling forward over my eyes and I couldn't see where I was going – I didn't have time to look up and crawl at the same time – so I just kept going as fast as I could until my head smacked into the ice-bank on the far side.

I crawled out and lay there, sick and dizzy, my chest heaving and blood pounding in my ears. That short burst of intense effort had probably taken no more than a minute but my body was thoroughly attuned to the marathon effort of long-distance sledge-hauling not a 100 metre dash, and the swelteringly hot, heavy and clumsy immersion suit made it even worse. I stripped it off and packed it away and to my relief, I encountered no more major leads that day. I stopped after only eight hours and fifteen minutes of sledge-hauling, but helped by my light sledge – now no more than sixty-five kilograms – the good ice and the following wind, I had covered 9.6 miles in that time. Just eighty-eight to go, and all the time I was cooking my supper, resting and sleeping that night, the southerly winds continued to push me northwards towards my goal.

The wind was still shrieking the next morning, Day 57, beating out a relentless rhythm on the taut fabric of the tent.

It sounded terrible but it was sweet music to my ears because the deep anticyclone to the west of me was still keeping the winds southerly. After checking my sledge and casting an eye over the leaden, snow-filled skies, I decided to take a rest day. I'd pushed myself so hard to get this far and now I just thought 'Time to chill out for twenty-four hours and let the wind do the work for me.' I could make some running repairs and gather my strength ready for the 'final push' to the Pole. I'd spent a good few days of the expedition stormbound, but this was the least frustrating one, because as I stayed warm in my sleeping-bag, every hour that passed saw the winds push me another two-thirds of a mile nearer to my goal. It was an unexpected bonus, because the Transpolar Drift Stream and especially the north-westerly winds that usually prevailed would normally have generated a south-easterly drift. But in line with all the snowdrift evidence I'd seen, the prevailing winds were still not making their presence felt.

I checked the forecast with Ian on the sat-phone that evening and discovered that the winds, though diminishing in strength, would stay southerly for at least another day, but with less strength. It was news that should have guaranteed an un-troubled night's sleep. With no negative drift to worry about and probably a few more miles of positive drift, I'd reach 89° North in the next day or so. I'd led dozens of clients of The Polar Travel Company on 'Last Degree' expeditions from 89°N to the Pole over the past few years, and though I was never blasé about reaching the Pole, it had become something of a routine event; but this time, I was sure, my arrival at the Pole would be a very different experience.

My sense of contentment was rudely shattered when I checked my sat-phone batteries after breaking the connection to Ian. My two main lithium thionyl chloride batteries – each capable of powering the sat-phone, the video camera or even both simultaneously, or recharging the two spare batteries of the sat-phone – were both as dead as hammers. I had run through the first battery by Day 35 in the coldest temperatures, and had therefore taken the view that the second identical battery, in the now much warmer climes, would last significantly longer – well past Day 70 – but I had obviously miscalculated or underestimated the amount of time that I had spent on the phone. I had no way of monitoring the power remaining in the battery, and while lithium batteries are legendary for their power even in extreme cold, when they start to fail they do so without warning and with dramatic speed. All that I had left were two small rechargeable lithium power packs, specific to the sat-phone, with an as yet unknown amount of charge remaining in them.

The batteries had been more than adequate for the tasks that had been scheduled at the start of the expedition, when the provisional plan I'd made with Ian was that I would talk to him daily for the first ten days, then every couple of days for the next ten, and then only every five to ten days thereafter. I would much rather have stuck to that because I didn't need daily voice communications to keep me moving north, and they just kept dragging me back to the outside world with all its associated additional pressures, stopping me from focusing on the expedition and getting 'into the zone'. But as interest had grown in the expedition and the website began to be deluged with visitors, I felt that it had to be updated daily and that required a detailed report from me every day. I had drastically cut back on my planned filming, and had assumed that would free up sufficient power for all the extra calls I was making; but foolishly I had not been monitoring my use of the satellite phone. It was miles above plan and, as a result, the batteries were now even more drained than I was. It was a real issue because if my phone failed, I would be reliant only on a prepared roster of numeric codes sent out by my Argos satellite transmitter.

I slept very badly that night and woke feeling very tired before I'd taken a step. I'd decided to switch from local time, based on my current longitude over to Greenwich Mean Time, so that I could synchronise my body-clock with England and time my arrival at the Pole to fit in with family and all the other interested parties back home, but in so doing I'd given myself very few hours of sleep. Even worse, the switch to GMT was an entirely pointless decision, because it would only have been relevant if I could have used the sat-phone to communicate. Since the batteries were almost flat, that was no longer going to be possible. I couldn't get to sleep, and my stomach had been upset, probably because the salami in my sledging rations had gone off. Even though I needed every calorie I could get, I had to take no chances and threw it away.

Despite my fatigue and my worries about my batteries, I made very good progress, sailing past the eighty-ninth parallel as I covered thirteen miles in nine hours. My progress was all the more remarkable because, although for much of the day I was crossing large pans of good, smooth ice, I also encountered by far the most open water I had seen all expedition. As well as a number of zig-zagging leads lying broadly north–south that were easy to circumvent, I also had to cross no less than fourteen large east–west leads in the course of the day and seven of them were whoppers 50 to 100 metres wide. With my stomach still very unsettled, I felt too weak and tired to risk swimming the leads and instead I had to detour to east or west to where the lead pinched out. Sometimes it took only a few minutes but on a couple of occasions I was walking for well over an hour before I found a crossing-point.

I was starting to look for a camping place at the end of the day when I hit the last and biggest lead of all. My normal rule was to cross any such obstacle before stopping for the night, ensuring a flying start in the morning, but I was simply too weak and tired to do so on this occasion. I stopped short of the lead and pitched my tent knowing that I'd have to put on the immersion suit first thing the following morning. I could only hope that I'd be well and strong enough to swim this and any other leads in my path. My rations were running dangerously low and I couldn't afford the time to keep detouring around leads. I simply had to set a straight course for the Pole and deal with any obstacles in my path as best I could.

I slept fairly well that night and woke on Day 59, Wednesday 14 May, feeling less queasy and a little stronger. It was just as well; I had to swim this dreaded lead. Fortunately the sun was shining and there was no wind to speak of as I donned my immersion suit and set out across the lead. As I did my customary sweep for bears before lowering myself into the sea, I noticed a dark smudge on the far bank, and I thought it looked mildly out of the ordinary. I looked at it for some time, trying to force a recognisable shape to emerge, but nothing came. As had been the case on several occasions before, I found myself attracted to this strange and distinctively different thing, perhaps in the same way the snow bunting had been attracted to me. For the first few metres I was moving over and then through very mushy ice, then there was a long stretch of open water, then more rotten ice and finally a broad expanse of very thin ice that I had to crawl across. I was exhausted and trembling with the effort by the time I reached the far side, and felt very shaky as I scrambled up the two-metre, crumbling bank on the far side.

In an instant I was on red alert, for about five metres ahead of me on a rising bank of snow was the dark patch that had attracted my attention – the scene of a brutal murder. Dry, blackened blood was spattered across the snow in an arc centring on the cadaver of a recently killed seal. The seal must have emerged from the water, just as I had done, and at once been ambushed and killed by a bear. It would have stoved in the seal's skull with one mighty swipe of its forepaw, and then ripped out its organs. Much of the seal was still perfectly intact, as if the bear had known exactly which parts it was interested in feeding on. A ravenous bear would have devoured the lot, so that was at least a little good news. I dragged my sledge up the bank in double-quick time and slung my gun over my shoulder, where it would remain for the rest of the day. Here I was, approaching 89° North, and I now knew with absolute certainty that there was a polar bear in the vicinity and until I was lifted off the sea-ice, I had better remember that fact – operable gun or not.

I'd be lying if I didn't admit to being on tenterhooks for the rest of the day, but the sun was still shining, the conditions underfoot were excellent and I was soon picking up the pace. With a small amount of positive drift to add to the day's total, it was beginning to look like my first fifteen nautical mile day until I hit another enormous lead. This one was well over a kilometre across, a huge, threatening, black gash slashed across the surface of the ice and all the more shocking to me because it was so unexpected. There was no way that I could sensibly commit to swimming a lead of that size, knowing that a polar bear, technically classified as a marine mammal, *Ursus maritimus*, was in the vicinity. Instead, I walked west and north-west for an hour and a half, trying to find a way around it. Finally I reached a place where it had shrunk to no more than forty metres wide, covered with a thin layer of new ice. I decided that there was little to be gained by looking further west, put on the immersion suit and got ready to cross it. I swam the first twenty-five metres, breaking the ice in front of me with my arms, and I then found that the ice over the last fifteen metres was solid enough to bear my weight, providing I leopard-crawled, spreading the loading over as large an area of ice as possible.

I felt even more exposed and vulnerable while making the crossing; the usual paranoia about Greenland sharks and polar bears being augmented on this occasion by the unshakeable belief that my immersion suit was leaking at the ankles and wrists and filling slowly with icy water. In fact my feet and hands were indeed sopping wet, but only because I was sweating buckets through my exertions.

Having got across, I ran out of steam completely and stopped for the night with fourteen miles on the clock for the day, leaving just fifty-four more to go to the Pole. I made a two-minute call to Ian that night and told him that, because of my failing batteries, I was going to cease using the sat-phone and save the remaining power for vital communications at the Pole and during the airlift out. From now on we would rely instead on our primary communication system – the Argos satellite transmitter. When I'd completed the call, I turned off the phone and switched my Argos beacon to Code 3, confirming that there was a problem with the phone. It was one of a series of ten pre-arranged codes that could convey the most important messages, including the vital weather information for the pilots of the chartered aircraft:

o All OK
1 Poor ice and/or weather conditions
2 Medical problem – manageable
3 Satellite phone problem – manageable
4 Satellite phone – permanent failure
5 Contemplating resupply
6 Resupply requested here. Weather conditions OK for plane
7 Contemplating pick-up
8 Non-urgent pick-up requested here. Conditions OK for plane
9 Looking for suitable ice or waiting for suitable weather for plane

The unit had been operating twenty-four hours a day since I had set off from Ward Hunt Island, sending an hourly transmission, including my position and selected code, via Toulouse to my base team. I could also set it to transmit an eleventh emergency code activating an alarm in the Argos office in Toulouse. They would then contact my base team, day or night, to alert them to my emergency, and in turn they would then contact our air charter operator to effect a rescue. It was something I had never had to do before, and I wasn't about to start now.

I thought back on everything that had brought me to this point: the death of my father; the long years of sacrifice; the financial debts and burdens; the endless grind of training; and, above all, the precious time with Mary and the children that I'd lost and the events, like Wilf's first day at 'big school' that I'd missed and that would never recur. I had not given up so much and come so far along so hard a road, to throw it all away now, within sight of my goal.

As if mocking such resolutions, Day 60 was a terrible day. There was rotten ice and water everywhere: huge leads, lakes and mazes of steep-walled, interlinking canals. In ten hours of gruelling going, foot-slogging through mushy ice and swimming an endless succession of leads in the immersion suit, I made no more than seven and a half miles. It got me down quite badly because I had only five days' rations left and at this rate it could take me a week to get to the Pole. For the last three hours of the day I was moving through an area of badly cracked ice, tracking a series of jagged small leads that were taking an erratic course in a broadly north-westerly direction. They were pushing me away from the due northerly course I wanted to take but I was reluctant to cross them in case they then jagged north-east again, forcing me to re-cross them. In the end I made camp beside them, leaving a decision for the cold light of day. I was so exhausted that I fell asleep while waiting for my first cup of tea of the evening to cool down – I'm always abandoning half-drunk cups of tea and coffee at home, but in the circumstances tonight I thought I could be forgiven.

If I'd thought things could not possibly get any worse, then Day 61, Friday 16 May, had a surprise in store. The day dawned with a heavy overcast and thick snow falling and within thirty minutes of setting out through this partial white-out, I was deep inside the worst area of pressure-ridging, interspersed with mazes of rotten ice, and small, medium and giant leads, that I had ever encountered. I wasted an hour trying to find a way around the whole area and instead just got deeper and deeper into it. Even worse, I got my boot drenched while crossing yet another giant rubble-ridge – a freak occurrence, because the rubble is normally under compression and not usually associated with water. After all these trials and torments, all I had to show for the first eight hours of the day was just over two nautical miles of northerly progress – the slowest rate of the entire expedition, even worse than the achingly slow haul with a fully laden sledge in the first few days out from Ward Hunt Island.

If it continued like this for the last forty nautical miles I would run out of rations and simply be unable to reach the Pole. Suddenly, all the stresses and strains that had been building up came to a head with the realisation that, after fifteen years of unremitting effort, having got this close to my goal, I was still being presented with ever greater challenges and obstacles. It was all too much. I could feel the tears welling in my eyes. I hated the fact I was cracking at this late stage, but my desperation to succeed seemed to have met an insurmountable obstacle, and something had to give. I leant forward, rested my hands on my knees, lowered my head and burst into tears. After a minute or so I found myself speaking out loud. It didn't start as a prayer, but as I said the words I knew it was becoming one: 'I am really struggling here, please help me . . .' There was a long pause before I finished the sentence '. . . God.'

I was admitting to myself that I had drained my own resources and now I needed to look beyond myself; I just could not do it alone. In that bleak moment I also drew strength from another source, a quotation from a Caribou Inuit, Igjugarjuk. I keep it pinned over my desk in my office at Wydemeet, and I've read and pondered it so often that I can recite it from memory: 'All true wisdom is to be found far from the dwellings of men in the great solitudes and it can only be attained through suffering. Suffering and privation are the only things that can open the mind to that which is hidden from his fellows.'

A few minutes passed. I remained leaning forward, head bowed and my hands on my knees, as my sobs slowed and stopped and my tears began to turn to ice on my cheeks. Finally, I straightened up and took a few deep breaths. I was a lot calmer now as I looked around me, telling myself that these conditions were purely a local problem. I just needed to push through them to the better weather and ice that would inevitably await me ahead. I remained motionless for a few more minutes, scanning the ice as far as the horizon for signs of a better route. Then I set off once more. The pause, the floods of tears and the prayers had vented the stress and helpless anger that I had been feeling, and, if I'd thought about it at all, I suppose I would now have expected to feel nothing more than a grim, teeth-gritting determination to get through this the best way I could. But, as I plodded onwards, I was startled to discover that, having plumbed the depths only a few minutes before, not only did I now feel much calmer, I was also completely relaxed and confident. In fact, more than that, I felt absolutely invincible. I practically laughed out loud. I now knew, beyond any doubt, that I would reach the Pole. Nothing, not rotten ice, open water, bad visibility, nor wind, snow or storm, was going to stop me now.

It took a long time to get clear of it all and I kept crossing and recrossing leads and large expanses of rotten ice, but in the last third of the day I was rewarded, by a return to good conditions – large pans of firm ice with only an occasional lead between them. In the midst of the morass of water and rotten ice, I'd told myself that I had to reach 89°20' North by the end of the day. I actually made it to 89°23', a total of 8.3 miles in the day, of which six had come in the last four hours. I stumbled through the motions of setting up my tent and cooking my meal, but if I was exhausted, I was also elated. I had reached rock-bottom mentally during the course of the day but come back from it. I was now within forty miles of the Pole and whatever conditions I now encountered, I was confident that I could reach it in three or four days.

If Day 61 had seen me at my lowest ebb, Day 62, Saturday 17 May, pushed me close to euphoria. The sun was shining from a cloudless sky and the air temperature of minus nine felt positively spring-like. There was a bit of movement and noise from ice activity and the ice conditions were very varied, with open rubble, rotten pans with cracks, thinly refrozen large lakes and hard, smooth pans alternating at regular intervals. It almost reminded me of Dartmoor in that the terrain would change completely every 100 metres or so, but, unlike the day before, the conditions didn't seem to slow me down at all. I was taking everything in my stride and moving north at a steady, relentless pace. In thirteen hours' walking I covered 16.5 nautical miles – a record day. As if that wasn't enough, ice-drift from the south-east presented me with a bonus of another three miles. I now had just twenty-one miles to go and by trimming my daily rations a little, I still had four days' supplies. I tried to imagine what Mary, my family and friends, who'd lived through the last fifteen years, might be feeling now as they realised that I was about to fulfil my dream.

I was pretty much running on automatic pilot. I couldn't hold a thought in my head for more than a few seconds. Even the simplest mental arithmetic took an age as I tapped and re-tapped out the numbers with my fingers on the ski-poles. As I walked, I chatted away with my 'team' of Baskers, Swerves and Curves, which seemed to do the job of keeping me on track. I was pushing really hard when it suddenly occurred to me that there was no point in thrashing myself to death. My grail was within my grasp. I wasn't in such a desperate hurry any more, it was time to savour the remaining hours left of my journey. This was my expedition, I was doing it on my terms, and I was on the brink of fulfilling the destiny I'd dreamed of since I was a boy. It was a delicious feeling – beyond words.

To celebrate this realisation, for the first time ever, I stopped bang in the middle of a seventy-five-minute sledge-hauling session, got out all my cooking gear in the open air and made myself two mugs of orange-flavoured water and a flask of tea for later on, and then set off again to complete my longest day yet. I was knackered physically and mentally when I finally stopped for the night, but not so completely burned out that I wasn't ready for another big push the next day. I was even thinking now that I could do it all in one last climactic hit if I just kept walking all night and into the next morning, but I did not want to reach the Pole in a completely exhausted mental or physical state. It had been a long, long wait and I wanted to enjoy and savour my moment of triumph, not let it pass in a blur of weariness. So wiser counsel prevailed, but, even though I was not intending to reach the Pole the next day, I was still planning the longest and possibly the hardest day of the entire expedition, aiming to cover fifteen to eighteen nautical miles so as to leave no more than a short burst over the last few miles for the following day. I could then enjoy the moment to the full.

Day 63, Sunday 18 May, dawned bright and sunny, and in the course of the day, for the first time since I had left Ward Hunt Island, the temperature briefly registered a fraction of a degree above freezing point. I ate an extra half bag of porridge for breakfast from my dwindling ration packs, as much for psychological as physical reasons, because I was staring down the barrel of another very long day and I doubted that the overnight rest had been anywhere near sufficient recovery time before another huge push. Because of the previous day's late finish, I started late as well, round about noon, and by the time I got to the fourth session I was already feeling very leg-weary. I was dreading the thought of another twelve to twenty hours to cover the necessary miles, so I decided to play a bit of a psychological trick on myself. I would do a normal-length day of nine sessions and then stop as if I was getting ready to camp for the night. I'd put up the tent, re-hydrate myself fully and have supper, but, instead of going to bed, I'd fill my flasks, make myself a breakfast, and then set off again to do the final four hours, or whatever it took to reach the Pole.

The ploy seemed to work because, although I was truly whacked, I was in a good rhythm and just kept pushing on and on. I kept myself going by belting out snatches of a few songs over and over again: KC and the Sunshine Band's 'Please Don't Go', Rod Stewart's 'Sailing' and 'You're in My Heart', Peter Sarstedt's 'Where Do You Go to My Lovely?' and Elton John's 'Candle in the Wind'. I could remember only snippets and phrases, so there was lots of loud humming to fill the gaps, and what I lacked in tunefulness, I more than made up for in volume and enthusiasm. In the end I didn't stop for the night until about four-thirty in the morning, so in all I had walked for over fifteen hours and covered seventeen nautical miles, a record day in both duration and distance. When I looked at my GPS, it read 89°56' and 53 seconds North. There was less than four miles to go.

I put up the tent after crossing two 100-metre leads in quick succession. They had only recently refrozen but to my vast relief, the ice was just thick enough to bear my weight and I was able to cross them both without recourse to the immersion suit. Despite our frequent collaborations, Mr O and I had never quite felt confident in each other's reliability in the water. Once the tent was up, I wolfed down three full mugs of orange drink, a chicken curry, a portion of porridge and half a bag of sledging nuts and chocolate. I felt I'd earned it now, and though I was physically very tired, I was pumped up for the last push and anxious not to delay it, taking advantage of the fine weather while it lasted.

I had planned to rest for three or four hours before making for the Pole, but I was too excited, and I was really concerned that, after fifteen years of effort, some last-minute problem could still prevent me from finally reaching the North Pole. I just wanted to get there and answer the endlessly recurring question: 'Will I or won't I make it this time?' I had to finish but there were still so many potential pitfalls in those last few miles and hours. Even at this late stage, anything could still happen to delay or stop me – the weather could close down, I could misjudge the ice in my weariness and drown, or that polar bear could catch up with me. I kept urging myself on: 'Don't hang around, don't have extra sleep, do the extra hours' sledge-hauling instead, get there as fast as you can.' But at the same time, I was haunted by the fact that if I pushed too hard, what I was dreading might very well happen; I might grow careless in my haste to reach the Pole. But I was now so near that, for the only time in the expedition, I allowed opportunism to supersede planning. This was the time to go for it as fast as I could. Once my life's mission was completed, I could relax and rest. So, with barely an hour's rest, I was packing up my kit and preparing to move out.

It was 6 a.m. on Day 64, Monday 19 May 2003. Within twenty minutes of setting off, I'd bent Curves, my left ski-pole, even more out of shape and lost the basket again, so while every instinct was urging me on, I had to force myself to stop, sit down and tie it back on again. Then a horrid, small, winding lead in the middle of a much larger, recently refrozen lead refused to let me head north. I detoured west along its bank, constantly seduced by its hints that, in just a few more metres, it would pinch out. Instead I found myself at an even larger lead and I had to join forces with Mr O one last time within three kilometres of the Pole. I was still using my tactic of breaking the remaining distance into manageable units and had now switched to thinking in metric units instead of nautical miles, so that I could picture the distance to go in the familiar terms of a running track: 3,000 metres was only seven and a half laps of the track – so nearly there.

I swam the lead, folded Mr O, hoping it was for the last

time, strapped it back on the sledge and then pressed on. I was now moving over an area of huge, one-kilometre-wide ice-floes – pocked with the remnants of old pressure ridges and nodules of ice. The thin snow cover was granular and crunched underfoot as I walked across it, my boots making a rhythmic, almost hypnotic sound. I was getting very close now, less than 1,000 metres from my goal – in fact I realised I was on the floe that was actually floating over the North Geographic Pole. Only now did I know beyond any doubt that I was going to reach the Pole. It was a strange thought, greeted with no surge of excitement. I was already wholly absorbed in my preparations to navigate my way to the exact point around which our planet rotates. I was moving slowly forward, holding both ski-poles in one hand and my GPS in the other, pulling the sledge, walking relatively upright, without the familiar assistance of my ski-poles. It wasn't very comfortable and the sledge suddenly felt heavy and unwieldy.

I had closed to within 100 metres of the Pole. The sun and compass were now useless and the GPS was all over the place as I sought the vital reading that would show I had reached the Pole. Before the introduction of GPS in the 1980s, polar travellers had to use sextants to calculate their position. It must have been torture for them because, even if they were actually standing at the exact North Pole as they began to take their readings, by the time they had waited for a clear sun-sight and then done their calculations, they would have drifted away from it again. Under those conditions, if you got a reading within a mile of the actual Pole, you'd be doing pretty well. Now, with GPS, it is possible to know your position to within three metres.

During those last few moments, I was concentrating so hard on my navigation, that I didn't have time to take in my surroundings or enjoy the anticipation of the moment I'd waited so many years to achieve. All my attention was on that tiny screen, because, even with a GPS, trying to nail down the actual location of the Pole can be fiendishly difficult if there's much drift going on. My longitude was constantly changing with the motion of the polar ice – since the lines of longitude converge at the Pole, they were now no more than a few metres apart – and, on top of this, precise as the GPS is, it can't actually compute 90° North – the Pole itself. The closest latitude reading it will give is 89°59'59 seconds and nine-tenths of a second.

Since each tenth of a second is equal to about three metres, that was as close as the GPS could get me to the Pole – close enough to reach out and touch it, if only I knew in which direction it lay, for nothing marked the spot on the ever shifting ice. I just had to navigate the last few metres by trial and error, walking backwards and forwards until I achieved the magic reading on my GPS. But one minute the Pole was ahead of me, the next behind me, then off to the left, then the right. I was moving and the ice-cap was moving under the usual influences, and the one constant – the North Geographical Pole – was proving very elusive. Finally, I just stood stock still for a few seconds, watching my GPS to see what was happening with the ice, to see if I could discern a trend from which I could orientate myself to the Pole.

As I stood there, to my amazement, I saw the display showing my latitude start to climb. I stood still. I was heading directly for the Pole. It read 89°59'59.6 seconds North . . . 59.7 . . . 59.8 . . . 59.9 . . . and *I was there*. By clicking a button, I could make a permanent record of the reading at that particular time and date – 09.54 Greenwich Mean Time on 19 May, 64 days after setting out from Ward Hunt Island. I pressed the button over and over again, making absolutely sure that I marked the waypoint with the date and time code burnt in. This far north, my Argos tracking beacon was also transmitting a signal of my position by satellite to my base camp every twenty minutes. It had been doing so ever since I left Ward Hunt and now, by an extraordinary coincidence, it sent another of its automatic transmissions as I was actually standing at the Pole. By the time it transmitted again, twenty minutes later, the ice-drift had already carried me some distance away, but it was wonderful to discover, when I later spoke to my base, that they had received that instant verification that, at 09.54 on 19 May 2003, my Argos beacon had sent a signal from precisely 90°00'00 seconds North. I had arrived.

13

When I realised that I had really reached the Pole, I didn't plant any flags, I just stood there motionless. I was alone. All was perfectly quiet. The sun was blazing away – and it was very warm. The sweat that had been dripping from my face had run into my eyes, stinging them. As I rubbed them with my bare hands, I could feel the layers of gritty salt crystals that had built up around my eyes in the final push. I stood there numb, not fully understanding what I had just done. The incessant drive to head north had suddenly gone. I could feel myself shaking. I'd had little sleep for days and had really been pushing myself hard to cover the final distance, but there was also the nervous tension that had been accumulating over months and even years. As my motivation had only ever been to reach the Pole in the purest way possible, I had no feeling that I'd conquered or triumphed over something. I was simply there. The Celestial North Pole conceived by the Greeks, an infinite extension of the Geographic Pole into the heavens, projected straight up through my body to the Pole Star and beyond.

I put the GPS, the Argos beacon and my mitts on top of my sledge. Next to them I placed the embroidered family motto that I had carried with me all the way. Then I took off my hat and sank to my knees on the ice, kneeling before my sledge as if it were an altar. My first thought was of my Dad and I murmured, 'I've done it, Dad. I've done it for you.' As I spoke, big tears were trickling down my cheeks.

When the moment had passed I looked up into the brilliant blue sky and another powerful emotion swept over me: relief, utter, utter relief. I had done it. It was over at last. This huge challenge I had set myself was now a part of my past. And as that last thought disappeared, a third, totally unexpected realisation starbursted into my head – I was free. I knew that I had fulfilled my destiny, and I was never again going to have to think about how I was going to achieve it. I had really done it. And it occurred to me – and it was all the more delicious a thought for never having been considered before – that all the preoccupations of the last fifteen, indeed almost thirty years, had been vaporised in those last footsteps. I no longer had to plan for this moment; it was here, it was now, and from this day on I would be entirely unencumbered by its demands. This moment of liberation was so heady that I almost felt I could fly.

I got back to my feet and looked around me for the first time. This ice-floe was the scene of my North Pole. I could have found it amidst a rubble-field during a blizzard or in the middle of open water in thick fog. But it had finally revealed itself in the centre of a large pan of first-year ice, on a near-perfect day. There was no wind, the air was clean and pure, and the freshly created ice ridges and weathered old pinnacles were gleaming a dazzling white as they were struck by the light of the sun, now high in the sky. I etched every detail into my mind, but even the stark beauty of the scene couldn't hold me for long. I knew that I had probably been at the exact Pole for no more than a few seconds before the inexorable ice-drift began to carry me away from it again. The Pole was already in the past; it was time to prepare for the future.

I used up a little more of the remaining life in my precious sat-phone batteries to make three calls. The first was to Mary; without her love, help and support, there would have been no expedition and no hope of success. It was the briefest of calls. 'It's me. I'm here. I've made it. I'm on my way home. I love you.' The second call was to Robert Elias of The Omega Foundation, who had also played a critical part in the success of the expedition. The third call was to Ian and was even more brief and very businesslike: 'I've made it, when's the pick-up?'

'Brilliant, Pen, well done. I'll call all the people that I know you planned to call. Now there's no plane available to pick you up today, the earliest they can get to you is tomorrow, Tuesday, afternoon. Let's speak again, GMT 09.00. Well done again. Bye for now.'

I was in shock as I broke the connection. I couldn't believe my ears. Weather permitting, it was imperative that a pick-up was made as soon as possible after reaching the Pole, but, in the absence of sat-phone contact, a summit meeting at Resolute between my base team and the aircraft operators had decided that Tuesday would be my most likely arrival date. I'd not worked with Kenn Borek Air anything like as much as I had with the ever reliable First Air, with whom I'd done most of my previous Arctic Ocean work, but they knew the critical importance of having a plane out of Resolute and on standby at Eureka so that it could be launched the moment I arrived at the Pole, maximising the possibility of a successful pick-up before any weather delays. I had made better-than-expected progress over the last forty-eight hours, but I had arrived comfortably within the time-window agreed with the air opera-tors before I set off – seven days inside my latest projected arrival date. The weather was perfect, I was on an excellent ice-floe offering several airstrip orientations and yet there was not going to be a plane for at least twenty-four hours. This was not good news. The weather had been fine for several days, but how much longer would it stay that way? And once it broke, it could be several days before a weather-window opened up again.

Stifling the frustration I felt, I put the phone away. Whatever power remained now had to be conserved. Despite all the attendant dangers, the most important time to have verbal two-way communications was not while trekking north, but now, when I needed to be able to report my weather and airstrip conditions to my major partner in the whole endeavour – the aircraft operator. I had worked in partnership with many pilots since 1994, and I was known amongst the First Air pilots for the efforts I made to fulfil my responsibilities on the ground. Prompted by the senior Twin Otter captains at First Air who felt such a document would be very useful for newcomers to the polar pack-ice, I had even gone so far as to prepare the only detailed notes in existence on 'The Selection, Preparation and Reporting of Sea Ice Airstrips'.

The pilots were 600 nautical miles away, often in completely different weather systems, and though there are satellite scans of the polar regions, the weather can change with such rapidity that there is no substitute for observations from the eyes on the ground – the person actually at the Pole. If my sat-phone was down, the pilots would have to decide whether to launch without the necessary information to make a fully informed judgement, and as soon as they took off, they would run up a very substantial bill – £35,000 if they came as far as 90°N – that I would have to pay. They would feel under a degree of moral pressure to pick me up if they'd launched the flight on their own initiative and they wouldn't want to charge me for an aborted pick-up, so I knew that they would try to make a landing in conditions that might be considerably less than ideal.

I did not want to put them in that position because it was unfair on them, but I was now facing the possibility of having to do so because the batteries on my sat-phone now had only minutes rather than hours of charge remaining. Although my Argos beacon was good for another 30 or more days, and continued to transmit my exact position within metres and my selected numeric code, I couldn't use it for verbal communication. If I could have guaranteed that I'd be picked up no later than my second or third day at the Pole, I would have been more relaxed about the sat-phone, but if the weather conditions were unfavourable and I was stuck there for two or even three weeks – a perfectly feasible scenario; it's happened before – then I would need to husband every scrap of power.

With that thought in mind, I began the search for an airstrip.

I knew that if I could find a decent one, I could then put up the tent, relax and just wait for the plane. I looked round for a couple of hours, but although I could see that there were possibilities for three orientations for a runway – so that they could land in different wind directions – I didn't mark them out, because by now I was stumbling with tiredness and my heart wasn't really in it. Since I'd already been told that the plane hadn't even left Resolute, I knew there was no prospect of it arriving that day. The earliest it could reach me would be in the late afternoon of the following day so there seemed no great hurry to secure an airstrip. I decided to put up the tent on the ice-pan and filled the valances with snow because I didn't know how long I would be there and I thought I would make it as secure an HQ as possible. I had nowhere else to go now, and would be there until the plane came, maybe tomorrow, but maybe not for several days. After I'd had some food and a good night's rest, I would resume pacing out an airstrip, checking for dangerous lumps and bumps and filling plastic sacks with snow to act as markers.

I hadn't gone to bed at all the previous night and was in desperate need of rest, so I lay down and closed my eyes. I thought of Mary, Wilf and Freya. Mary would be frantically busy in her attic office, fielding the avalanche of enquiries from family and friends, supporters and journalists, Freya chomping her way through her sticky biscuits at elevenses, and Wilf sitting in class with his friends at his wonderful school in Widecombe-in-the-Moor. How excited he'd be today to race home and find out from his Mum that I'd made it. Then he could pin the paper flag in its proper place on his wall-chart and know that at last I was on my way back to him. Lots of friends and relatives would soon be descending on the house for a celebration party, and letting off the giant firework that had been stored against the day when I finally reached the Pole. With those happy thoughts, I drifted off to sleep.

I slept for about eight hours, woke up that evening and had

some food and then went back to sleep again for another five or six hours. Over the next three days, while I was recovering from the prodigious physical effort during the final dash to the Pole, I probably slept for about twelve to fourteen hours in every twenty-four; after that, I managed no more than six extremely sporadic hours a night, kept awake by a restlessness born of extreme boredom and haunted by the desire to be reunited with my Mary, but with no idea of how long it might be before the plane would come. Tired as I was, my tour of duty did not end until the plane took off with me aboard and there could be no complete relaxation until I had played my part in bringing that about.

I woke the next morning after one of the longest, deepest sleeps of my life, but I found that the weather was changing fast and by Tuesday afternoon, when the aircraft could have reached me, thick cloud was obscuring the sun and stinging snow flurries were scudding over the ice. The wind was strong enough to whip the pools of meltwater from the surface and drive it over the ice as wraiths and tendrils of mist. There was no point in even trying to identify an airstrip in such conditions. The heavy overcast and the absence of shadowing, contrast, definition and perspective in such flat, monochromatic-grey light made it impossible to discern the ridges, mounds and ice-boulders, large or small, projecting from the surface of the ice-pan. They would be fatal for an aircraft attempting to land, and no pilot would ever attempt to do so in such weather.

My GPS showed that I had now drifted four miles away from the Pole – I was to drift about thirty-five nautical miles before I was finally picked up. My Argos beacon was automatically sending out my position every twenty minutes as my ice-pan moved away from the Pole. As I'd planned with Ian before the start of the expedition, the meaning of my ten numeric Argos codes had changed as soon as I reached the Pole. Codes 6 'Food finished, fuel only' and 7 'Estimate can hold out for 15 days with remaining fuel, living off water alone', related to my personal state, but the remainder were designed to give the pilots a running commentary on the all-important weather conditions. For example, Code 1 now meant 'Weather marginal for flying and deteriorating', Code 3 'Weather marginal for flying and improving', Code 5 'Weather conditions good for flying at present', Code 8 'Airstrip selected and marked out' and Code 9 'Weather conditions bad for flying/no airstrip at present'. Having checked the weather, I re-set the Argos beacon to Code 9 and then lay back down in my sleeping-bag to begin the long wait. Once, twice or sometimes even more times a day, I drained a little more of my battery power to make the briefest of reports on the conditions. I wrote out all the information before I made the call, so that there was no umming and aaahing; I was on air for the absolute minimum time, and every time I said, 'This might be my last call, don't worry if you don't get another one.' The LED battery indicator display went from three bars to two and then one, and every time I used it, I thought that it would be the last one, but somehow it held out until almost the last act.

I rattled off a description of the sun – whether it was shining from a bright blue sky, discernible but obscured or completely obscured – and if the latter, whether it was consistently obscured or occasionally obscured by broken or scattered cloud. I also gave the atmospheric pressure, the wind speed and direction, and the visibility (how far I could see, what the ground visibility would be for an aircraft pilot), the degree of shadow, contrast and perspective (good, average or poor) and the degree of cloud cover: its approximate altitude, type and thickness, and what area of the sky by octa (eighths) was covered by cloud. I also estimated whether each factor – sunlight, cloud cover and visibility – was increasing or decreasing. When relevant I would also have to give the details of any potential landing strips, including their orientation as a true bearing, the length and width, details of any important features on the sides and ends, the nature of the surface ice-cover or snow and its depth, whether markers had been laid at the corners and along the sides, and a windsock erected or a fire lit so that smoke would indicate ground wind speed and direction.

The weather information was the key. If the pilots knew that they had good weather, then they could find their own airstrip if they had to, but if it was marginal and they decided that it was the only or best opportunity to fly, then it would all hang on whether I had a good, well-prepared airstrip. In such circumstances, it was impossible to overstate the importance of giving the pilots accurate information about the quality of the strip. If I said that it was a great strip they would come up in more marginal weather. When they arrived, they would check the strip visually if they could, and if I'd prepared it badly or given them misleading information about it, they might just turn round and go home again. I would then not only have two seriously stressed pilots on my hands, who would never take my word for anything again, I would also have to find an extra £35,000 for another flight out of a budget that was already overspent. If the visibility was too poor for them to see the runway, the consequences could be even more severe; they might just take my word for the quality of the strip and try to land. If the strip then turned out to be rubbish we could easily have a disaster on our hands.

So it was very important that I told them exactly how it really was. If the best I could do was a rubbish strip, they'd just say 'OK, we're going to wait for good weather, come up and find our own strip' – something they were perfectly capable of doing from the air, providing there was direct sunlight and good visibility. They could then make informed decisions themselves without reference to me and take responsibility for their own and my safety. But I always regarded it as a point of honour at the end of an expedition to do my best to find a realistic airstrip for the pick-up plane.

While I was waiting for the weather to lift, the pilots were working from static satellite images of the Pole taken every six hours, trying to identify areas of open sky up to 100 miles away from my position and observe their direction and speed of travel, so that they could predict when one of those areas would be passing over my ice-pan and how long it would take to traverse it. A small patch of blue sky was useless because the likelihood of being able to predict its arrival over the target area just as the plane arrived ready to land was vanishingly small. At a minimum, they needed a break in the clouds large enough to give thirty minutes of blue skies over my ice-pan. And it had to be predictable a minimum of four and a half hours in advance, because that was the flight time to the Pole from Eureka at 80° North. So the pilots were in the predicting game, and of course I couldn't give them very much useful information because I had no way of seeing this blue sky coming towards me. My role was purely to keep them informed of any changes in my local weather so that they could try to match that to the cloud cover images on the computer screen at Eureka and work out if their projection was still looking promising.

Over the succeeding nine days I drifted steadily further from the Pole and the flight to lift me out still failed to materialise. For five of those nine days there were strong winds, poor visibility, snowfall and thick cloud, and for three of them there were gale-force winds. The tent was taking a real pounding as the gales continued all day and all night – hammer, hammer, hammer on the tent. Even when the wind finally died away, I was still in partial white-out conditions with poor visibility and low definition because of the lack of direct sunlight. In that sort of diffuse light, unless I physically walked every metre of the length and width of any proposed airstrip, I could easily have missed even a large obstruction that could wreck a plane.

Before the two Twin Otter planes could take off, the weather had to be viable at three different points: at the Eureka weather station, where the pick-up team were waiting, at the refuelling point between 85° and 86° North where one of the planes would wait with the necessary aviation fuel to refill the other plane on its return, and at the point on the ice-cap where I was waiting for them to land. As each day passed, the three never coincided. On Days 66 and 67, I had good weather and had my beacon set to Code 5: 'Weather conditions good for flying at present', but there was heavy cloud and snow at Eureka and no flights were possible. By the afternoon of Day 67, I had to switch my beacon back to Code 9, effectively barring them from taking off. By now I was on half-rations, eking out the last of my food for a couple more days.

The following day, Friday 23 May, Day 68, the Twin Otters actually took off in response to my Code 3 signal: 'Weather marginal for flying but improving'. But their flight was aborted because, after a couple of days in the weather station during poor weather, the pilots had emerged to find the wings of both aircraft covered in ice. Even with all four pilots clearing the ice, there was a lengthy delay. They were then unable to find the open sky visible on the weather station's computers to lead them to the proposed refuelling stop out on the sea-ice between 85 and 86° North, and had to return to Eureka. By Sunday and Monday we were back to Code 9 at my end, and a wait for good weather in those three critical locations.

I was at the Pole, I'd achieved my life-time ambition. Yet as day succeeded day and I remained in my tent, waiting in vain for the aircraft to lift me out, I had no interest at any level in reviewing the events of the previous ten weeks in my mind, nor revisiting them emotionally, nor going through my expedition diary, adding observations and recollections to it while they were still fresh in my mind. There were endless opportunities – there was nothing else to do – but I simply had no interest in it at all. I couldn't even bear to look at it.

When I arrived at the Pole, I was exhausted from lack of sleep because I had pushed myself so hard for the last few days, but that sleep deficit was soon recovered and my physical strength regained. However, I was also utterly drained mentally, and recuperation from that proved to be much slower. Just as a long-distance athlete times his run to the finishing post so that he is completely spent when he crosses the line, putting everything he's got into achieving the best time or the best position, I had timed my run to the tape and there was nothing left. At the start of the expedition I was doing calculations in my head – and there is a hell of a lot of basic maths that you can do every day – distances done, running totals, averages over the period of the expedition and so on. By the end I could barely add three and five – I had to count on my fingers – and that shows how mentally exhausted I was.

So I lay in my tent in a state of total mental lassitude. I had a line running from one end of the tent roof to the other, threaded through two safety pins. As the tent fabric tautened, slackened and flapped around in the wind, the line would swing to and fro and the safety pins would revolve around the line, going round and round, sometimes in perfect synchronicity, one way and then the other, and sometimes in opposite directions to each other; then they would start moving apart doing the same thing and then they would come back together, like some complex dance routine. I watched this performance for hours on end – that's how switched off I had become.

I also stared at the green roof of the tent for hours, watching the movement of the ripples of material in the wind, and, like a surfer trying to spot the next big wave, I would try to predict the size of the ripples in the material from the noise of the next gust of wind when it came. It was all completely pointless, self-absorbed nonsense, getting me absolutely nowhere. The only useful task I performed in all that time was to sweep the fresh snowfall from my Argos transmitter unit; the rest of the time I was lying as still as a corpse – and with about the same level of brain activity.

In the last five days or so of the expedition leading up to the Pole, based on the knowledge that there was a direct correlation between calories consumed and miles on the clock, if I felt I needed more food, I took it. I had double nosebag rations on the last two big days, for example, and by the time that I arrived at the Pole, all I had left was one nosebag of nuts and chocolate, three breakfasts and three and a half suppers, two sachets of chocolate powder, a small amount of dried milk, fourteen teabags and a dozen sugar lumps. I had a supper on the day I arrived at the Pole, and a breakfast, the last nosebag and a full supper on the Tuesday, so by the Wednesday morning I was down to two breakfasts and one and a half suppers. Even though I knew that bad weather could see me stuck at the Pole for well over a week – nine days was my previous worst with a group of clients – I suppose the fine, settled conditions when I arrived lulled me into thinking that it would probably be no more than two or three days. So I'd already eaten a lot of food before the weather turned and I started serious rationing. After the second day I ate only half a breakfast and a quarter of a supper every day until Sunday morning when I ran out of porridge altogether. There was no more porridge in the morning and almost every day I was halving my intake of supper again to try and keep eking out this ever dwindling supply. So by Monday, Day 71, I was down to one cup of water in the morning and one at tea-time, drunk cold to save fuel, and two cups of hot water, one to replace breakfast and the other in the evening, into which I sprinkled a few grains of freeze-dried supper rations – just enough to give the water a little flavour. As I was not trying to establish a record for the number of days spent without food in a tent in the Arctic, I cannot say I enjoyed the pangs of hunger that gnawed at my stomach all day and all night, but I was quite intrigued to discover what it would be like to live on water alone for two or three weeks.

I had been able to make a few brief calls on my sat-phone to Gary Guy in Resolute, the timing of the next call always dependent on the anticipated changes in the weather advised by Eureka. Some days I would not call at all, letting the Argos tell my story instead. During one of these calls, I learned a little of the full-blown global media madness that had now erupted around the expedition. Unfortunately the coverage was giving the impression that I was starving and at the point of death and needed 'rescuing' from the Pole, and there had been an avalanche of emotional stuff about the family waiting at home who I might never see again. I heard this with mounting horror, worried about the effect it would have on Mary and the children, and my mother, family and friends, and also furious at the lurid, overblown treatment of what was a perfectly routine occurrence. It was nothing more than a weather delay to a pre-arranged, pre-contracted and fully paid-for flight, not 'a life or death mercy dash' as the tabloids were apparently describing it. There were even networks of churches around Britain, and maybe around the world, all praying for me, which, though I was exceptionally touched and grateful, I found excruciatingly embarrassing when there were so many other causes infinitely more worthy than mine. I wasn't remotely concerned for my life. If necessary, I could survive for another twenty days without any food at all – such privations come with the territory of extreme polar endeavours – but in any case, air-dropped supplies could have been put in at any time, in almost any weather.

What would have greatly unsettled me was the knowledge that a satellite news channel was running an interview with the general manager of Kenn Borek Air, the gist of which appeared to be that I was stupid to have been travelling on the ice so late in the season, and that by doing so I was increasing the risk to his pilots when attempting a pick-up. Given that I'd arrived at the Pole well within the time-window of 15–25 May that was agreed with his own base manager at Resolute, I found the news puzzling. It wasn't even *that* late in the season and I suspected that the poor man was getting understandably nettled at being besieged by media demanding to know when he was going to 'rescue' Pen Hadow. Out on the ice, though, I was unaware of the fuss and, in the end, the efforts of his pilots showed action spoke louder than words.

Ian, Martin and Ginny had all flown up with the planes from Resolute to Eureka in the expectation of coming on the pick-up flight, but Gary now told me that the pilots were switching to Plan B, and would fly with minimum payload to give them maximum flexibility in choosing if and how to make a landing at my position. Even if they could not land to lift me out, they could always overfly me and drop supplies, and in that way I could remain on the ice-cap almost indefinitely. On the morning of Tuesday 27 May, Day 72 of the expedition, the pilots took the decision on their own initiative to try and pick me up, taking advantage of a brief spell of clear weather that they estimated would drift over my position later that day. I had rubbish weather and couldn't see the least sign of improvement in the sky, but they predicted a large break in the clouds and timed the arrival of their flight to coincide with it. The battery of my sat-phone had lasted up to now, but the moment Gary at Resolute confirmed that the planes had taken off from Eureka and would be over my position in four and a half hours, it finally gave up the ghost. I now had only my Argos beacon.

Four hours later, about half an hour before they were due to land, I could see that the sky was definitely lightening from the north-east, but when I at last heard the engine note, faint at first then swelling into a throaty roar as they passed low overhead, the blue skies had not arrived on schedule. In poor visibility they could not risk a landing, but the plane circled a couple of times as they dropped a bundle of food supplies in a vivid fluorescent orange container and two five-litre cans of fuel – one of which burst on impact – in case they were forced to fly back without me. Even better, they also dropped an HF radio, allowing me to communicate with them. As I set up the antenna, they were flying on for another forty miles into an area where the skies had cleared and they put the plane down there to save fuel while they waited.

The chief pilot, rather worryingly called Stephen King – I hoped I wouldn't feature in an Arctic horror story – then called me on the radio to say that they could wait for no more than two hours. After that, because of the maximum duty time allowed for pilots in the air, they would have to take off again and fly home. I could only hope that the blue sky would edge its way over my position before the time ran out. I reported the current conditions to them every thirty minutes, but the weather remained stubbornly cloudy. With just half an hour to go Stephen said, 'Look, Pen, it's not looking good, the blue sky should be over your position now and it's stalled, and in fact the weather is starting to close out where we are. So our only hope is for you to find and mark a strip. We'll check it out as we overfly your position and if it's good enough, we might be able to try and pick you up. If not, we'll have no option but to leave you there.'

As he was speaking, I was doing some lightning calculations in my head. It was going to take me five minutes to get from the tent to the area of the most likely of my three potential strips, another ten minutes to walk to the far end of it and ten minutes to walk back, and another five to get back to the tent to report in. That was the full thirty minutes, without allowing any time to walk up additional lines in the strip looking for, and doing something about, any potentially hazardous surface features or to fill sacks with snow to act as markers. The absolute minimum was four – one at each corner of my runway – but several others at intervals down the sides was much better. This was going to be a one-shot deal. If I started to prepare a strip only to find a problem somewhere along its length, I'd have no time to find and prepare a second. I knew Stephen was in earnest when he said that they'd have to head home empty-handed if I had no strip ready for them. So I said to him, 'I'm very grateful to you for giving me the option, but can you give me forty-five minutes? I just can't do it in thirty.' There was a long pause, then a single word, 'OK.'

I was already stumbling out of the tent, my heart hammering from the adrenalin rush. I had been lying motionless in a tent for over a week and had eaten virtually nothing in the last forty-eight hours, so I was really weak and wobbly on my legs, and floundering badly in the soft, new-fallen snow, but there was no way that I was going to blow this chance for lack of effort; after nine days of nothing, major guns were blasting. I had to find a strip and at least create the best opportunity I could for the plane to land. If I didn't, it was going to pass straight overhead and just keep on going and it might be another week or even longer before I saw it again . . . and when I did, it would be bringing me an invoice for another £35,000.

Within five minutes, heart pounding, I was at the area where the ice looked generally smooth. I could just make out the pressure ridges all around the perimeter of my floe – the visibility wasn't that good, but at least it wasn't snowing or foggy. There were low ridges and dome-shaped mounds of buckled ice scattered over the surface of the pan, and with no shadows or meaningful contrast or definition in the flat, white light, they were virtually invisible until I was practically falling over them.

I had just one chance, and nowhere near enough time to survey the whole pan, so I had to come up with my best option first time. If ever there was a time for a flash of inspiration it was now . . . and necessity being the mother of invention, it came to me right then. I dropped to the ground and began doing press-ups every five degrees through a complete circle. I got my eyes right down to the snow level, so low that my nose was actually buried in the snow, and if I could still see the pressure ridge at the end of the ice-pan when my nose was in the snow, the chances were that there were no meaningful humps or bumps between me and it. There were three lines that looked promising and by a combination of 'eenie, meenie, minie, mo' and a bit of intuition, I decided that one might be better than the other two. It seemed slightly broader, giving a bit more latitude if I found a deformation on one side or another. The minimum size for the runway was 400 metres long and 20 across. That was the deal. I knew and the pilots knew that if the circumstances allowed, they could land in shorter distances, but those were the ground rules I had to follow. I immediately set off along one edge of my proposed strip, pulling my sledge behind me. Every fifty metres I stopped, shovelled snow into one of the blue nylon bags that I had been using for storing food and clothing and placed it on the edge of the landing strip. I needed the bags not only to mark the edges so they were visible from the air, but also to create objects of sufficient height to still be visible to me right the way down the strip so that I could create straight sides to the runway.

In the same way, still working at absolutely top speed, I marked the quarter, halfway, three-quarter points, and the far end. I swung left through ninety degrees and marked out the base line, then turned again and began working my way back down the other side. I stole a glance at my watch – twenty-five minutes gone. After so long at rest, I was gasping from the effort and my body was clammy with sweat, but there was no time to worry about anything other than filling the next bag and covering the next stretch. All the time I was pacing it out, I was also looking across to the far side, straining my eyes to detect any crack or mound in the ice that might pose a danger to the plane. The runway was only twenty metres from side to side, but it was like being inside a ping pong ball – a soft, unfocused, white light with very little definition or contrast and no shadows. Although I could see the bags on the other side, it was almost impossible to detect any change in the ice-surface, and I was constantly tripping and falling.

As I neared the middle of the strip, I was aghast to find a mound of ice directly ahead of me and had to detour inwards to avoid it, narrowing the centre portion of the strip. It was too late to worry about that; I just had to mark it with a bag and realign the rest of the strip to this new, thinner dimension. But as I again glanced across towards the other side, I was mortified to glimpse another low, conical mound of ice right in the middle of the runway. It was about seventy-five centimetres high and a metre across at its base. There was a crust of snow covering it, but beneath that, it was solid, rock-hard ice. If the aircraft hit that, it would be a wreck. It was no good calling Stephen and saying, 'There's a big lump of ice in the middle, so watch out for that.' Planes can't do doglegs mid-landing or take-off. If the strip was to have any chance of being usable, the mound of ice had to go.

I didn't have time to stop and think, I just grabbed my shovel and started to attack this thing. I was very pumped up and I didn't want this to fail for the sake of one stupid lump of ice, so I put the shovel to the ultimate test, wielding it like an ice axe, ramming and smashing it down on the concrete-hard ice-block, sending showers of crystals and jagged shards of ice flying through the air in every direction. I was going at it like a madman, not pausing for a second even though I was feeling sick and faint with the effort. Nine days of nothing and then this, but I couldn't have worked harder; I was a man possessed. The plane had now already taken off from where it had been waiting; I just had to get rid of this thing. I don't know how long it took, but I managed to reduce the mound until it was almost level with the surrounding ice. I didn't pause for a second, but wheeled around, stumbled back to the side of the strip and hurried down to the far end.

I turned and looked back. There were several blocks and mounds to either side, but the runway itself appeared clear, though it narrowed to an hourglass shape in the middle, barely wider than the skids of the plane that would have to land on it, and it was much shorter than the ideal length, perhaps 280 metres instead of 400. It would have to do, there was no time left. I stumbled back through the snow to the tent, my legs leaden. I was shaking and trembling, with cold sweat on my brow, and my fingers fumbled agonisingly slowly with the keypad of the HF radio.

My chest still heaving and gasping for air, I had to compose myself to deliver all the information he needed. I was very aware that how I spoke to him was just as important as what I said. If I had given him a garbled account in a desperate tone of voice, and had been excessively positive about the strip, both those things would have combined to make him think twice. He had a marginal situation and the poor visibility meant that he couldn't use his own eyes to verify what I was saying, so he had to decide whether to trust the information that I was giving him. We had never met but he knew of me and my work, and that I took these things seriously and was aware of the potentially dire consequences of supplying inaccurate information. All these things were very important. If he damaged the plane and couldn't take off again, he was in serious trouble, not to mention the danger to the lives and limbs of himself and his co-pilot.

I took a couple of deep breaths, trying to slow myself down from the frenzy of effort I had just put in, and gave him the basic details of the strip. 'I've got a strip. It's not great and it doesn't come with any guarantees, but I've looked at it as best I can and I have measured it out. It's on a pan of first-year ice with an eight-foot pressure ridge thirty metres back from the northern end. The ice is firm underneath a slightly soft crust. It's not a full-length strip; it's about 120 metres short and it's narrow at the centre, but it's maybe two metres wider than the plane's skis and it's marked with bagged snow; you'll see it when you overfly it. The only usable line is down the middle. I'll light a fire with some rubbish and put some snow on it to give some smoke, so you'll see the wind speed and direction, and I'll also put a wind sock on a ski at the downwind end of the runway.'

'Too late for that,' he said. 'We're about to come over your position now.' As he said it, I heard the engine note on the wind. I rushed outside the tent. The orange and white plane was just visible, a tiny dot in the distance that suddenly swelled into a huge shape as it came overhead. They circled around my ice-pan and then did two laps of the neighbouring one to see if there was anything better, but the visibility was so poor that there wasn't any other option to take; the choice was to use my strip or not land at all.

Stephen then came back to me on the HF radio and I knew he was wondering if I was trying to sell the strip to him or just giving him the facts in a measured, objective way. I kept my voice flat and unemotional as I repeated the information. 'Like I said, there is no guarantee with this strip. It's all I could do in the time available. It has this waisting in the middle and a significant hump of ice to either side if you don't stay between those two markers. But it is my belief from what I can see – and I have walked up both ways, looking across all the time – that it is otherwise sound.' That was all I could say. It was now up to him. It was a partnership, a collaborative thing to an extent, but only he could make the final decision. He didn't want me to incur a bill of £35,000 for an aborted flight, so there was pressure on him as a professional to get the job done, but there was an even greater responsibility to himself, his co-pilot and his employer not to jeopardise the safety of the aircraft and themselves. It was an uncomfortable situation for a pilot to be put in and he said afterwards that, paradoxically, what had decided him was that I was clearly negative about the strip and he thought on balance that I was probably being overcautious and therefore the strip was likely to be better than I thought. On that basis alone he decided to come in.

He made two low passes first. The plane came down lower and lower until it was no more than ten or fifteen feet above the surface of the ice and I could see the pilots' faces framed in the cockpit as they checked the strip visually – how long was it, any cracks, lumps or unseen obstacles, were they going to land in the first part of the runway and stop about halfway or use the second half of it? Even in that poor visibility they might see things from the air that were invisible to me on the ground, and patterns of cracking like fault-lines might be visible suggesting hidden areas of weakness. There can have been no obvious problems, because the third time they came in, flying into the wind, they went lower and lower until suddenly I saw twin flurries of snow as the skids touched down. At once, Stephen put the props into full reverse thrust. The engine note rose to its familiar throaty roar and the blast sent snow clouds billowing upwards, half-enveloping the plane before the wind and slipstream whipped them away. The plane braked from almost 90 mph to a dead stop within 150 metres. I saw it pause for a split second, rocking on its skids as the engine note died down, and then there was a roar as the props began to accelerate again and it swung around and began to taxi back to the start of the runway ready for take-off into the wind. It swung round once more and then the engine note died away. The two pilots got out. They were both wearing dark clothing – the first dark objects I had seen in months. They wore big 'moon-boots' with their trousers stuffed into the top of them, so their legs looked quite stumpy, and thick padded jackets; from a distance they looked like two Russian dolls tottering comically towards me. We walked towards each other. They both congratulated me and offered to help me pack my stuff and take the sledge to the plane, but after pulling it over 400 nautical miles, I wanted to do the last 400 metres as well. I had to get all my kit together, but it was reasonably relaxed; there was no 'Do it now. Go, go go!'

There was no problem about taking what little I had left at my camp back on the plane, and there was no question of Baskers, Curves, Swerves and poor broken-backed Mavis, who had been through a lot with me, being simply dumped in the snow. It took ten or fifteen minutes to finish clearing up and loading my stuff into the plane and by then there were inky dark clouds massing and a sudden haste to be airborne. There was no time even for a last look round and a few 'famous last words'. We scrambled aboard and I strapped myself in.

On the seat next to me were some things that the pilots had brought up from Resolute for me. There was a package of treats and a letter from Mary, cards from Wilf and Freya, pressed flowers from the garden, a cake iced with the words 'Cool Dude', a couple of paintings of Daddy at the North Pole and a lurid purple badge proclaiming 'I've done it and I've done it good', which I put on at once and wore with pride all the way home. There was also a telegram from Her Majesty the Queen: 'We were pleased to learn of your success in completing your remarkable, unaided journey to the North Pole. You have defied great odds and extreme conditions in your endeavour. Your courage, perseverance and determination have been an inspiration to us all. We offer you our warm congratulations.'

As I read those words, the engine whined and fired and the props began to revolve, disappearing into a blur of motion. A few seconds later we were bumping and rattling over the ice, accelerating and then lifting off with a final thud as the skids rose. Looking down from the plane as we banked to head south, I could just make out the line of blue bags marking the strip. Then it disappeared from view, swallowed up in an ocean of ice.

As I took in the fact that I was finally airborne, the biggest smile I have ever had spread across my face. The job hadn't been finished when I'd reached the Pole, huge relief though that was. I had completed the main mission, but I couldn't allow myself to relax until I was in the aircraft and off the ground. Now, for the first time in seventy-five days, my destiny was in someone else's hands. I felt my whole body relax as the realisation sank in; it was finally all over. I was on my way home.

Epilogue

I flew back into England early on the morning of Thursday 29 May 2003, but it was not until late that night that we returned to Dartmoor and all I saw of the moors and tors were their dark, slumbering shapes, etched in deeper black against the night sky. As we turned off into the narrow, winding valley that leads to our house, the headlights caught the ghostly shape of a barn owl hunting over the fields by the river. I got out to open the gate at the bottom of the drive, and then walked up to the house, re-attuning myself to those familiar but half-forgotten sounds: the river tumbling over the rocks in the bottom of the valley and the wind soughing through the trees. A soft summer rain had been falling during the evening and the smell of damp earth mingled with the warm, comforting stables smell from the barn where Mary kept her horse. I felt a cold nose press into my hand and there was Baskers, wagging his tail. Even PC, our semi-feral pest control cat, put in an appearance.

Wilf had fallen asleep in the back of the car on the journey home and I picked him up and carried him into the house, his face nestled into my shoulder. As I laid him down in his bed, he stirred, murmuring in his sleep and grasped my fingers in his chubby hand. I tried to ease away but though he was still fast asleep, he clung tight to my hand and I stayed crouching by his bed for a few more minutes, comparing his sleeping features with the mental snapshot of him that I had imprinted on my mind before I set off for the Pole.

The next morning, I woke just before dawn and found that Wilf was already dressed and standing silent at my bedside. As soon as he saw my eyes flicker open, he put his arms round my neck and whispered in my ear, 'Can we go up on the tors, Daddy?' We tiptoed out of the house, leaving Mary and Freya asleep, and set off up the moor with Wilf riding on my shoulders, his strong legs gripping my sides. Baskers' enthusiasm at my return did not extend to coming with us. As soon as he realised that Mary's horse, Philbo, would not be accompanying us, he ducked behind some rocks and sneaked back to the house to resume his interrupted sleep.

It was cool and damp in the grey light of pre-dawn and my boots left dark prints in the dew-sodden grass. There was not a breath of wind, the air so still that tendrils of mist still clung to the surface of the river. A heron stood motionless in the shallows, keeping its lonely vigil. As I looked up, the tors above us were haloed with the first golden light of dawn. We didn't speak much as we climbed up out of the valley, just happy to be together again. I was revelling in the sights, sounds and smells filling my senses, so long starved by the sterile Arctic sea-ice. The turf was springy under my feet, the air full of the heady scent of bluebells and flooded with the sound of the dawn chorus of birdsong from the woods flanking the river.

Every hundred yards or so we entered a different micro-landscape – from pasture, to woodland, to marsh, to open moorland – and saw fresh vistas of rolling hills open up before us, with the tors standing sentinel above. We followed the rough track down to the ford, pausing to watch a couple of Dartmoor ponies running over the damp grass, full of sheer exuberance at the breaking day, then climbed the other side of the valley. At the top we reached a cluster of granite crags, as old and timeless as the moor itself.

We'd often been up there before, scrambling over the rocks, looking for shelters and hiding places, and spotting features in the landscape from our favoured cliff-top places in the rock formations. If Wilf was struggling to climb one of the crags, I'd often encourage him – just as my Dad used to do, standing with his stopwatch in the lane by the church while I ran my sets of 400 metres – 'Come on, son. You can do it.' Wilf went on ahead of me this morning, determined to show me how well he could climb, and I stood and watched him. As he pulled himself up and over the rocks, I heard him muttering to himself, 'Come on, son.' He reached the top and turned to look down on me, beaming with pride at what he had achieved. As I followed him up, I missed my footing for a second and my boot slipped off a ledge. I heard him say, half to himself and half to me, 'Come on son, you can do it!'

At the top of one of the rock stacks, we found our favourite granite 'seats' and sat there watching the line of the sunrise inching down into the valley. That tranquil scene was, in every sense, a world away from the place I had left only a few days before, though already it seemed an eternity. Indeed, it was as if the whole endeavour had been a dream. There were no monochromatic vistas here, no confusing perspectives, no ice and snow, no black, frigid waters, no harsh, blinding light. Everything was softer and gentler, and the moors and valleys around us were coloured a thousand shades of green and bursting with life.

After a while I put Wilf up on my shoulders again and we walked back down the lane towards Wydemeet. The cries of a circling buzzard pierced the silence of the morning and when we reached the valley bottom the sun was already dappling the river and swallows were skimming the surface. I was back on Dartmoor in the home I loved, with the people – Mary, Wilf and Freya – who meant more to me than anything in the world, and, for now, this small world was all I wanted or needed.

I had half-thought and half-hoped that in completing my solo journey to the Pole after fifteen long years of unrelenting effort, I would have fulfilled my destiny, but in the same instant that I at last stood at 90° North and felt the profoundest sense of relief, I also realised that the Pole had never really been the finishing post. But one thing had changed forever, for the first time in my life, I was free.

Acknowledgements

Let no one be in any doubt that while much of my adult life, has been focused on achieving this endeavour, solo, it is only the act of putting one footstep in front of the other on the sea-ice that is truly done alone. An idiosyncratic feat like this requires the patience, interest, support and generosity of a huge number of individuals and organisations, without whom I simply would not have reached my goal. I owe you all more than I will ever be able to express.

I know that in truth this has been a monumental team effort rather than an individual act, involving small spontaneous gestures, substantial on-going commitments, and all levels of support and collaboration in between. Casting a net over my life, I know I will have accidentally omitted some people whose contribution to keeping me sane, safe and on-track has been of immeasurable importance, so please accept my apologies and my sincere thanks here.

I feel the most important paragraph in the whole book is this one, to thank you for all you have done for me; however achingly inadequate the word 'thank' is in the context of what you have given me. But for now it must suffice. Please just know this. I have stood on the edge of the abyss and stared abject failure in the face. But it was with *your* support that I was able to win through.

The Omega Foundation

Fundamental to the success of The Omega Foundation Arctic Ocean Research Expedition was the comprehensive and unwavering support of The Foundation – both operationally and financially. My case study into the psychology of operating alone on a long-range and extreme undertaking, and my study of the drift movements and surface conditions of the sea-ice were both relevant to The Foundation's on-going support of scientific research in high latitudes; and my commitment to introducing a wider audience to the nature and global significance of the Arctic Ocean fitted The Foundation's objective to broaden public awareness and understanding of the polar regions. To have had the patronage of an organisation such as this behind me was a privilege for which I am exceptionally grateful.

My Most Special Thanks

If you have ever wondered what a list of giant's names would look like, your search is over. The people here are all giants upon whose shoulders I have climbed. Some are national figures and some are my close family, some are leaders in their field and some are friends you'd want to have by your side in the trenches. I consider myself fortunate in the extreme to have been the beneficiary of their counsel, commitment and time. Without them I had no chance.

Philippa Arding
Serena Chance
Camilla Coulson
Ann Daniels
Ginny Dougary
Robert Elias

Mike Ewart Smith
Sir Ranulph and Ginny
   Fiennes
Tina Fotherby
Dawn French
Gary and Diane Guy

Henry and Adele Hadow
Caroline Hamilton
Martin Hartley
Sebastian and Flora Lyon
Howard Marshall
Peter and Elizabeth Martin
Simon and Jennifer Murray
Jo Musgrove
Esther Nicholson
Peter Noble-Jones

Robert Owen
Ben Preston
Vaughan Purvis
Jack Russell
Rebecca Seeley Harris
Robert Thomson
Ian Wesley
Sara Wheeler
Phil White
Andy Woodward

Key Long-Term Sponsors and Suppliers

Some of these commercial organisations have supported my expeditions since 1989, and The Polar Travel Company's expeditionary activities since 1995. Often events and circumstances have made it difficult to return satisfactorily the compliment they paid me in making the extra effort to modify their equipment, or deliver at short notice, or provide additional services. Many supplied equipment, products and expertise at cost or free of charge for little or no reward. Let my unequivocal recommendation here of their services be a start in redressing the accumulated debt of thanks I owe.

Acapulka
Antarctica – Bespoke Tents
Asnes Ski
AST Connections
Be-Well Nutritional Products
Brenig
Campbell Irvine
Cebe Eyewear
Cercles Polaires Expéditions
    – Cerpolex

CLS – Collecte Localisation
    Satellites
Devon and Cornwall
    Constabulary
Digitising Direct
Eureka HAW Station
Excel (London)
First Air (Bradley Air
    Services)
First Ascent

First Choice Expedition
  Foods
The Imperial Match
  Company
Mammut
Marc Lawson and Co.
Mary Nicholson Public
  Relations
Multicell International
Perseverance Mills

Personal Development
  Coaching
Polar Ice Expeditions
Silva (UK)
Snowsled
Suunto Wristop Computers
Taunton Leisure
Tetley GB
Trail Venture (Ashburton)
Viking Saddlery

Key Long-Term Technical Supporters

The majority of those named here either own, or work for, and have led the interest of, the companies listed above. Their passion for their respective specialist fields, and their sheer depth of knowledge have been of inestimable value as I strove to develop polar-specific products, supplies, activities and research studies over the years.

Hugh Anderson
Alan Axon
Alex Bierwald
Steve Chadwick
Chris Court
Nigel Darling
Roger Daynes
Dr Peter Edwards
Chris Fenn
Jackie Harris
Helge Hoflandsdal
Laurence Howell
Ian Irvine

Tim Langton
Juliette Lloyd
Toni Manik
Christian de Marliave
Louis Mesnier
Graham Ogle
Zena Osborn
Mike and Debbie Owen
Hervé Riffault
Justin Roberts
Oliver Shepard
Geoff Somers
Clive Tovey

Johan Ulvede   Greg White
Brian Welsby   Ian Williams
Tony Whale   Shane Winser

Key Additional Sponsors and Suppliers for 2003 Expedition

These are the companies who were new to the supporting team of suppliers, becoming involved during the preparations in 2002 or in post-expedition activity in 2003: from the British manufacturer of the 'lilo' (a.k.a. sledge-to-boat conversion kit) to the Canadian air charter operator effecting the drop-off and pick-up; and from the television documentary film-makers to my chocolatiers from Dartmoor. All were an integral and vital part of the team that either enabled my progress north or enabled a wider audience to learn more about the Arctic Ocean.

Alan Cooper Laboratories   Helly Hansen Spesialprodkter
Alpha Secretarial Services   Henshaw Inflatables
Anglo-Romanian Bank   Hilleberg The Tentmaker
Bigpeaks.com   Icelandair
British Airways   Kenn Borek Air
Browne's Handmade   National Geographic Channel
    Chocolates   Peter Hutchison Design
Creative Touch Films   (PHD)

Key Additional Specialists and Supporters for 2003 Expedition

As part of the total operational review of every aspect of the expedition to maximise my likelihood of succeeding in 2003, a significant number of new working relationships and friendships were made with professionals, inventors, specialists, designers, manufacturers, managers and editors.

Edward Alcock
Chris Allen
Arnold Asnes
George Brock
Andy Brown
Chris Chapman
Alan Cooper
Mark Dyson
Al Gaudet
Bill Gawletz
Sarah Gray
Tony Gumbs
Peter Herbert
Chris Hornidge
Peter Hutchison
Dr Chris Johnson

Steve King
Nadine Lucas
Troy McKerral
Andrew Miles
Perran Newman
Sandra Parsons
Andy Pollard
Nick Price
Michael Radoi
Shirley Sawtell
Kate Snell
Gerry Taylor
Richard and Sue
    Taylor-Young
Paul Tomlin
Jane Wheatley

Significant Past Sponsors

The high Arctic and Arctic Ocean are extremely expensive operating environments in which to organise and conduct expeditions, so the financial support of sponsors, whether on the basis of patronage or in return for commercial rights, has always been an absolute necessity in order to put my plans into action. The contribution of these companies has been critical in enabling me to organize an array of expeditions, including my first and second attempts, but the rewards were not always what we had all hoped for, so it is with particular gratitude that I acknowledge what their support has finally enabled – for without them there could have been no success in 2003.

3M
7-E Communications
Angela Mortimer

Bantex
Bayer Pharmaceutical
BetzDearborn

Bradstock, Blunt and
   Thompson
Canadian Airlines
   International
Carrington's Performance
   Fabrics
Celestion
Daily Mail
Dartmoor Best Bitter
FPD Savills UK
Greencat
Hot Lunches
Intavent-Orthofix
JW Groombridge
Kodak
McVitie's Penguin
The National Express Group
Neutrogena Norwegian
   Formula
Nexus Choat Public Relations
Polar Bears – The Dry
   Diving Specialists
The Prince's Trust
Rhino Products (UK)
Sector Sport Watches
Shell Unleaded Fuel
Sony
Stratec Medical
Stringfellows
Suzuki Marine
Thermawear (Damart)
Vander

And a Very Special Thanks to . . .

The funny thing is some of these people have no idea how important they are to me – it's the way life works. Sometimes even I didn't realise till many years later. Some of their number have now died, some are still youngsters. Some have been my mentors, some have stepped into the breach at critical points and offered a helping hand, but most have simply offered their time, support and friendship. I will remain in your debt always.

Paul Ackford
Karen Addison
Dick and Denise Allen
Nick Arding
Nikki Ball
Anne Barclay
Peter Beardow
Corinne Bell
Hafdis Bennett
Jen Benton
Leslie Bishop
Lauritz Bloch
Freya Bloor
Hugh Bourne

David Burckett St Laurent
Mark Carr
Julia Charles
Penny and Prue Charles
Stephen and Jenny Charles
Anton and Alison Coaker
Crispin Coghill
Alison Congo
Tarquin Cooper
Mark Cross
Paul Deegan
Andrew Dick
Rob Dixon
Christian Duff
Mark Firth
Rosie Firth
Fiona Fountain
Jack Fountain
Nicky Gaisford
Dick and Sue Gerrard-Wright
Alan and Caroline Godwin
Lucie Gooch
Robert Gooch
Judy Gordon Jones
Lucinda Green
Julie Greenwood
Hector and Monty Hadow
Jane Hamilton
Julian Hanson-Smith
Simon Harris-Ward
Robin Hawse
Julia Hayward
Ron, Elizabeth and James
    Heath
Jane Heatlie

Gill Hemburrow
Judy Henderson
Donna Hetheringon
Simon and Nicky Heyworth
Catherine Hickson
Zoë Hudson
John and Ann Ingram
Stephen Jones
Chrissie Keeble
Andrew Keith
Jane Kingsley
Paul and Nicola Krusin
Charlotte 'Gig' Lees
Oliver and Mary Lough
Alastair and Jemima Lyon
Michael McGrath
Lewis McNaught
Caroline Marks
Matty Marsland
Denise Martin
Madelaine Mason
Ginny Michaux
Suzie Mumé
Revd Derek Newport
Archie, Amelia, Violet and
    Bertie Nicholson
Colin and Martha Nicholson
Peter and Jane Nicholson
Michael Oliver
Pom Oliver
Tim Oliver
Katie Owen
Jeremy Palmer-Tomkinson
Alex Prenn
Lise Prentice

George and Joanna Radford
Gina Rawle
Tim and Harriet Reilly
Julia Richards
Angela Richardson
Sarah Richardson
Tom Riddell-Webster
Steve Roberts
Rupert and Catherine Russell
Brigitte Sabard
Dave Sargent
Sue Self
Lindsey Sexton-Chadwick
Jo Shephard
Michael Shirley-Beavan
Keith Simpson
Barbara Sinclair
Robert Somerville
Adam and Carrie Southwell
Djazia Spowers
Hugo Spowers
Rosie Stancer

Sue Stratton
Ben and Emma Stubbs
Anthony Talbot
Dave Thomas
Myles Thompson
Donna Timmis
Ian Todd
Hilary Townsend
Mark and Deborah Treneer
Paul Turner
Ivor Underhill
Charles de V Shaw
Dr Claudio Vita-Finzi
David and Kate Watson
Bernadette Wayte
Simon Whalley
Steve Whittaker
Dee Wilkinson
David Williams
Nic Williams
Tom Williams
Peter, Joy and Daniel Wright

And for the Preparation of Solo

I now know what it takes to write and produce a book, and exactly like the solo feat itself, it is far from an individual effort. So I would like to offer my whole-hearted thanks here for the prodigious energy, talent and encouragement of my supervisory team at Michael Joseph and Penguin General Books, and those who contributed to making this book possible.

Kate Brunt
Sarah Day

Chantal Gibbs
Sue Hall

Neil Hanson
Debbie Hatfield
Belle Hepworth
Alex Hippisley-Cox
Pete Metcalf
John Plumer

Sophie Richmond
Keith Taylor
Tom Weldon
Rowland White
Araminta Whitley

Permissions

Quotations by Fridtjof Nansen are taken from *Farthest North* (Duckworth, 2000) vol. 1, pp. 62 and 263; the quotation by Barry Lopez and an interesting observation about polar bear behaviour are taken from his *Arctic Dreams* (Picador, 1986) pp. 20 and 84–5; quotations by Robert Peary and Frederick Cook are taken from Fergus Fleming, *Ninety Degrees North* (Granta Books, 2002) pp. 32–5; the quotation by Captain Robert Falcon Scott is taken from Stephen Gwynn, *Captain Scott* (Penguin Books, 1939) p. 156. Information on the physical effects of cold is primarily drawn from James A. Wilkerson, Cameron C. Bangs and John S. Hayward (eds), *Hypothermia, Frostbite and Other Cold Injuries* (Mountaineers Books, 1986).

Postscript

Baskers, the most loyal of friends, died after a short illness the day I signed off the final proofs for *Solo* – he had seen my endeavour through to the end.

Index

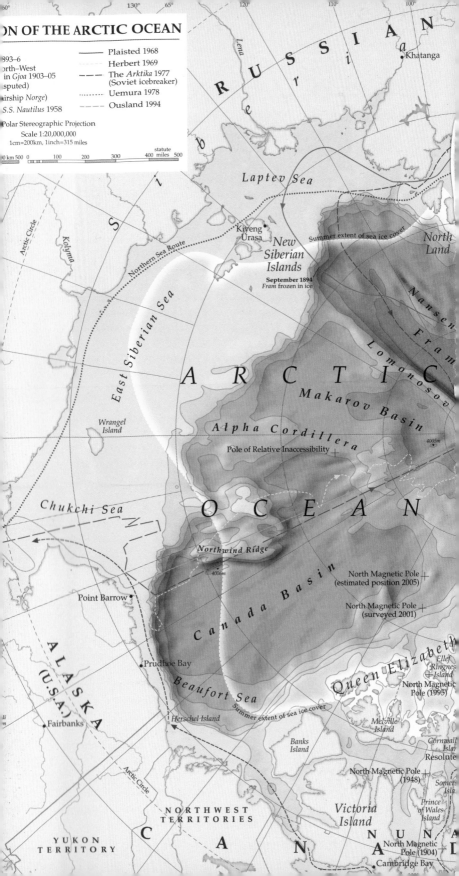

393–6
orth–West
in *Gjoa* 1903–05
sputed)

airship *Norge*)

S.S. Nautilus 1958

Polar Stereographic Projection
Scale 1:20,000,000
1cm=200km, 1inch=315 miles

	Plaisted 1968
	Herbert 1969
	The *Arktika* 1977 (Soviet icebreaker)
	Uemura 1978
	Ousland 1994

0 km 500   0   100   200   300   400   500
statute miles

R U S S I A N

Lena   *a*   Khatanga

Siberia

Laptev Sea

Kiveng
Urasa

New
Siberian
Islands

September 1894
Fram frozen in ice

Summer extent of sea ice cover

North
Land

Nansen

Fram

Northern Sea Route

East Siberian Sea

A R C T I C

Lomonosov

Makarov Basin

Wrangel
Island

Alpha Cordillera

Pole of Relative Inaccessibility   +

4005m

Arctic Circle

Kolyma

Chukchi Sea

O C E A N

Northwind Ridge

400m

North Magnetic Pole
(estimated position 2005)   +

North Magnetic Pole
(surveyed 2001)   +

Point Barrow ●

Canada Basin

A L A S K A
(U.S.A.)

Prudhoe Bay ●

Fairbanks ●

Beaufort Sea

Summer extent of sea ice cover

Herschel Island ●

Arctic Circle

Banks
Island

Queen Elizabeth

Ellef
Ringnes
Island   +

North Magnetic
Pole (1995)

Melville
Island

Cornwall
Island

Resolute

*Victoria
Island*

North Magnetic Pole
(1948)   +

Somer
Isla

Prince
of Wales
Island

N O R T H W E S T
T E R R I T O R I E S

Y U K O N
T E R R I T O R Y

C

A

N

A

North Magnetic
Pole (1904)   +

Cambridge Bay ●

130°   65°   120°   110°   100°

140°

EXPLORAT

0   100   200   300

Ueler
Bering Stra
Wales

metres below sea level

0
250
500
1000
2000
3000
4000